Railroads of Pennsylvania

Railroads of Pennsylvania

FRAGMENTS OF THE PAST IN THE KEYSTONE LANDSCAPE

Lorett Treese

STACKPOLE
BOOKS

For Mat

Copyright ©2003 by Stackpole Books

Published by
Stackpole Books
5067 Ritter Road
Mechanicsburg, PA 17055
www.stackpolebooks.com

Printed in the United States of America

10 9 8 7 6 5 4 3 2 1

First Edition

Cover design by Caroline Stover

Photos by the author and illustrations from the author's collection, unless otherwise noted.

Front cover: *Pittsburgh Promotes Progress,* the 1954 Pennsylvania Railroad calendar art. Painter Grif Teller depicted a red two-unit diesel passenger locomotive leaving Pittsburgh, which was then reclaiming its downtown, or Golden Triangle, from railroad warehouses during its celebrated urban-renewal renaissance. COLLECTION OF DAN CUPPER

Back cover: *The Horseshoe Curve,* the 1952 Pennsy calendar art. Grif Teller's painting depicts diesel-hauled passenger and freight trains about to pass one another, while a train pulled by a steam locomotive is relegated to the distance. Horseshoe Curve remains one of the world's best-known railroad engineering features and a very popular tourist destination. COLLECTION OF DAN CUPPER

Library of Congress Cataloging-in-Publication Data

Treese, Lorett, 1952–
    Railroads of Pennsylvania : fragments of the past in the Keystone landscape / Lorett Treese.—1st ed.
        p.   cm.
    Includes bibliographical references (p.) and index.
    ISBN 0-8117-2622-3 (pbk.)
    1. Railroads—Pennsylvania—History.   I. Title.
HE2771.P4 T74   2003
385'.09748–dc21

2002011395

CONTENTS

SECTION TWO: Hershey/Gettysburg/Dutch Country

Sampling the Region's Railroad History

The Region's Rail Trails   139

PREFACE

In 1812, John Stevens, sometimes called the father of American railroads, published *Documents Tending to Prove the Superior Advantages of Rail-Ways and Steam-Carriages over Canal Navigation.* It was a groundbreaking pamphlet because it proposed the construction of a railroad at a time when America had no steam locomotives or passenger cars. Stevens envisioned a railway constructed of timber—its "moving power to be a steam-engine"—that would burn wood. He thought that a railroad could be built more quickly and with fewer casualties than a canal, and that it would be no more expensive than a turnpike.

Although Stevens expected to be "stigmatized as a visionary projector," he argued, "Sooner or later, then, the improvement now proposed will be brought into general use, and, if I mistake not, long before the projected canal [the Erie Canal] will be completed." He might have been somewhat optimistic, but Stevens was right. Within another two decades, railroads were springing up all over the eastern United States, first as feeders to canals, then alongside the canals they were replacing.

Railroads may have been the best thing that ever happened to America. They opened markets, making it possible for geographically distant regions to be closely tied economically. Railroads greatly expanded the volume of trading on Wall Street and provided opportunities for many Americans to work, apply their ingenuity, and perhaps even make a Gilded Age fortune.

In Pennsylvania, railroads transported natural resources like coal, oil, and lumber, as well as agricultural products, to urban consumers, while they brought manufactured goods and machinery to rural areas. Cities like Philadelphia, Pittsburgh, Reading, and Harrisburg developed as railroad hubs, while towns like Altoona were founded to maintain railroad property. Railroads made the Commonwealth one of America's leading industrial and richest states.

Pennsylvania's railroad mileage began to diminish around the time of the First World War. Passenger traffic began declining during the 1920s, and railroad freight volume joined the downward trend soon after World War II.

During the 1930s, the changing face of rail transportation—and a growing awareness that historic railroad artifacts were slipping away—sparked

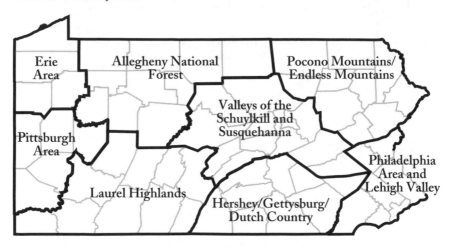

an era of heritage preservation that continues to this day. The Common-wealth has nearly twenty tourist railroads actively engaged in selling nostalgia, offering riders a scenic round-trip to nowhere. More than nine hundred miles of abandoned tracks have been converted to recreational paths in the program created by the Commonwealth's Rails-to-Trails Act. Pennsylvania has three major railroad museums, plus numerous local repositories of railroad equipment and documents. Those participating in these preservation efforts, often on a volunteer basis, are saving not only physical objects but a decidedly romantic spirit of the past.

Pennsylvania also has a lot of railroad artifacts that distinguish the modern landscape. In his science fiction time travel classic *Time and Again,* Jack Finney uses the word "fragments" to describe New York's vintage buildings and neighborhoods when he refers to them as "fragments still remaining . . . of days which once lay out there as real as the day lying out there now: still-surviving fragments of a clear April morning of 1871, a gray winter afternoon of 1840, a rainy dawn of 1793." Pennsylvania's railroad artifacts are such fragments of the economic system and way of life of an earlier America.

I was reminded of Finney's novel when I first glimpsed the railroad viaduct stretching across the entire visible horizon of the valley in Nicholson, Pennsylvania. Finney also came to mind when I toured the Italianate mansion in Jim Thorpe that had been the home of the founder of the Lehigh Valley Railroad, a self-made millionaire. And I thought of *Time and Again* when I rode the Monongahela Incline and gazed down at the railroad station and buildings now preserved to serve another purpose on Pittsburgh's South Side.

This book is not a comprehensive history of transportation in Pennsylvania, nor does it provide complete information on every railroad that ever operated in the Commonwealth. *Railroads of Pennsylvania* is part history and part travel guide, intended to place many of the Commonwealth's railroad artifacts, or fragments, in historical context. It covers the period when railroads were among the nation's biggest and most important industries, as well as the more recent era of railroad heritage preservation. It is a collection of short essays about giants and humble beginnings, historic firsts and spectacular failures, world famous landmarks and things that are no longer.

The text is organized into eight sections, roughly corresponding to the regions of Pennsylvania, as defined by the Pennsylvania Office of Travel and Tourism (the visitors guide published by this agency lists accommodations and other attractions in the same regions). For the convenience of travelers, I wrote the text so that readers could open the book anywhere and start reading.

In the section entitled "Great Railways of the Region," readers will find brief histories of major railroads associated with the region, how they were organized, how they grew, and what happened to them. They will also find the names of museums and historical societies that interpret their history. The full bibliographic citations for material quoted from published histories of railroads appear in the bibliography. "Rail Stories of the Region" includes various tidbits and footnotes of railroad history, as well as the names of the local chapters of the National Railway Historical Society, whose members are often actively involved in rail heritage preservation. "The Region's Railroad Giants" includes brief biographies of those who made their names or fortunes with the region's railroads. Information on museums and tourist railroads, as well as other places where readers can go to find railroad artifacts, is in the "Sampling the Region's Railroad History" section. "The Region's Rail Trails" section includes information on the state of rail trail construction in the area.

I am grateful to all those who helped me research and write this book. My husband, Mat Treese, accompanied me on all my rail heritage treks and shared his opinions on what we found. I appreciate the professional support and advice of transportation historian Dan Cupper, who reviewed the manuscript. The staff and collections of the Mariam Coffin Canaday Library at Bryn Mawr College were tremendously helpful, particularly the patient members of the interlibrary loan department. I also thank the staff at the Hagley Museum and Library and the staff of the Railroad Museum of Pennsylvania, especially Kurt Bell. Finally, I thank Stackpole Books and my editor, Kyle Weaver, for taking a chance on a railroad book that was "just a little different."

Philadelphia Area and Lehigh Valley

Great Railways of the Region

The Pennsy

On October 7, 1834, the line that would become the heart of the giant Pennsylvania Railroad's system was officially opened. At 8:00 that morning, two trains left Columbia, on the Susquehanna River, carrying Pennsylvania's governor George Wolf and various state officials and guests. Locomotives named the Lancaster and the Columbia pulled the cars all day and finally brought them to Philadelphia around 6:00 in the evening. According to an account in a local newspaper, the *Columbia Spy*, reprinted in *Hazard's Register of Pennsylvania*, they were "welcomed by a multitude of citizens" who were no less enthusiastic than the throng that had welcomed the trains to the depot in Lancaster.

The trip was not without incident. The *Columbia Spy* briefly mentioned an unfortunate accident that had taken the life of an old-timer identified only as "Lint." After the first train had departed from Lancaster, this man stepped onto the tracks to watch it roll away. Because he was deaf, he never heard the second train coming.

Nevertheless, the newspaper ended its account on an optimistic note: "We have only time to express the confident belief which we entertain that, as in its incomplete state it has given glorious promise of repaying all the expense that has been lavished upon it, so when it gets into full operation, that promise will be bountifully performed."

In their history of the Pennsylvania Railroad published over a century later, in 1949, George H. Burgess and Miles C. Kennedy describe the route of this eighty-two-mile-long railroad. Its double tracks began at the corner of Broad and Vine Streets, ran north on Broad and then west to Twenty-first Street. After crossing a bridge over the Schuylkill, they mounted a steep hill with the help of an engineering feature called an inclined plane. Trains then chugged through the Chester Valley, stopping at Downingtown, Coatesville, and Lancaster and finally terminating at Columbia, where a second inclined plane lowered the cars to the level of the Susquehanna River.

Hazard's Register of Pennsylvania, an early-nineteenth-century serial publication containing articles excerpted from various other state and national newspapers, often reflected the pride that Americans had in their new nation and their own accomplishments. An 1835 article discussed some of the engineering wonders this railroad had added to the

The Pennsylvania Railroad's bridge across the Schuylkill River as it appeared around 1875 in *Philadelphia and Its Environs.*

Philadelphia area's undulating landscape. It described the "six piers of hammer-dressed masonry" that supported the Schuylkill viaduct, allowing trains to proceed "30 feet above the surface of the water." It also described other viaducts constructed farther west, such as the towering five-span structure over Valley Creek and those that bridged the east and west branches of the Brandywine River.

An 1833 article on the Commonwealth's expanding transportation facilities hinted that this railroad would do more than move freight. Its description of Pennsylvania's scenery invited the reader to take a train ride for its own sake, predicting the impact that railroads would one day have on tourism in America. The author mentioned the historic nature of the land between Philadelphia and South Valley Hill, near the Warren Tavern (still operating as the General Warren Inne near Paoli) and Paoli Tavern, which was the scene of the bloody Battle of Paoli during the Revolutionary War. As for the Warren Tavern, "We know that a good bed awaits us there, and as to supper, let fat Dinah, the cook, alone, for getting up the eatables." The author commended the Chester Valley for its "beautiful scenery, and especially for that in which smiling and well cultivated fields are a main ingredient." The author also noted that the train passed right by the road to the fashionable summer resort known as the Yellow Springs.

This new railroad, originally called the Philadelphia & Columbia Railroad, was just one part of a larger rail and canal transportation system linking Philadelphia and Pittsburgh that had been constructed by the Commonwealth at a cost to the public of millions of dollars. Unfortunately, while the citizens of Pennsylvania were still celebrating its novelty, it was already becoming apparent that the system was unlikely to earn back the cost of its construction.

The system's key weakness lay not along the tracks between Philadelphia and Columbia, but west of the Susquehanna River, where freight moving in either direction had to be transferred from canal to railroad and then back to canal. Since railroads had proven themselves vastly superior to canals during the previous two decades, the logical way to burst this bottleneck would be a single continuous railroad between Harrisburg and Pittsburgh. A piece of legislation signed by the governor on April 13, 1846, bestowed the right to build that railroad to a new entity called the Pennsylvania Railroad (PRR), which would someday be known as the Standard Railroad of the World.

Since the Pennsylvania Railroad was a private venture, its initial task was raising capital, so its commissioners opened subscription books in Philadelphia and other Pennsylvania municipalities. When this traditional fund-raising method generated less than was needed, Burgess and Kennedy reported, "The City of Philadelphia was divided into blocks, which were to be canvassed from house to house, if necessary, by persons assigned to the work. Subscriptions of as little as one share were to be solicited." After $3 million had been subscribed, the Pennsylvania Railroad was formally organized in March 1847 under the leadership of Samuel V. Merrick with a board of thirteen directors.

For their chief engineer, board members elected J. Edgar Thomson, who had made surveys for the Philadelphia & Columbia Railroad. By 1849, the Pennsy was operating trains between Harrisburg and Lewistown, and it expanded its service to Hollidaysburg the following year. In 1854, the railroad's greatest topographical challenge, the Allegheny Ridge, was finally addressed by the magnificent Horseshoe Curve and nearby Allegheny Tunnel. According to Burgess and Kennedy, the Pennsy's officers and directors declared the line "complete" on November 1, 1855.

The Pennsy's new rail line between Harrisburg and Pittsburgh made the prospect of traveling the same distance over the Commonwealth's canal-rail-canal system far less attractive and therefore even less profitable. Pennsy officers were frustrated by the comparatively poor condition of the Philadelphia & Columbia Railroad, which was still owned by the Commonwealth and which their trains had to use to reach Philadelphia. An increasingly obvious solution was to get the Commonwealth out of the transportation business by selling its entire system to the Pennsylvania Railroad. In 1855, J. Edgar Thomson, who was then president of the Pennsy, offered Pennsylvania's secretary of state $7.5 million for "the main line from Philadelphia to the Monongahela and Allegheny Rivers." The sale was completed at an auction held at the Philadelphia Merchant's Exchange in 1857.

Its original charter made provision for a single major branch line to be built from Pittsburgh to Erie, and gave it permission to build smaller branches into any county through which the main line passed, but the Pennsy quickly skirted these restrictions and expanded by acquiring or leasing other railroad properties. As early as 1848, it leased the Harrisburg, Portsmouth, Mountjoy & Lancaster Rail-road, connecting its own terminus at Harrisburg with the Philadelphia & Columbia Railroad. By the end of the 1860s, the Pennsy had become a through line to the territory west of Pittsburgh with its acquisition of the Pittsburgh, Fort Wayne & Chicago Railway and the "Panhandle" lines to Chicago and St. Louis. By the 1870s, a traveler could ride Pennsy trains from New York harbor at Jersey City to Washington, D.C. By the turn of the century, the Pennsy system included more than a hundred active companies.

In 1902, the Pennsylvania Railroad's deluxe Pennsylvania Special, which would become famous later as the Broadway Limited, began taking passengers from New York to Chicago. The name, changed in 1912, honored the Pennsy's four- and six-track main line, which had been dubbed by the company its "Broad Way of Commerce." In later years, advertisements promoted the Broadway Limited as the fastest long-distance train in the world and the "Leader of the Fleet of Modernism," often mentioning its "club-like" surroundings and onboard staff, which included a valet, barber, manicurist, and secretary.

Only in a roundabout way can the Pennsy claim the first dining car: it acquired the Philadelphia, Wilmington & Baltimore Railroad, which had placed a car fitted for food service on its regular trains during the Civil War. By the turn of the century, the Pennsy was famous for its diners, where professional waiters in starched white jackets served the railroad's signature dishes, including meaty two-rib lamb chops and a creamy mayonnaise-based salad dressing. Each dining car had a steward hired for his extensive restaurant and hotel experience who supervised the waiters and guaranteed overall customer satisfaction. An article published in 1926 in the railroad's house organ, *Pennsylvania Railroad Information,* explained in detail the intricate and well-organized procedure for equipping the dining cars at the company's commissary not only with food but also with laundered table linens and cooking equipment that was carefully arranged in standard locations so that any chef could board any dining car and know where to find the spatula. "Pennsylvania Railroad dining cars are not dedicated to profit but to that intangible asset, goodwill," the article proudly proclaimed.

By the time the Depression swept the United States, the PRR was the largest transportation system in the world, a corporation that had been described by former president Samuel Rea, in a pamphlet published in 1928, as "a self contained system traversing the great central belt of the country." The Pennsy survived the 1930s without entering receivership or bankruptcy, and even managed to continue to pay its stockholders dividends that decade, keeping its record of continuous payment unbroken. It rose to the challenge of competition from other developing forms of transportation by beginning to electrify certain lines and introducing container cars and, eventually, diesel locomotives and intermodal "piggyback" trains that carried truck trailers on flat cars.

According to Burgess and Kennedy, in its centennial year (1946) the system encompassed 10,690 miles of lines stretching from Canada into the South and from the Mississippi River to the East Coast. At that time, it handled 9.38 percent of the nation's freight traffic and 16.69 percent of its passenger traffic. However, the conclusion of their book included the ominous sentence, "Nonetheless, when normal times return [when World War II is well behind us] they [the PRR managers] will again face the competition of the truck, the bus, the airplane, and the private automobile." The company recorded its first deficit that year.

Like so many other American railroads, the Pennsy met its end later in the twentieth century. Heroic attempts to save it by the creation of the Penn Central fell flat when the company went bankrupt in the 1970s. The railroad became part of Conrail, and the remainder of this corporation became an insurance firm.

Since 1974, the Pennsylvania Railroad Technical and Historical Society has been collecting and preserving information about the Pennsylvania Railroad and its subsidiaries. Local chapters and national meetings allow interested participants to share information and organize programs and excursions. The society publishes a journal called *The Keystone* and is restoring the 1849 Lewistown Junction passenger station to serve as its archives and research library.

The Lehigh Valley

By the 1840s, there were a number of entrepreneurs mining coal in the area surrounding the Lehigh Valley. That coal made its way through the valley to markets in New York and Philadelphia by canal. Despite complaints about the canal's high rates and the familiar disadvantages of canal transportation—its lack of speed and cessation of operations when the temperature dropped below freezing—the Lehigh Coal & Navigation Company maintained its monopoly on through transportation in the Lehigh Valley and delayed the building of major railroads in this area for about twenty years after they had been initially proposed.

Inspired by the success of the fledgling Philadelphia & Reading Railroad, Edward R. Biddle joined with other Philadelphia businessmen to incorporate the Delaware, Lehigh, Schuylkill & Susquehanna Railroad in 1846. The project languished for want of funding until Asa Packer took it over, renaming the business the Lehigh Valley Railroad.

Under Packer's direction, construction began in 1853 on a track that would follow the course of the Lehigh River to Easton, linking the existing Beaver Meadow Railroad (a short-line coal-hauler that the Lehigh Valley Railroad later acquired) with New York harbor via the Central Railroad of New Jersey, and Philadelphia via Trenton on the Belvidere Delaware Railroad. By 1855, the Lehigh was open between Easton and Mauch Chunk (now Jim Thorpe), with passenger depots in Easton, Mauch Chunk, Allentown, and Bethlehem, where passengers waited in a house belonging to Asa Packer.

In his history of the Lehigh Valley Railroad, Robert F. Archer describes a hectic period of expansion during the 1860s. Packer and his associates connected their anthracite railroad to upstate New York and Lake Erie at Buffalo, making its original forty-six miles just one link in an extensive through route. In all its history, the Lehigh confined its operations to Pennsylvania, New York, and New Jersey. It also remained first and foremost an anthracite railroad, where moving passengers always took second place to moving coal.

Although Lehigh Valley is not very far from Philadelphia, the connection of the Lehigh Valley Railroad with the city of Philadelphia was always tenuous. The Camden & Amboy Railroad and Transportation Company had provided significant funding to the Lehigh in exchange for assurances that would protect its own interests in Philadelphia. Also, at the same time that the original route of the Lehigh Valley Railroad was under construction, the North Philadelphia Railroad was laying tracks between Philadelphia and Bethlehem for a line that opened in 1857. Eventually these two railroads shared a passenger station, an alliance that continued after the North Pennsylvania came under control of the Philadelphia & Reading Railroad in 1879.

For a long time, the Lehigh Valley Railroad had its headquarters near Asa Packer's mansion in Philadelphia, but following Packer's death in

The 1875 book *Philadelphia and Its Environs* included a drawing of the railroad station on the south side of the river in Bethlehem.

1879, a new headquarters building was constructed south of Bethlehem in a neighborhood where other Lehigh Valley Railroad officers had chosen to reside. Just down the road from their homes was the company that would become Bethlehem Steel, which manufactured steel rails to support heavier trains and increased traffic, taking in raw materials and shipping finished steel by rail.

In his 1981 book, *Urban Capitalists,* Burton W. Folsom describes the debacle made of this railroad's management by Packer's descendants, primarily his nephew Elisha P. Wilbur, who was left in charge after the early deaths of Packer's two sons. Wilbur attempted expansion, but ran short of cash and leased the line to the Philadelphia & Reading Railroad, which went into receivership in 1893. His failure to recognize the Federal Railway Union resulted in strikes. After financier J. P. Morgan gained control of the Leigh Valley's stock, Elisha P. Wilbur relinquished his presidency in 1897.

In a 1927 book about anthracite railroads, Jules Irwin Bogen writes of the rehabilitation of the Lehigh's physical plant that followed this change and the railroad's new policy of "liberal, and perhaps unusual, expenditures on both roadbed and equipment, in order to adapt the property to the most economical operation." The executive offices were moved to New York about this time, "representing the end of control by independent Philadelphia capital."

In 1896, the Lehigh Valley Railroad launched its own glamour train, the Black Diamond Express, on a daylight run from Buffalo to Jersey City, New Jersey. The Black Diamond had elegant dining cars, club cars, and observation cars, and it survived until 1959. Unfortunately, its route was slower than those of its two major competitors, and despite the promotion of its scenic nature, traveling between New York City and Buffalo by way of Bethlehem and the upper Susquehanna River valley cost passengers time.

By the 1920s, the market for anthracite coal was shrinking, and during the 1930s the Lehigh Valley Railroad would begin to divest itself of branches and scramble for general merchandise freight. The Lehigh tried to reinvent itself as an "industrial carrier" in the 1950s with modernized freight cars, but it faced a new competitor: the New York State Thruway. The Pennsylvania Railroad, which had maintained a controlling interest in its stock since 1928, took full control of the Leigh Valley Railroad in 1962. The Lehigh Valley Railroad lived on as part of the Penn Central system and was incorporated into Conrail in 1976. Its history is now interpreted and preserved by the Lehigh Valley Railroad Historical Society in Manchester, New York.

Rail Stories of the Region

Pennsylvania's System

The town meeting held in Philadelphia in January 1825, which had been called to investigate building a canal between the Susquehanna and Allegheny Rivers, dissolved in confusion when its attendees kept introducing other ideas. It did, however, prompt legislation, passed that spring, appointing canal commissioners charged with the objective of establishing "navigable communication between the eastern and western waters of the state and Lake Erie."

Philadelphia, which had once been the leading seaport on the Atlantic coast, was then facing serious competition from New York City and Baltimore. In 1817, New York had started building the Erie Canal, which would provide New York City with a water route to the Great Lakes and Midwest. The following year, Maryland completed its National Road between Baltimore and the Ohio River. Pennsylvania had a fairly decent turnpike between Philadelphia and Lancaster, but traveling west of the

Susquehanna meant a tedious trek on primitive wagon roads like the Forbes Road and the Kittanning Path, which could take several weeks.

In 1818, John Stevens, an avant-garde thinker who had scoffed at the Erie Canal, asked the Pennsylvania legislature to look into building a railroad between Philadelphia and Pittsburgh. After this suggestion was regarded as too visionary, Stevens obtained a charter in 1823 to build a shorter railroad between Philadelphia and Columbia. Stevens made a rudimentary survey, but he encountered vigorous opposition from those who were unwilling to look beyond canals and he was unable to raise sufficient investment capital to start building.

Part of the problem was that few Americans had ever seen a railroad. Pennsylvanians tried to address this issue in 1824 by creating the Pennsylvania Society for the Promotion of Internal Improvements in the Commonwealth. In 1825, they resolved to send William Strickland, an architect and engineer, to Europe to study the various transportation systems being developed there and to determine whether canals or railroads would be more cost-effective in the long run. In his monumental study of American transportation, J. Luther Ringwalt quoted some of the society's formal directions to Strickland: "Of the utility of railways, and their importance as a means of transporting large burdens, we have full knowledge. Of the mode of constructing them, and their cost, nothing is known with certainty."

Pennsylvanians did know something about canals from those being built or already operating in the Commonwealth. The Conewago Canal on the Susquehanna River had been getting vessels around the Conewago Falls since 1797. Between 1821 and 1828, the Union Canal Company built a canal between Reading on the Schuylkill River and Portsmouth (now Middletown) on the Susquehanna. In 1825, the Schuylkill Navigation Company completed work on a canal designed to make the Schuylkill River navigable between Port Carbon and Philadelphia. Since the Schuylkill Canal joined the Union Canal in Reading, Pennsylvania had a rudimentary water route between Philadelphia and the Susquehanna.

In 1826, Strickland published a report—today acknowledged as one of America's first great engineering texts—highly recommending railroads. Nevertheless, Pennsylvania's legislature voted in favor of a program of public improvements centering on a "Main Line Canal." This evolved into a "Main Line of Public Works" (more commonly called the "State Works") through legislation signed by Pennsylvania's governor on March 24, 1828, which also repealed John Stevens's charter in favor of a state railroad linking Philadelphia and Columbia.

Parts of Pennsylvania's transportation system were operating as early as 1832, including canals between Columbia and Hollidaysburg, and Pittsburgh and Johnstown. In 1834, the Philadelphia & Columbia Railroad opened, and so did the Allegheny Portage Railroad, which addressed the problem of getting freight over the steep Allegheny Ridge. While the main line of the State Works was primarily intended to facilitate traffic flowing east and west, it was supplemented with other canals, including one that followed the Susquehanna from Duncan's Island to Northumberland and others that followed the north and west branches of the same river.

Traveling the entire length of the State Works main line entailed an 82-mile train ride from Philadelphia to Columbia, followed by 172 miles by canal to the base of the Allegheny Mountains, 36 miles on inclined planes over the mountains, and 104 miles by canal to Pittsburgh. The 394-mile journey averaged four and a half days. Pennsylvania's system required both freight and passengers to be transferred from one type of conveyance to another, creating huge logjams of traffic. The cost of maintaining its inclined planes was high, and its canals were subject to the inconveniences of ice in the winter, floods in the spring, and low water in the summer. It became clear that the State Works, which cost the Commonwealth nearly $18 million, would never pay for itself.

In 1845, as America recovered from a general depression, more than five hundred citizens signed a petition for another mass meeting in Philadelphia to support what John Stevens had envisioned and advocated. Their movement would result in the creation of the private Pennsylvania Railroad Company in 1846 and the demise of the State Works in 1857.

Thomas Leiper's Railroad—The Nation's First?

In earlier local histories, authors sometimes proudly claimed for Pennsylvania the first real railroad built in America. They were not referring to the Philadelphia & Columbia Railroad, but to a small workaday line built in 1806 by Thomas Leiper outside of Philadelphia, south of the present town of Media, to carry stone from the Leiper Quarries on Crum Creek to a landing on Ridley Creek. This railroad had been designed by a civil engineer named John Thomson, who was coincidentally the father of J. Edgar Thomson, a man who became one of the most famous and influential presidents of the Pennsylvania Railroad Company.

Before Leiper had this railroad constructed, he had taken the precaution of constructing a test railroad about sixty feet long in a vacant yard near the Bull's Head Tavern in the Northern Liberties section of Philadelphia. Rails of oak were secured on stone blocks placed about eight feet apart. According to the history of Delaware County written by George Smith, published in 1862, many people gathered to witness the trial run of this contraption and placed wagers that no horse could pull a loaded carriage up a grade of one and a half inches to the yard. However, "the horse moved off with ease amid the plaudits of the assembled multitude," and railroading got its start in America.

The Belmont Plane

Early accounts of travel on the original railroad connecting Philadelphia and Columbia, built between 1828 and 1834, include descriptions of what was locally known as the Belmont Plane. This engineering feature employed a stationary steam engine that hoisted or lowered railroad cars on ropes up or down a steep hill. The Belmont Plane was a half mile long and had a 7 percent grade. In 1836, a locomotive called the George Washington amazed skeptics by proving it was powerful enough to haul a loaded train up this same hill.

The plane took its name from Belmont, the country estate of the late Judge Richard Peters, built by his father, William Peters, around 1746 on the west side of the Schuylkill River. In his history of Philadelphia, published in 1911, Ellis Paxson Oberholzer explains that this area was by that time losing its appeal for country estates because it was declining steadily into an industrial district.

The Belmont Plane was abandoned around 1850 due to its high cost of operation. The Pennsylvania Railroad replaced it by building a new railroad track from what is today Ardmore to the Schuylkill River just south of Market Street. The original Market Street Bridge was strengthened, and the system was connected to Philadelphia's existing street railroad.

According to the Burgess and Kennedy history of the Pennsylvania Railroad, the old line, complete with its Belmont Plane, was sold to the Philadelphia & Reading Railroad Company. The Belmont estate became part of Fairmount Park in 1869. The Peters mansion and the hill are still standing, but the Belmont Plane is long gone.

The Philadelphia, Germantown & Norristown Railroad

By the 1830s, Germantown, once the site of the country estates of wealthy Philadelphians, had become a peaceful village populated by merchants whose business took them regularly to Philadelphia. Edward H. Bonsall became the chief promoter for an independent railroad that would carry these early commuters between Philadelphia, Germantown, and eventually Norristown.

Chartered in 1831, the railroad began operations in 1832. In an article about opening day printed in the *U.S. Gazette,* reprinted in *Hazard's Register of Pennsylvania,* Bonsall reported that thousands flocked to the depot on Buttonwood Street in Penn Township to admire "the splendid cars, which were placed in file along the track." At 12:15, the cars began to move: "some slight difficulties were experienced, owing to the horses not being used to the employment."

By 1:00 in the afternoon, the cars reached Germantown. Speeches were made, and the passengers repaired to Mrs. Heft's tavern for a "sumptuous repast." At 3:30, the cars made their return trip.

On the following day, the railroad began its regular schedule of six round-trips daily at a cost of twenty-five cents each way. Germantown became the city's first true railroad commuter suburb.

A second article, published in *The Pennsylvanian* in 1835, told of the August opening of the line to Norristown. Two to three hundred passengers left Philadelphia and arrived in Norristown in less than an hour and fifteen minutes. There they celebrated with an outdoor dinner under a tent. At 4:00, the cars returned, while "thousands of cheerful faces smiled,

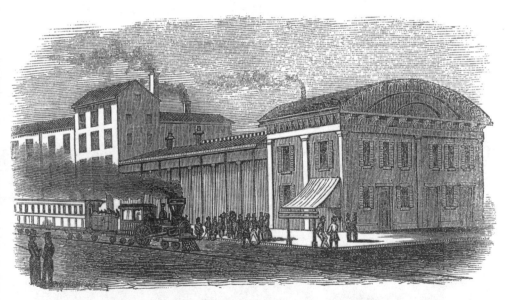

The depot for the Philadelphia, Germantown & Norristown Railroad as it appeared in an 1852 book titled *The Pictorial Sketch-book of Pennsylvania,* by Eli Bowen. Bowen acknowledged that railroads were actually creating suburbs with his observation: "[The railroad] has been the instrument of scattering along the route it traverses an active, intelligent, and enterprising population."

and hundreds of well turned ankles were moving in harmony to the band of music on the cars." The road from Manayunk to Norristown was no doubt the most scenic portion of the line, for it ran along the bank of the Schuylkill River. The article also described the gardens, mansions, and luxuriant grain fields the train passed.

The opening day voyage arrived back in Philadelphia at 6:00 that evening, and its participants offered the toast, "Success and prosperity to the president and managers of the Philadelphia & Norristown Railroad!"

The West Chester Railroad—The First Branch Railroad?

During the 1830s, while construction of the State Works was still under way, Dr. William Darlington, chairman of the West Chester Railroad Committee, wrote a member of the Pennsylvania state senate, proposing to build one of the nation's earliest branch railroads. Darlington noted, "The thriving condition of our Town, the fertility of the surrounding country, and the productive industry of the people, all induce us to believe that a branch railway to intersect the Pennsylvania road, will be of inestimable value to all concerned; and we have been highly gratified on finding that nature has not denied us a chance of participating in the advantages to result from the grand scheme of Internal Improvements."

It was a great day for West Chester when a branch railroad linked the rural town to Philadelphia. This photo of the railroad's trains appeared in *History of the Pennsylvania Railroad Company* by William Bender Wilson, published in 1899.

By 1832, nine miles of track had been constructed linking West Chester, the county seat of Chester County, to the Philadelphia & Columbia Railroad at a place that would one day be called Malvern, but then was simply known as "The Intersection." The first train to travel from Philadelphia arrived in West Chester on Christmas Day in 1833. Horses pulled the carriages until steam locomotives were introduced in 1845. As early as 1835, the company had its own passenger station and inn on Broad Street, below Race Street.

In order to make the commute between West Chester and Philadelphia even more convenient and perhaps to free the West Chester Railroad from dependence on another line, a company was formed in 1847 by professional men favoring a "direct railroad" from West Chester to Philadelphia via Media in Delaware County. The new railroad opened in 1858, and the old line became part of the Pennsylvania Railroad system.

The connection with Philadelphia, so astutely made by early boosters, meant that in the later part of the nineteenth century West Chester could and did promote itself as a residential alternative to Philadelphia Main Line communities like Haverford and Bryn Mawr.

The Baldwin Locomotive Works

By 1832, the Philadelphia, Germantown & Norristown Railroad thought it was time to retire the horses that pulled its cars and turn to high-tech steam locomotives. PG&N contacted Matthias William Baldwin, whose firm manufactured machinery, including stationary steam engines, and who had also constructed a working scale model of a steam locomotive for Franklin Peale, the manager of a Philadelphia museum. In Baldwin's shop in Lodge Alley, between Seventh and Eighth Streets, Old Ironsides was constructed, and a locomotive empire was born.

The vast operations of the Baldwin Locomotive Works in Philadelphia, depicted for *Philadelphia and Its Environs,* published in 1875.

By 1835, Baldwin was making enough locomotives to warrant a move to Broad and Hamilton Streets, where his firm stayed for nearly a century, occupying more than seven city blocks in a busy industrial district. The Philadelphia & Reading Railroad purchased Baldwin locomotives, and so did the Pennsylvania Railroad, whose president, J. Edgar Thomson, became a great friend of Matthias Baldwin.

In an article in the *Pennsylvania Magazine of History and Biography,* Malcolm C. Clark says, "Before his [Matthias Baldwin's] death in 1866, the railroads were to purchase 1,500 engines which bore his name. For his persistence and skills, Baldwin reaped a generous reward as the founder of Philadelphia's famous enterprise."

In 1906, Baldwin Locomotive Works opened a plant south of Philadelphia in Eddystone, and by 1928, all Baldwin operations were located there. As the age of railroads ended, Baldwin ceased production in 1956. The old Baldwin Locomotive Works office building remained; it now houses a major paper company that employs about nine hundred people. To accommodate their daily commute to Eddystone, the Southeastern Pennsylvania Transportation Authority (SEPTA) may reopen the old Baldwin railroad station.

The Penn Central Debacle

The end of World War II marked the beginning of steady and consistent losses in passenger service for American railroads. Automobiles and highway improvements gave travelers more flexibility. Airplanes made long-distance travel a lot faster. America's population began to gravitate away from the Northeast, which was generously supplied with railroads, to the Sunbelt. By the 1960s, most passenger railroads were losing money, and by 1967, even the U.S. post office had ceased to ship the nation's mail by train.

Railroad executives began to look for ways to offset their losses by the savings that could be effected through mergers. In the late 1950s, the Pennsylvania Railroad and the New York Central Railroad began to put in motion the machinery for these two old rivals to merge. Following approval by the Supreme Court, the two lines joined to become the Penn Central Railroad on February 1, 1968, in the largest railroad merger in the nation's history.

The railroads merged, but they never functioned as a single corporate entity. They continued to use separate signal and computer systems. The top managers never worked well together, and the workers continued to hold allegiance to, and follow the rules of, their former railroads. In 1969, Penn Central Railroad somewhat successfully introduced its profitable but technically troubled high-speed Metroliner, which covered the 226 miles between New York City and Washington, D.C., in less than three hours with well-appointed passenger cars, but most of the rest of the railroad's passenger trains continued to be old, filthy, and often late.

The losses of the Penn Central totaled $56.3 million in 1969 and another $62.7 million in the first quarter of 1970 alone. In their book, *The Wreck of the Penn Central*, Joseph R. Daughen and Peter Binzen wrote, "On June 21, 1970, with a sickening crash that frightened Wall Street, jarred both the United States economy and its government, and scared off foreign investors, the nation's largest railroad went broke." The book sums up the debacle: "The railroad went broke because of bad management, divided management, dishonest accounting, diversion of funds into unprofitable outside enterprises, nonfunctioning directors or a basic disinterest in running, or even an inability to run, a railroad. . . . In the end, possibly even in the beginning, there wasn't anything anybody could do about it."

Now that three decades have passed since its demise, the history of the failed and short-lived Penn Central Railroad is being preserved by the Penn Central Historical Society in Lock Haven.

Conrail

No one wanted to buy the bankrupt Penn Central, so in 1976, Congress stepped in to create the Consolidated Rail Corporation, or Conrail. Conrail was conceived as a private, for-profit freight railroad consisting of the remains of six railroads, most of which had played a part in Pennsylvania's railroad history. Besides the Penn Central, Conrail included the Central Railroad of New Jersey, the Lehigh Valley Railroad, the Reading Company, the Erie Lackawanna Railroad, and the Lehigh & Hudson River Railroad.

In 1980, as Conrail continued to lose money, Congress passed the Staggers Rail Act, which deregulated railroads to some degree, enabling them to behave in a more competitive fashion when it came to issues like abandonments and rate setting. Within two years, Conrail was making a small profit.

The Northeast Rail Service Act stipulated that Conrail be returned to the private sector when it was once again profitable, and by 1985, bids were coming in. Conrail was ultimately sold to the public in 1987 through what was at the time America's largest initial public stock offering.

Conrail made the news again a decade later, in 1997, when two other railroads, Norfolk Southern Corporation and CSX Corporation, filed a joint application to assume and split Conrail's routes and assets. With the approval of the Surface Transportation Board in 1998, Norfolk Southern Corporation acquired 58 percent of Conrail, with the other 42 percent going to CSX Corporation. Within three years, both railroads reported that they had solved logistical problems and integrated the segments into their systems.

All the mergers and changes occurring in the freight railroad industry in the two decades since the Staggers Rail Act was passed resulted in many abandonments of parallel lines or branches that incurred higher maintenance costs. While those routes may have been unprofitable to large railroads, they were often important to local commerce. A perhaps unintended consequence of late-twentieth-century rail legislation has been a new rise of regional railroads, born when local individuals or businesses with or without government support organize to operate such abandoned railroads.

Whither Amtrak?

In 1925, William Wallace Atterbury, then the new president of the Pennsylvania Railroad, was quoted in the company's house organ: "I have never believed that the public could run the railroad business. Indeed I have never believed that legislatures or railroad commissions could run the railroad business." In 1971, the government was prepared to try by creating the National Railroad Passenger Corporation, with a national intercity passenger service marketed under the name Amtrak. Existing railroads were able to pay the federal government to assume their passenger operations; the government ended up with more than twenty thousand miles of routes, most of them running over some other railroad's tracks.

By 2001, Amtrak was operating in forty-five states and serving more than twenty-three million passengers per year with 260 trains reaching 512 stations. Over the years, it had begun adding freight cars to some of its trains to increase revenues. Hopes have been high for the long-awaited Acela Express high-speed service Amtrak adopted in its Northeast corridor and promised for a number of other corridors, including the Keystone corridor, which runs between Philadelphia and Harrisburg.

However, Amtrak has never in its history come close to making a profit. In 2001, Amtrak was $3 billion in debt and had to seek permission from the secretary of transportation to apply for a $300 million mortgage on New York City's Pennsylvania Station to offset a shortfall in operating funds. In July 2002, it came within days of shutting down before another congressional agreement kept it rolling.

In a 1997 book titled *Derailed: What Went Wrong and What to Do About America's Passenger Trains,* Joseph Vranich, who had worked to create

Amtrak, called for its demise. In his opinion, its major problem is that it is "a government-created, government-protected, and government-guided legal monopoly" that is unprogressive, while at the same time remaining protected from competition. In 2001, Senator John McCain called for a national debate over what to do with Amtrak.

Just as the debate was getting started, the events of September 11, 2001, grounded the nation's airplanes for several days and imbued many Americans with a new fear of flying. Despite a general economic downturn, it appeared that Amtrak's ridership and revenues were significantly increased in the week following the terrorist attacks. High-profile commentators began calling for high-speed rail service to replace short intercity flights, and within a month, Amtrak asked for $3 billion in federal aid to improve and expand its services.

Congress bailed Amtrak out in 1997, but stipulated that Amtrak become self-sufficient by December 2002 or submit plans to restructure of liquidate itself. The Amtrak Reform Council, a federal panel, was created to monitor Amtrak's performance, and in early 2002 it voted to give private companies a chance to compete with Amtrak to operate America's passenger trains. By mid-year, the Bush administration published its own vision for American passenger rail service, which included opening intercity rail service to competition and divesting Amtrak of its infrastructure in the Northeast, making it strictly a train-operating company.

In Pennsylvania, a Transportation Advisory Committee has already been assessing passenger rail service needs, identifying routes between the Commonwealth's population centers, and looking into public-private partnerships.

It will take several years for the various scenarios to be proposed and examined. The future of passenger rail service will be one of the most interesting debates of the first decade of the twenty-first century.

Local Chapters of the National Railway Historical Society

In an article about the formation of the National Railway Historical Society printed in its journal, *National Railway Bulletin,* long-time Philadelphia-area railroad historian Francis G. Tatnall writes that in 1935, officers of the Lancaster Railway & Locomotive Historical Society and the Interstate Trolley Club of Trenton decided to consolidate their clubs and create a larger organization that could operate through local chapters to "preserve steam and electric railway historical material; to encourage the building of model railways; to secure data on the history of transportation; and to encourage rail transportation." It was one of a number of organizations created and initiatives undertaken to preserve and celebrate railroad heritage while the Depression was taking its toll on the industry.

Additional chapters were added in 1936 and through the course of the Second World War. By 2002, the National Railway Historical Society had nearly two hundred chapters worldwide and about seventeen thousand members. Today, its headquarters are located in the Robert Morris Building in Philadelphia at Seventeenth and Arch Streets, where members of the research staff are on hand one day per week to help patrons use its extensive library. Local chapters are frequently associated with individual preservation efforts, such as local rail museums or the operation of railroad equipment and rolling stock.

The Philadelphia Chapter hosts monthly dinner meetings with educational entertainment such as lectures and slide shows delivered by the chapter's members or invited guests. The chapter holds an annual auction of railroadiana and publishes a newsletter called *Cinders*. Since SEPTA operates in this region, the chapter occasionally organizes excursions over its rails.

The Delaware Valley Chapter plans regular trips, hosts regular meetings, and publishes a newsletter called *The Observation Car*. The Lehigh Valley Chapter publishes *Lehigh Lines,* hosts regular programs, and sponsors at least one field trip per year. The Hawk Mountain Chapter publishes *The Hostler*. Besides its regular meetings, it hosts an annual event called Picnicrail.

The Region's Railroad Giants

Herman Haupt (1817–1905)

Following his graduation from West Point in 1835, Herman Haupt spent very little time in the army, leading historians to speculate that he had ended up in a military academy at the urging of his widowed mother, not because he was interested in a military career. However, the engineering skills he acquired there launched his railroad career by gaining him employment with several smaller Pennsylvania railroads.

Haupt joined the Pennsylvania Railroad in 1847 as assistant to J. Edgar Thomson. He was promoted to general superintendent and then chief engineer, in which capacity he managed the completion of the Pennsy route over the Allegheny Mountains. A book he wrote, published in 1852, titled *The General Theory of Bridge Construction,* became a popular text for engineering schools. He left the Pennsy in 1856 and went to work on the Hoosac Tunnel in Massachusetts.

In 1862, he was invited to Washington, D.C., where he assumed the rank of colonel and designed and built the railways and bridges that the Union needed to win the Civil War. He was also responsible for moving troops and equipment efficiently by rail during the conflict.

Haupt continued his career in executive positions for a number of other American railroads.

J. Edgar Thomson (1808–1874)

J. Edgar Thomson learned the basics of surveying from his father, who got him a job making surveys for the original Philadelphia & Columbia Railroad. He moved on to work for railroads in New Jersey and Georgia before the Pennsylvania Railroad hired him as chief engineer.

Thomson began locating the Pennsy route between Harrisburg and Pittsburgh in 1847. Horseshoe Curve, a two-mile engineering feature that allowed locomotives to pull heavy loads up the Allegheny Ridge, was probably his crowning achievement. The curve remains in use today and is also one of the world's best-known railroading tourist attractions.

Thomson was elected president of the Pennsylvania Railroad in 1852, and under his leadership the Pennsy expanded, becoming the largest transportation company in the world. Early in the twentieth century, the empire whose blueprint he had drawn adopted the slogan, "Standard Railroad of the World." Thomson leased the Pittsburgh, Fort Wayne & Chicago Railway and purchased a system called the Panhandle lines, ensuring that Pennsy trains could run west from Pittsburgh to Chicago, Cincinnati, and St. Louis. He also leased the New Jersey railroads that took Pennsy trains to the Hudson River.

The terms of Thomson's will established a trust fund for the orphaned daughters of railroad men who had lost their lives while working for any railroad company, but particularly the Pennsylvania Railroad. In 1871, he purchased the lot adjoining his mansion in Philadelphia's Rittenhouse Square, planning to use it for a boarding school for these orphans. Thomson died before the structure was built, but his trustees saw to it that the institution, originally called St. John's Orphanage and later the J. Edgar Thomson School, opened in 1882 in several adjoining residences on Rittenhouse Street.

In a 1927 history of Rittenhouse Square, Charles Cohen recorded a personal conversation with the widowed Mrs. Thomson, who was one of the trustees: "I ventured to call her attention to the importance of the erection of homes for orphans in a rural district where plenty of air and ground could be obtained, and where the successful operation of an institution as contemplated could be assured. There is no certainty that the comment had any influence, but later the estate disposed of the lot and Mr. Samuel Price Wetherill has erected a beautiful dwelling thereon, an ornament to the neighborhood."

Thomson's orphans were moved to Kingsessing Avenue, and later the trustees decided that they would be better cared for not in an institution, but in the home of some surviving relation. The J. Edgar Thomson Foundation still exists, providing limited financial assistance to the female orphans of deceased fathers who had been in the employ of a U.S. railroad.

Thomas A. Scott (1823–1881)

Thomas A. Scott obtained his education on the job, clerking for several stores and other employers, including the toll collector on the turnpike between Philadelphia and Columbia. In 1850, he joined the Pennsylvania Railroad as its agent at Duncansville (near Hollidaysburg), where a new portion of railroad joined the Allegheny Portage Railroad. Here he supervised the transfer of freight between the two systems.

Within ten years, he was promoted to general superintendent and then vice president. A 1976 article for the *Pennsylvania Magazine of History and Biography* by James A. Ward describes the celebrated "symbiotic partnership" between Thomas A. Scott and J. Edgar Thomson during the Pennsy's greatest period of expansion. Scott is generally acknowledged to have balanced Thomson's technical know-how with a sense of daring, a charismatic personality, and a great deal of political savvy. The partnership lasted until a falling out that occurred around 1873, not long before Thomson's death.

When the Civil War started, Scott went to work for the governor of Pennsylvania, using the railroads to deliver equip-

Thomas A. Scott
LIBRARY OF CONGRESS

ment and state troops where they were needed. In 1861, he took control of the Union's railroads and telegraph lines and became assistant secretary of war.

Scott was elected president of the Pennsylvania Railroad in 1874 after Thomson died. He resigned in 1880 because of failing health.

Alexander J. Cassatt (1839–1906)

The son of a Pittsburgh banker, Alexander J. Cassatt moved with his family to Philadelphia and then Paris. After attending private schools abroad, he graduated from Rensselaer Polytechnic Institute in 1859 with a degree in civil engineering.

Cassatt joined the Pennsylvania Railroad in 1861 and worked his way up through a number of engineering jobs before being named superintendent of motive power in Altoona. He advocated a number of technological improvements, such as the use of standard designs for locomotives and the adoption of air brakes.

Cassatt resigned from the Pennsy in 1882, but remained active in the railroad industry, forming what was popularly known as the "Cassatt Line South," or the New York, Philadelphia & Norfolk Railroad. This daring business venture built a railroad straight down the length of the Delmarva Peninsula, where fast-moving barges took railroad cars across the choppy waters of the Chesapeake Bay to Norfolk and direct rail connections to the South. By 1885, this line was in full operation, making it possible to bring southern produce to northeastern markets more quickly and in fresher condition than ever before.

Cassatt devoted much of his retirement time to his Chester County farm, Chesterbrook, where he raised prize race horses and sheep, pigs, and cattle. He rode to hounds with the Radnor Hunt and was one of the nation's earliest collectors of impressionist paintings.

Alexander J. Cassatt returned to the Pennsylvania Railroad in 1899 as president. One of his first accomplishments was the standardization of freight shipping rates and the elimination of the secret rebates that had always been demanded by large shippers. Under his administration, the Pennsy spent millions to rebuild major components of the railroad.

The greatest monument to Cassatt's presidency should still be standing in New York City, but it has vanished. The magnificent Pennsylvania Station, with its pink granite walls and its main waiting room modeled after the Roman Baths of Caracalla—built by the influential architectural firm of McKim, Mead, and White—was demolished in 1964, just over a half century after it was erected. It was replaced by an underground facility that sits beneath Madison Square Garden.

Cassatt placed another feature on the Pennsy line between New York and Philadelphia, one still in use and familiar to millions of today's Amtrak riders: twin tunnels constructed beneath the Hudson River, which make it possible for passengers and their baggage to be carried directly into Manhattan without having to transfer to a ferry for a time-consuming and often tedious ride.

William Wallace Atterbury (1866–1935)

After graduating from Yale's Sheffield Scientific School in 1886, William Wallace Atterbury joined the engineering department of the Pennsylvania Railroad. He held various engineering positions and assisted in making standard locomotive designs a reality. Starting in 1902, he occupied a number of executive positions in the railroad's operations.

When Gen. John Pershing asked for America's best railroad man, Atterbury went to France in 1917 to take charge of the French railways needed to move American troops and supplies during the First World War. His service alerted him to the possibilities of commercial air travel and convinced him that the major railroads needed to become involved with this new opportunity.

The administration of William Wallace Atterbury as president of the Pennsylvania Railroad lasted from 1925 to 1935, a decade of boom and bust for the entire American economy and a period of general decline for the railroad industry. In their 1949 history of the PRR, George H. Burgess and Miles C. Kennedy wrote, "The railroads had passed through trying times before, but never had they been faced by the combination of circumstances which now confronted them, and it is to the great credit of the Pennsylvania's management under General Atterbury that the company was not only able to maintain its solvency and its credit, but to go forward with great improvements even when conditions were at their worst."

Some of those improvements included the electrification of the line between New York and Washington, D.C. Atterbury also carried out the construction of new passenger terminals in Philadelphia, including the city's Thirtieth Street Station.

Had he lived longer, Atterbury might have led the entire transportation industry in a bold new direction. The Pennsylvania Railroad invested in the development of a new company organized to provide coast-to-coast transportation in forty-eight hours or less using planes in the daytime and trains at night. In a 1929 article published in the PRR house organ, Atterbury was quoted as saying, "I have no fear whatever for the railroads. They will share in the increased prosperity which the development of air transport will bring."

Asa Packer (1805–1879)

In his own day, the founder of the Lehigh Valley Railroad was just as famous as Andrew Carnegie for personifying the nineteenth-century ideal of the self-made man. Packer moved from his native Connecticut to Pennsylvania, where he found work as a carpenter's apprentice, a canal boatman, and later a canal boat builder and merchant. In many published accounts of his career, various authors note that he made his original journey to Pennsylvania on foot with but a few coins in his purse and a knapsack on his back that contained all his worldly possessions.

By the 1840s, he was already a wealthy man and one of the original incorporators of the Delaware, Lehigh, Schuylkill & Susquehanna Railroad, the initial attempt to supersede the canal being protected and defended by the Lehigh Coal & Navigation Company. In 1851, Packer

Asa Packer
ASA PACKER MANSION

announced that he had purchased most of this railroad's outstanding stock, essentially gambling his entire personal fortune on this venture. He hired Robert H. Sayre as his chief engineer and saw to it that the enterprise, which he renamed the Lehigh Valley Railroad, was successfully constructed and operating profitably to transport anthracite coal to markets in New York and Philadelphia.

Although he served only briefly as president, Packer maintained a controlling stock interest in the Lehigh Valley Railroad throughout his life. In his history of this railroad, Robert Archer calls Packer the "undisputed ruler" of the Lehigh Valley Railroad during his lifetime.

At his death in 1879, Packer was Pennsylvania's richest man, with a personal fortune around $17 million. After the early deaths of Packer's two sons, his nephew Elisha P. Wilbur, who had initially been Packer's private secretary and chief accountant for the company, became president.

In his lifetime, Packer was also known as a generous philanthropist. Among the institutions that he founded and funded are Lehigh University (which he modestly declined to name Packer University) and St. Luke's Hospital. Both institutions are currently thriving in the area south of Bethlehem known as Fountain Hill.

Sampling the Region's Railroad History

The Pennsy in Downtown Philadelphia

Early railroad managers found it convenient to have their trains stop near existing inns and taverns, where passengers could gather and wait. Soon, railroads began building their own inns at regular stopping places, and eventually the concept of a railroad station emerged.

The Philadelphia & Columbia Railroad's first official station opened in 1850 and was located in Philadelphia at Eighth and Market Streets. The Pennsylvania Railroad opened its own downtown passenger and freight facilities and built a main depot at Thirtieth and Market Streets in 1864. Since America's centennial celebration in 1876 was expected to bring thousands of visitors to a huge world fair in west Philadelphia, the Pennsy opened a new passenger station at Thirty-second and Market Streets. This Moorish-style building contained a restaurant, saloons, offices, baggage rooms, and waiting rooms. It remained standing until 1896, when it burned down.

As the Pennsy grew in influence and economic importance, the railroad constructed its Broad Street Station in 1881, a Gothic Revival edifice that

A Pennsylvania Railroad station that is no longer part of the Philadelphia landscape: the freight terminal at Thirteenth and Market Streets that later became the site of John Wanamaker's flagship store, as it appeared in William Bender Wilson's *History of the Pennsylvania Railroad Company*.

**The old Broad Street Station from the *History of the Pennsylvania Railroad Company*
by William Bender Wilson.**

recalled a European cathedral in both style and scale. One of its less popular features was its "Chinese Wall," a viaduct of brick arches that carried trains into town above street level. The Chinese Wall also divided the city with an unattractive structure that impeded traffic and took up valuable downtown space. The station was expanded with an adjacent building in 1893, but was ruined in 1923 by a devastating fire that burned for two days despite the use of almost every piece of fire-fighting equipment in Philadelphia.

Since the Broad Street Station handled 530 trains and eight thousand passengers each day, the Pennsy needed a new station to replace it. The railroad planned its new "Suburban Station" to be located on a site just north and west of the old Broad Street Station. The commuter train lines to the suburbs, whose trains would dominate this terminal, had by that time been electrified. Thus, the incoming tracks could be built underground and the old Chinese Wall could be demolished, allowing the city's new "Parkway" to extend to city hall. Above the train station concourse there would be a building with office space that could be leased or occupied by Pennsy executives.

Construction began in 1927, and the building opened for service in September 1930. Underground tunnels linked it to the city's subway system, while pedestrian passages made it possible to walk underground between Eleventh and Eighteenth Streets.

Because construction had coincided with the onset of the Depression, not all the ambitious redevelopment plans were realized immediately. In their 1949 history of the Pennsylvania Railroad, Burgess and Kennedy stated, "The city's finances came to such a pass that it was unable to proceed with its portion of the work. The old Broad Street Station remains, and is still used for the New York–Philadelphia trains and certain others, and as a terminal for the Pennsylvania Greyhound Lines. The 'Chinese Wall' remains and the new boulevard has not been built, nor the Parkway extended." The Chinese Wall remained until 1953, when it finally succumbed to the project that created Penn Center Plaza, but retained the earlier Suburban Station complex.

When Suburban Station first opened, it was described as classic in design. Today, its gray limestone facade ornamented with black and red marble and bronze makes its exterior an excellent example of the Art Deco architectural style. Although the mezzanine has suffered from renovation efforts that have obliterated much of its Deco decor, fragments of former glory remain, like the metal grills around the ticket windows, some of the banisters and railings, the doors to the women's restroom, and a sign that reads "Men's Bootblack" at the entrance to an alcove where passengers can still get their shoes shined.

The year 2001 saw the beginning of a $30 million improvement project for Suburban Station that is scheduled to take several years. Among other changes, it will bring the station a convenient new entrance at Fifteenth and Market Streets.

Thirtieth Street Station

In their 1949 history of the Pennsylvania Railroad, Burgess and Kennedy wrote, "It was finally decided to locate the main passenger station on the west side of the Schuylkill, where it had been prior to 1881. At this location, the New York–Washington trains would pass directly through the station, and it would be possible, if found desirable, to bring in the New York–Western trains and turn them on a loop track, so that no back-up movements would be necessary."

In 1925, the PRR joined with the city of Philadelphia in what was called the Philadelphia Terminal Improvements Project to significantly change the city's transportation infrastructure and give Philadelphia two train stations. The second, which was at first called Pennsylvania Station, came to be known as Thirtieth Street Station, though its location in west

Philadelphia made it more suburban than the Pennsy's Suburban Station, which was in the heart of town.

Thirtieth Street Station was designed by the architectural firm Graham Anderson Probst and White after more than 130 plans were considered. It opened to the public in 1933 with the intention of being more than a train station: it was supposed to be a state-of-the-art transportation center with facilities for taxis and buses and a flat roof, where someday helicopters could land.

Thirtieth Street Station is one of the best places in the world to experience the excitement of arriving in or departing from a really magnificent place. Its coffered ceiling rises about a hundred feet above a marble floor, making the main concourse an elegant cavern, lined with gilded Corinthian columns, where passengers can hear the drumbeat of hurried footsteps and the booming reverberation of loudspeaker announcements.

The dimensions of the main concourse are dramatized by a towering sculpture by Walker Hancock, installed in 1952, that is popularly called the Railroad War Memorial. The figure of an angel with wings stretching skyward is holding a corpse, as if to lift a soul to heaven. Around its base in alphabetical order are the names of all the Pennsylvania Railroad employees who lost their lives in World War II.

Thirtieth Street Station harbors yet more works of art in what used to be the main waiting room behind what still functions as the ticket lobby. Here one wall is dominated by a bas-relief titled *The Spirit of Transportation*, by Karl Bitter. This sculpture depicts humanity on parade, contrasting older forms of transportation with the trains and riverboats of the nineteenth century. It also includes an innovation which may have seemed to be the wave of the future when this work of art was installed in Broad Street Station in 1895: A child leading the parade is holding what appears to be a zeppelin dangling a boxcar.

Elsewhere in the old waiting room are plaques commemorating the service of J. Edgar Thomson, William Wallace Atterbury, and George Gibbs, whose work led to the development of the Pennsy's distinctive class of streamlined electric locomotives called GG1s.

Since Thirtieth Street Station handles a passenger volume second only to Amtrak's Pennsylvania Station in New York, Amtrak recently spent millions restoring it. Its walls and ceilings were cleaned and repainted. New lighting features were carefully chosen to blend with the interior. A few moveable panels sometimes positioned in the old main waiting room provide information on the building's history and its restoration.

Two major universities nearby have lately done much to improve the area, and both Amtrak and Philadelphia hope for its continued development as "Center City West."

Reading Terminal and Its Market

After the Liberty Bell and Independence Hall, Philadelphia's most popular tourist destination is the Reading Terminal Market, which is visited by eighty thousand people every week. There they find merchants selling all kinds of food and cooking ingredients, from sushi and Peking duck to homemade shoofly pie. Sometimes visitors even pause to ponder the name of the place. What does the market have to do with the town of Reading, and why is it called a terminal market?

Back in 1889, officers of the Philadelphia & Reading Railroad decided to build a new train shed and office building in Philadelphia at Twelfth and Market Streets, to be named Reading Terminal. City residents loudly protested the loss of the markets that had long been operating in that very location, where they had regularly purchased their meat, dairy products, produce, and other foodstuffs. For the sake of good community relations, railroad executives announced that rather than displace the

Before the Philadelphia & Reading Railroad built its "new" terminal (which now houses the Reading Terminal Market downtown), the railroad was headquartered on Fourth Street below Walnut in this building depicted for *Philadelphia and Its Environs*.

The Philadelphia & Reading Railroad left room in its downtown terminal for the food markets that had long been operating at the site. Today the Reading Terminal Market is one of the city's most popular destinations.

markets, they would relocate them under the new train shed.

The new market opened in 1892. Its unique location was a lucky coincidence that made it the perfect place to receive and store food products and attract customers. The Reading Terminal Market became famous as the largest American food market under one roof, and in short order, it also became a Philadelphia tourist attraction, one that has outlived its sponsoring railroad.

By the 1970s, the market had suffered several years of neglect, while bankruptcy had overtaken the railroad that owned it. For a while, it was rumored that the market would be closed and the building sold. Once again, public outcry saved the market, and in the late 1990s, a massive renovation project was successfully carried out.

Today, scores of merchants do business in the Reading Terminal Market every Monday through Saturday, and the market can claim to be one of the best food markets in the nation. It draws visits from world-famous chefs and cookbook authors. Speakers and cooking demonstrations (not to mention first-rate food at great prices) keep the locals coming back.

The old train shed has been incorporated into the new Pennsylvania Convention Center. As for the adjacent pink granite Italianate head house of the Reading Terminal, opened in 1893, it is still standing and is now occupied by an avant-garde restaurant and a downtown hotel.

Rittenhouse Square—Home of the Pennsy's Presidents

Just a few blocks away from Suburban Station in Philadelphia, the neighborhood known as Rittenhouse Square remains as stylish as it was when several presidents of the Pennsylvania Railroad lived there. The square itself has not changed much, but the elegant homes they inhabited have been generally replaced by apartment houses and commercial buildings.

After the death of Alexander J. Cassatt's widow, Lois, the trustees of the Protestant Episcopal Church of the Diocese of Pennsylvania acquired the Cassatt town house at 202 South Nineteenth Street. The brick structure had a plain exterior, but it had been enhanced by the improvements that the luxury-loving Cassatt had lavished upon it. The property was replaced by an apartment building and given a new address: 1900 Rittenhouse Square.

It is likely that the residents of the apartment building at 1830 South Rittenhouse Square do not realize that their building occupies the footprint of Thomas A. Scott's home. Scott had acquired property where a stable once stood and built a four-story brick mansion that covered two city lots. He later purchased the corner property at 1830 South Rittenhouse Square and made his house even larger. After his death, Samuel Price Wetherill purchased the entire parcel and replaced Scott's residence with apartments.

J. Edgar Thomson's mansion at the northeast corner of Eighteenth and Spruce Streets was renovated after the death of his widow, but this elegant residence with classical colonnade and fenced lawn is now the site of a nondescript commercial building. The lot next door, which had been intended for an orphanage for the daughters of slain railroad workers, was disposed of by Thomson's widow and became the location of a residence constructed by Samuel Price Wetherill. One of the few individual mansions remaining in the vicinity of Rittenhouse Square, it now houses the Philadelphia Art Alliance.

The Philadelphia Main Line

Soon after the Pennsylvania Railroad had purchased the old State Works in 1857, the Pennsy began operating six passenger runs daily between Philadelphia and Paoli in cars that were heated with coal and illuminated with oil lamps. It might have seemed hardly worth the effort, since people who lived outside the city and commuted to Philadelphia generally chose to reside north of the city in villages like Germantown. In a history of Montgomery County published in 1859, William J. Buck noted that Athensville (now Ardmore) then had twenty-eight houses, while Humphreysville (now Bryn Mawr) had only twenty-one. Residences that could be classified as country estates were at that time clustered near the "City Line," where the train tracks crossed a creek, prompting the locals to refer to the place as "Overbrook."

But during the middle years of the nineteenth century, some Philadelphia residents were beginning to summer in suburban hotels like the

White Hall, which stood opposite the present location of the Bryn Mawr Hospital, or the Wildgoss Boarding House, near the Quaker institution known as Haverford College.

In his book, *The Old Main Line*, first published in 1919, J. W. Townsend explains that in the sixties the Pennsylvania Railroad, "wishing to eliminate a long detour past the old White Hall Hotel, found it necessary to make a deep cut through the high ground covering the proposed cut-off. This was considered to be injurious to the neighboring farms and heavy damages were claimed for the right of way, so it was found to be cheaper to buy a large farm with some adjoining tracts and utilize it for a real estate operation." The acquired land was divided into building lots. New train stations designed by architect Joseph Wilson were erected at Haverford, Athensville, and Humphreysville, and the latter two communities gradually came to be known by the classier Welsh-sounding names that the railroad had bestowed upon their train stations, Ardmore and Bryn Mawr.

The station at Bryn Mawr had a signal tower and elevated footbridge that allowed travelers to cross the tracks safely and watch for trains from a vantage point high above the hill that the trains climbed in their approach from Philadelphia. The name Bryn Mawr means "big hill" in Welsh, and the area was promoted for its cool and healthy "high" air.

Joseph Wilson was also the architect chosen to design the Bryn Mawr Hotel, constructed in 1871 at the intersection of what is now Montgomery and Morris Avenues. Townsend states that Pennsy officers were frequent

The passenger train station that the Pennsylvania Railroad named "Bryn Mawr," as depicted in *Philadelphia and Its Environs*.

visitors. So were the parents and the artist sister of Alexander J. Cassatt. The Bryn Mawr Hotel burned down during the winter of 1889–90, but it was replaced by a structure designed by the firm of architect Frank Furness. The new hotel sported the ornament associated with Furness's Romantic Revival neo-Gothic style, rather than the blockier appearance of the earlier stone structure, which had more or less resembled the Wilson train stations (the station at Haverford and the Bryn Mawr baggage station are still standing).

In his book, Townsend recalled, "The population of Bryn Mawr and its neighborhood soon began to grow by leaps and bounds. The hotel had made it socially popular and the railroad had added many more trains." Prominent Philadelphians purchased property, and lower Merion township boomed. George W. Childs, editor of the Philadelphia newspaper *Public Ledger,* built a home in the Bryn Mawr area, as did several executives from the Baldwin Locomotive Works and the Strawbridge and Clothier Department Store. Alexander J. Cassatt, then a vice president of the Pennsylvania Railroad, settled his family in Haverford.

Once the wealthy had established their residences, the hotels and boarding houses ceased to be so popular. Starting in 1896, the second Bryn Mawr Hotel leased off-season space to Florence Baldwin for her school students.

The first Bryn Mawr Hotel built by the Pennsylvania Railroad, as it appeared in *Philadelphia and Its Environs*. The hotel helped to give birth to the Philadelphia Main Line.

The second Bryn Mawr Hotel, designed by Frank Furness, now houses the Baldwin School.

She purchased the entire structure in 1922 and converted the Bryn Mawr Hotel into the present Baldwin School.

The Pennsylvania Railroad made a number of improvements to enhance the neighborhood, such as planting maple trees along the wide avenues. Alexander J. Cassatt got the legislature to enact a law permitting townships of a certain size to elect commissioners who could order the construction of amenities like sewers, sidewalks, and street lights. Cassatt also made it his business to see that local roads were improved.

In 1880, George W. Childs and Anthony Drexel planned a real estate development in a town west of Bryn Mawr called Louella, which they renamed Wayne. According to Townsend, when Childs was asked why

The station at Strafford on Philadelphia's Main Line has recently been restored as part of SEPTA's Historic Stations Rehabilitation Project.

the new development was so far away from the city, he replied that this would give commuters more time to read the *Public Ledger* on the train.

By the turn of the twentieth century, Pennsy commuter trains made all the same Main Line stops that SEPTA's R5 does today. Commuters on the Paoli Local waited in attractive brick, stone, or frame train stations. In Strafford, they boarded from a tiny building that had been originally constructed as an information booth for the Centennial Exposition of 1876 and, after the exhibition closed, was moved by the PRR first to Wayne, then to its present location in 1887. Many of the same stations are in use today. The Wayne Station Historic Preservation Association, a local preservation society, recently secured grants and donations to restore Wayne's Main Line station. The Overbrook, Strafford, and Radnor stations are part of SEPTA's Historic Stations Rehabilitation Project.

In his book, Townsend aptly described the suburb that the railroad had made: "Beyond Bryn Mawr, there follows a succession of small villages with country places interspersed and spreading out for two or three miles on each side of the railroad. Rosemont, Villa Nova, Radnor, Wayne, Devon and other well-known names, follow 30 miles out from the city, covering a beautiful rolling country with high hills and deep valleys, of which the city wealth has made a vast garden."

Christopher Morley Travels

Christopher Morley was a well-known author whose sketches for Philadelphia's *Public Ledger* were collected in a book titled *Travels in Philadelphia,* published circa 1920. In his sketch *The Paoli Local,* he wrote:

> One who was nourished along the line of the Paoli Local, who knew it long before it became electrified with those spider-leg trolleys on its roof and before the Wynnewood embankments were lined with neat little garages, sometimes has an inner pang that it is getting a bit too civilized. And yet no train will ever mean to us what that does! The saying that was good enough for Queen Mary and Mr. Browning is good enough for me. When I die, you will find the words PAOLI LOCAL indelibled on my heart. When the Corsican patriot's bicentennial comes along, in 1925, I hope there will be a grand reunion of all the old travelers along that line. The railroad will run specially decorated trains and distribute souvenirs among commuters of more than forty years' standing. The campus of Haverford College will be the scene of a mass-meeting. There will be reminiscent addresses by those who recall when the tracks ran along Railroad Avenue at Haverford and up through Preston. An express agent will be barbecued, and there will be dancing and song and passing of the mead cup until far into the night.

Chestnut Hill

The Philadelphia Main Line may have nationwide recognition, but through most of the late nineteenth and twentieth centuries, Chestnut Hill has actually been more exclusive. In a book titled *Philadelphia Gentlemen,* published in 1958, E. Digby Baltzell reported that a Chestnut Hill resident, after having dined on the Main Line, referred to the experience as "slumming."

David R. Contosta wrote a history of Chestnut Hill, *Suburb in the City.* He described how this farm village west of Germantown became such an elegant suburb, currently supplied with two railway lines that go to the same place and terminate within one block of one another (SEPTA's Chestnut Hill East Line and Chestnut Hill West Line).

In the early nineteenth century, the few residents of the Chestnut Hill village had to go to Germantown in order to find railroad transportation to the city. The village acquired its own rail service when the Chestnut Hill Railroad opened in July 1854. This line continued to operate as part of the Philadelphia & Reading Railroad system after being leased to it in 1870, and its presence encouraged the development of a neighborhood known as North Chestnut Hill (now Chestnut Hill East), where ample houses sprang up in the vicinity of Summit Street (which was also known for its healthful "high" air). Most of the houses, which were designed to resemble the dwellings of the Italian countryside, still stand as genteel scenery, inviting visitors to explore this quiet residential street. On nearby Gravers Lane, a railroad station built by Frank Furness is still standing.

The area originally known as Wissahickon Heights, later St. Martin's, and now Chestnut Hill West, was nurtured by the efforts of financier Henry H. Houston and his son-in-law George Woodward. Houston worked for the Pennsylvania Railroad from 1851 and served as a director from 1881 to 1895. He invested in land along the Wissahickon Creek, and in 1884, at his urging, the Pennsy opened a subsidiary line called the Philadelphia, Germantown & Chestnut Hill Railroad. Houston saw to it that Chestnut Hill, like Bryn Mawr, acquired an elegant resort hotel, built by the architectural firm of William D. Hewitt and George W. Hewitt, who had once been a partner of Frank Furness. It was called the Wissahickon Inn and is now part of Chestnut Hill Academy. Houston built his own mansion on a bluff overlooking Wissahickon Creek about three blocks from St. Martin's railroad station.

Port Richmond

The Philadelphia & Reading Railroad was responsible for the development of a different kind of suburb in that part of the city, which was officially created by the 1847 Act to Incorporate the District of Richmond in

The Philadelphia & Reading Railroad created a Philadelphia neighborhood when it opened its receiving and shipping terminal at Port Richmond. This drawing from *The Pictorial Sketch-book of Pennsylvania* shows the area circa 1852.

the County of Philadelphia. A few years earlier, the railroad had constructed its main coal terminal on the waterfront in this area, which took its name from Richmond Hall, the estate of its original settler, William Ball, a relation of George Washington.

At Port Richmond, workers guided the railroad's coal cars along tracks on piers extending out into the Delaware River, where their contents were loaded onto waiting ships. Over the years, more sophisticated mechanized car dumpers were installed, and the Port Richmond complex grew into one of the busiest commercial ports on the Atlantic Coast.

Since the laborers needed convenient dwellings, developers constructed blocks of cheap row houses in this area between the mid-nineteenth and mid-twentieth centuries. Originally an Irish working-class neighborhood, it acquired its share of Poles, Lithuanians, and Italians when the railroad began recruiting more recent immigrants to replace striking workers.

A railroad viaduct over Richmond Avenue just below Somerset Avenue, now overgrown with weeds and dwarfed by the elevated I-95 highway, once carried railroad cars to the piers. Easy public access to the old piers is now prohibited by chain-link fences, barriers across crumbling streets, and the private property signs of those who purchased the railroad's waterfront real estate. The adjacent old residential neighborhood of row houses and narrow streets, however, now often clogged with double-parked vehicles, remains neat and appealing. And thanks to the ethnic mix of its residents, it has interesting small ethnic businesses such as Czerw's, the self-proclaimed "manufacturers of the finest quality old-fashioned Polish kielbasa for over 65 years."

Bridge History on the Schuylkill

Pennsylvania's many rivers and streams meant that the Commonwealth would need a lot of bridges, regardless of the form of transportation its citizens preferred. The railroad industry challenged American bridge engineers with much heavier vehicles than had ever moved over bridges before, causing the science of bridge building to evolve hand in hand with the development of locomotives.

The earliest railroad bridges tended to be the same masonry arch bridges in use for centuries, which were sturdy, but costly and time-consuming to build. Nineteenth-century engineers experimented with other time-honored forms, like timber truss bridges (which were sometimes covered) and suspension bridges, but these turned out to be ill suited for railroads. Bridges built of metal trusses, first iron and later steel, were constructed by many railroads, the very first for the Philadelphia & Reading Railroad in 1845. The late nineteenth century saw a revival of

To most Philadelphians, the official "Falls Bridge" is another structure upstream, but this bridge constructed by the Philadelphia & Reading Railroad carried its trains over the water at the falls of the Schuylkill River.

the arched railroad viaduct, constructed of masonry, concrete, or a combination of both materials.

The stone arch Falls Bridge, built by the Philadelphia & Reading Railroad over the Schuylkill River in 1855, was meant to carry coal cars to Port Richmond. It is the third bridge at this location of the falls of the Schuylkill River, which was by then a thriving industrial community. The bridge crosses the river diagonally with its piers parallel to the flow of water.

The Pennsylvania Railroad gave the city something more dramatic: a reinforced concrete viaduct with dramatically tall arches that crosses over the Schuylkill River and the Schuylkill Expressway near Manayunk, completed in 1918. In recent years, it has been called the Pencoyd Viaduct, but most people know it simply as the Schuylkill River Railroad Bridge.

When the Schuylkill Expressway was built to fit beneath it, the gentle S-curve and the arches of this bridge became a familiar sight for millions of commuters. In 1981, the National Railway Historical Society's *National Railway Bulletin* carried an article by Malcolm L. Bruno and Patrick E. Purcell about the Pennsylvania Railroad's Schuylkill Division that mentioned the bridge "leaping over the Reading freight line, the four-lane Schuylkill Expressway, the Schuylkill River, various side streets of Manayunk and the Reading passenger line." SEPTA ran trains into Manayunk over this viaduct until 1990.

Marvels below Ground

By the 1860s, the need for longer, deeper railroad tunnels spurred the development of new tunneling equipment such as nitroglycerin, dynamite, and compressed-air drills. Two tunnels in the Philadelphia area were constructed using the more tedious, older method of drilling holes in solid rock with hammer and chisel, then blasting out a section with black powder and removing the debris with wagons and carts.

The Pennsylvania Railroad's "Arch Bridge" spans the Schuylkill River, the Schuylkill Expressway, and the old Schuylkill Canal in Manayunk.

The Black Rock Tunnel was built by the Philadelphia & Reading Railroad between 1835 and 1837. This view is from *Pictorial Sketch-book of Pennsylvania*.

The Philadelphia & Reading Railroad built the Black Rock Tunnel beneath Phoenixville between 1835 and 1837 under the supervision of W. Hasell Wilson. Over 1,900 feet long, it was the second railway tunnel to be built in the United States after a tunnel built in western Pennsylvania for the Allegheny Portage Railroad. Opened for service in 1838, it is the nation's oldest railroad tunnel still in use.

In 1835, *Hazard's Register of Pennsylvania* reprinted a private letter signed "W" (for Wilson the engineer?) that describes the route of the Philadelphia & Reading Railroad through Phoenixville while it was still under construction: "In traveling over the road when finished, the passengers will pass over the [Schuylkill] river at a considerable height–from off a stupendous stone bridge, and immediately enter an extensive tunnel. The top of the tunnel will be 122 feet below the surface of the ground, and the grade of the road 17 feet below, making it 139 feet from the grade of the road, to the surface of the ground."

In a travel book written in 1852, Eli Bowen refers to Black Rock Tunnel as "one of the heaviest sections of railroading ever executed in the United States." A history of southeastern Pennsylvania written in 1943 by J. Bennett Nolan refers to the costly nature of this engineering feature, speculating that "it was said this was done because numerous influential stockholders lived in that region and it was desired to gain the freight business of Phoenixville's iron industries."

Yet so historic a structure gets literally no tourists at all. The curving tracks hide the tunnel from view on the south side, while signs warn visitors from coming too close to the river at the point where they could see the portal on the north side. Rail fans are discouraged from walking along the tracks for safety reasons. However, Phoenixville is in the process of embracing its industrial past in order to become more of a tourist destination. Perhaps someday the sights will include a clear view of the venerable Black Rock Tunnel.

On the other hand, the Flat Rock Tunnel is seen by thousands every day; it is wedged beside the eastbound lanes of the Schuylkill Expressway precisely where commuter traffic is often slowed during the morning rush hour. Flat Rock was the original name for the area that became the industrial village of Manayunk. There is still a Flat Rock Dam in the Schuylkill and a Flat Rock Road in Manayunk. The Philadelphia & Reading Railroad began work on Flat Rock Tunnel in 1836, and the tunnel was open for service by 1840. It was less than half the length of Black Rock Tunnel, and it cost less to build.

Philadelphia's Commuter Rail Tunnel

On November 12, 1984, the Southeastern Pennsylvania Transportation Authority (SEPTA), which currently operates the region's commuter trains, finally accomplished what the Penn Central said could not be done and something that the Pennsylvania Railroad would never have done. SEPTA opened a commuter rail tunnel linking the downtown stations of the former Pennsy and Reading railroads.

SEPTA grew out of SEPACT I (Southeastern Pennsylvania Transportation Compact), a federally assisted commuter rail demonstration project formed in 1962 to prevent commuter rail service from literally being abandoned in the Philadelphia area. At that time, both the Pennsylvania Railroad Company and the Reading Company had been trying to offset increasing deficits by cutting commuter service and raising the fares. According to a 1969 report issued by SEPTA, SEPACT I was formed to "demonstrate the effectiveness of improved service and reduced fares" and to initiate more regional cooperation between the city and its suburbs.

SEPTA succeeded in keeping the trains running in Philadelphia, and so far the tunnel has been its crowning achievement. It took six years and $330 million to build the 1.7-mile tunnel that took historically separate rail systems and created "the first totally unified regional rail system in North America," according to SEPTA's train operations director, who was quoted in the *Philadelphia Inquirer* on its opening day. The tunnel meant that passengers could ride between any of SEPTA's 167 train stations. The tunnel also deposited passengers beneath an urban mall, which has subsequently sparked a great deal of development in that area of center city Philadelphia.

The completion of the tunnel also triumphed over more than a quarter century of carping and naysaying. Originally proposed during the 1950s, the tunnel concept first faced an incredulous "Who needs it?" attitude. In their book about the Penn Central, Daughen and Binzen quoted a Penn Central executive: "If you get the money and build the center city tunnel you're not going to have anything to operate on it. I said eighty percent or more of this equipment can't operate in that tunnel. Because it will have over a two percent grade and they won't go up the hill. Empty."

Luckily, the tunnel idea won a powerful champion in Philadelphia's colorful mayor Frank Rizzo, who made it a priority and got it under construction. Commuters traveling between Suburban Station and Market Street East now take one of the most useful additions to Philadelphia's modern railroad landscape for granted.

The New Hope & Ivyland Railroad

Despite the noisy traffic on nearby Street Road, the tiny Lahaska station on the New Hope & Ivyland Railroad (NH&I) retains the feel of a rural whistle-stop station, where passengers waited a century ago for the milk train to arrive. A suitably plaintive whistle can be heard while the train is still miles away. Then a cloud of steam precedes the 1925 Baldwin locomotive known as Old Number Forty as it rounds a distant curve and finally comes into view.

The NH&I got its start as the Northeast Pennsylvania Railroad. Its trains began running between New Hope and Philadelphia in 1891. Later incorporated into the Reading system, the NH&I became a classic milk route, providing freight and passenger service to the residents of a rural area, many of whom were dairy farmers.

The NH&I was saved from abandonment in the late 1960s by a group of Philadelphians who continued to provide freight and passenger service, but in 1970, it filed for reorganization under the Bankruptcy Act just two weeks before the Penn Central did. It shared the Penn Central's problems of high operating costs and low returns, but unlike the Penn Central, it was seeking to increase its passenger service and make the transition to a tourist railroad. An article in the July 25, 1970, issue of *Business Week* noted that traffic had increased 15 percent since the tourist runs had been started in 1966.

Today, most riders of this tourist railroad get on at the popular tourist destination of New Hope and simply make a trip to Lahaska and back, which takes about an hour, including the time required to switch Number Forty from one end of the train to the other. On the trip, families and rail fans will ride through the Aquetong Forest, where they'll see fewer glimpses of dairy farms than the country mansions of wealthy Bucks County residents. The NH&I also passes a number of sites that are not so much scenic as they are landmarks of film culture. The train crosses Pauline's Trestle, the spot where actress Pearl White, star of the silent series *The Perils of Pauline,* was tied by the villain to the railroad tracks to wriggle and writhe until she was rescued from an oncoming locomotive by her hero. The train also passes the sawmill where another movie finds Pauline strapped to a conveyor belt, but saved from a buzz saw in the nick of time.

In the height of the summer tourist season, the NH&I makes seven runs per day. It also features special entertainment trips, including a 1930s Bonnie and Clyde Train Robbery, its fall foliage tours, and a North Pole Express, as well as occasional breakfast, lunch, and dinner trains. An additional route from SEPTA's Warminster Station runs on weekends through the villages of Ivyland and Rushland to Wycombe.

The West Chester Railroad

In December 1996, SEPTA leased an unused portion of the former Pennsylvania Railroad branch to the borough of West Chester so that a new West Chester Railroad could begin to operate its tourist trains in the seven miles between the borough and an old station at Glen Mills. The newsletter of the Philadelphia Chapter of the National Railway Historical Society announced that this promising venture had purchased locomotives and passenger cars and had begun bringing the old tracks up to par for trains that would be operating at fifteen miles per hour.

The tourist trains would not be following the route of the original West Chester Railroad, which had connected to the State Works at Malvern, but rather the direct route that replaced it in 1858. The trains would be operated by 4 States Railway Service, Inc., a railroad management, maintenance, and operations company.

The new West Chester Railroad has regular fall foliage runs and other themed rides, including a Halloween Mystery Dinner, a Great Pumpkin Express, and a Great Train Robbery that takes passengers back to the

1920s. During the 2000 Republican National Convention, U.S. Senator Pete Domenici took the delegates from New Mexico on a scenic West Chester Railroad trip to the old Westtown train station.

West Chester Railroad trains generally travel between West Chester and Glen Mills, where they stop at a restored Victorian train station that is believed to have been designed by Frank Furness and now functions as a museum for a local historical society. The railroad plans to add additional stops at Westtown, Cheyney, and Locksley.

Railroad Hall at the Franklin Institute

When the Franklin Institute opened its new museum in 1934, one of its largest exhibits was the Baldwin steam locomotive called the Number 60,000, built in 1926 as an experimental model. After it was retired from testing on some of the nation's leading railroads, Samuel M. Vauclain, chairman of the board of the Baldwin Locomotive Works and a member of the institute's board of managers, offered it to the Franklin Institute. Matthias Baldwin, founder of the Baldwin Locomotive Works, had been an original member of the Franklin Institute.

Getting the locomotive into the museum was a monumental project that fascinated the citizens of Philadelphia in the autumn of 1933. While the museum was still under construction, an enormous hole was left in one of its walls. However, getting the Number 60,000 to the museum from the nearest set of railroad tracks, which were four blocks away at Twenty-fourth and Vine Streets, was still a problem. The John Eichleay Jr. Company was hired to move the locomotive.

To keep the streets of Philadelphia from collapsing under a locomotive that weighed 709,000 pounds, the movers distributed its weight by carpeting the street with planks over which temporary tracks were laid. Laura Lee, reporting for the *Evening Bulletin* newspaper September 22, 1933, wrote about the slow progress of the Number 60,000: "An ordinary size truck has been pulling it," she explained, continuing, "one day, on account of the truck strike, a horse was used, much to the amusement of the crowds of onlookers who have lined the streets ever since maneuvers began."

The Number 60,000 finally reached the hole in the museum's wall and rolled in. Miss Lee reported that its smokestack "just grazed through," to sighs of relief from the museum director and the movers.

In 1937, the Franklin Institute reported in its newsletter that "of the more than 4,000 action exhibits at the Museum of the Franklin Institute, the famous giant locomotive, is perhaps most representative of the spirit of the entire building." Visitors loved climbing into its cab and working the levers, which actually caused it to roll forward or backward a single rotation of its wheels. The Franklin Institute had pioneered the hands-on interactive science exhibit, and the largest object with which visitors interacted was definitely the Number 60,000.

The Baldwin Number 60,000 represented modern technology back in 1934 and it made an interesting contrast with another locomotive in the same exhibit hall, called the Rocket. The Rocket had been built in Britain for the Philadelphia & Reading Railroad. When it arrived in Philadelphia in 1838, it accidentally plunged into the Delaware River, where it remained until a crane capable of fishing it out could be found. Nevertheless, the Rocket served its railroad for forty-one years before being retired to a display area at the Reading Terminal.

The Franklin Institute has refurbished its Railroad Hall every decade or so, most recently in 2001, with a project that changed its name to the Train Factory. Curators were not able to move the enormous Baldwin Number 60,000, whose weight is supported by special scaffolding beneath the floor, so they chose to give back its historical perspective by building a circa 1926 locomotive erecting hall around it. Today's visitors enter the engine's darkened cab, where recorded voices and train noises suggest that it is on its trial run. Drama is added by another installation where visitors are invited to figure out why another experimental locomotive crashed when it was being similarly tested at the same factory. The Baldwin Number 60,000 begins to move, traveling the same few feet it has traveled for more than sixty years, but the new installation still gives this feat the same level of excitement it generated when the museum opened.

Fountain Hill—Lehigh Valley Railroad Country

"It's a thrill to live on the hill," proclaim the banners lining the main thoroughfare of the neighborhood known as Fountain Hill, stretching along the south bank of the Lehigh River below Bethlehem. In 1854, officers of the Lehigh Valley Railroad (LV) began buying land there for their mansions and their railroad's headquarters, and there they nurtured the institutions founded by Asa Packer and other local entrepreneurs, such as Lehigh University, St. Luke's Hospital, and the Episcopal Church of the Nativity.

A study of the Lehigh Valley written by M. S. Henry and published in 1860 described Bethlehem proper as historically the "principal settlement of the Moravians," an isolated and insular religious community nestled in a sylvan rural landscape. But Henry mentioned that below the river one could find "large manufacturing establishments," together with a "large number of dwellings erected for the accommodation of employees."

Robert H. Sayre, chief engineer for the Lehigh Valley Railroad, built this house, which now serves as a bed and breakfast, in the Fountain Hill section of Bethlehem.

One of those manufacturing establishments would have been a plant founded in 1857 to produce iron rails so that the Lehigh Valley Railroad would not have to import them from England. This enterprise grew to become Bethlehem Steel, which by the 1930s covered 720 acres with a complex of steel mills and coke plants surrounded by the modest dwellings of thousands of Irish, Welsh, and Eastern European steel workers.

Bethlehem Steel ceased metal production at its South Bethlehem headquarters in November 1995, but remained involved with the community in deciding what to do with what had become an ugly, sprawling brownfield. The result was a project called Bethlehem Works, intended to attract tourists and local residents to a "mixed-use development" that would include facilities for recreation and entertainment, retail stores, and restaurants.

The central component of the Bethlehem Works site will be a 300,000-square-foot National Museum of Industrial History, currently planned to open in 2004 or 2005, to be operated in affiliation with the Smithsonian Institution. Since the Bethlehem Steel site is so large, the new museum will be able to accommodate hundreds of Smithsonian artifacts, including the industrial machines that were on exhibition in the Smithsonian's Arts and Industries Building in Washington, D.C. It will certainly include America's railroad history. In 1999, Pennsylvania's governor presented $4.5 million for a preview center to showcase some key artifacts.

Other Lehigh Valley Railroad relics on Fountain Hill include the mansion built by Robert H. Sayre, Asa Packer's chief engineer, who later held a number of executive positions with both the Lehigh Valley Railroad and Bethlehem Steel. The mansion is a bed and breakfast that is a popular choice for wedding receptions. The old LV headquarters building now functions as an apartment complex called Brighton Court. Across the street, Elisha P. Wilbur's own mansion has been incorporated into a complex owned by the Free and Accepted Masons.

Asa Packer's will made provision that health care for the Lehigh Valley Railroad workers would be free at St. Luke's Hospital. Elisha P. Wilbur served on its board, and Robert H. Sayre became a major contributor. The institution has grown into St. Luke's Hospital and Health Network, with about twelve hundred physicians in five hospitals.

Both Sayre and Wilbur, together with the descendants of Asa Packer, contributed to Lehigh University, which Packer had founded, making it one of the best-endowed educational institutions in America for a time. The university is still known for producing excellent engineers and scientists, the sort of professionals that Asa Packer believed were critical to the development of the nation and its major industries.

The Region's Rail Trails

During the late nineteenth and early twentieth centuries, Pennsylvania began to experience a new trend: railroad abandonments. In northwest Pennsylvania, where petroleum had first been commercially drilled, railroads were abandoned as soon as better sources of oil were discovered in other states and foreign countries. Other railroads built to serve the logging industry were abandoned as Pennsylvania's northern forests were depleted. Even more railroads were abandoned in the years following World War II, as travelers and shippers increasingly turned to the highways and Americans began turning to fuel sources other than Pennsylvania's anthracite and bituminous coal.

Out of the Midwest, another region with a lot of abandoned railroads, came the notion of preserving railroad corridors while removing the tracks, so that the railroad beds could function as trails for walking, jogging, bicycling, or other recreational uses. The National Trails System Act of 1983 allowed these corridors to be "railbanked," or used as trails while they were also being preserved for possible reclamation for rail transportation at some future date. The Rails-to-Trails Conservancy was formed in 1986 to provide assistance for local rail-trail conversion efforts.

In 1990, Pennsylvania passed its own Rails-to-Trails Act to facilitate the conversion of abandoned railroads. Today, the Commonwealth's Rails-to-Trails program is funded through Pennsylvania's Department of Conservation and Natural Resources (DCNR) Keystone Recreation Park and Conservation Fund, as well as a recent environmental spending package called Growing Greener. Other funding comes from the Federal Transportation Equity Act and the Commonwealth's general fund.

Pennsylvania has become the nation's leader in rail trails, with 113 trails currently open. Between 1995 and 2000, the number of open rail-trail miles more than doubled, from 432 to 923. The DCNR maintains a website (www.dcnr.state.pa.us/rails/) with maps showing the locations of all the Commonwealth's rail trails, as well as information on their corresponding abandoned lines.

In Chester County, the Struble Trail begins just north of Downingtown. Its suburban location means that it gets a lot of use from families, particularly on weekends and holidays. It runs parallel to the east branch of the Brandywine, and for much of its open length, it is a shaded gravel lane, very easy to negotiate, offering glimpses of the river as well as access points where users or their canine companions can take a dip.

Like many of the Commonwealth's rail trails, the Struble Trail is considered a work in progress. When complete, it will extend sixteen miles through central Chester County, passing near Springton Manor, a quiet model farm preserved to educate the public about the county's agricultural past.

The Schuylkill River Trail currently stretches twenty-two miles from the Philadelphia Museum of Art to Valley Forge National Historical Park. Since the Schuylkill River Trail is so long, it is necessarily the project of many partnerships, including Montgomery County, the city of Philadelphia, and the various municipalities through which it passes. So far, it is popular with bike touring groups and organizations. In the future, the Schuylkill River Trail will be extended the entire length of the Schuylkill River, a distance of one hundred miles.

In 1991, representatives from Chester County, Montgomery County, and Pennsylvania's Department of Transportation conceived the Chester Valley Trail, which will extend from Downingtown, across Chester County, to the Montgomery County line, linking a number of local parks and trails. In 1997, the Chester County Parks and Recreation Department obtained rights for the development of an old Conrail line running roughly parallel to Route 30, or Lancaster Avenue. Construction began in 2002 and will be completed in phases.

The region's other rail trails include the Perkiomen Trail, the Towpath Bike Trail, the Northampton Bath Recreation Trail, the Forks Township Recreation Trail, the Bristol Spurline Trail, and the Plainfield Township Trail.

SECTION TWO

Hershey/Gettysburg/ Dutch Country

Great Railways of the Region

The Western Maryland

Although major Pennsylvania railroad systems would eventually serve this region's counties on both sides of the lower Susquehanna, its residents would remain equally familiar with and dependent upon the Western Maryland Railway (WM). The Western Maryland's tracks remained just below the Mason-Dixon Line through much of the nineteenth century, but the railroad eventually entered the Commonwealth, where for a time it served as an intermediate link in a multi-railroad route connecting New York, New England, and the Midwest.

The entity that would become the Western Maryland Railway was granted a charter by the Maryland General Assembly in 1852. Its objective was to compete for the trade of the Cumberland Valley with Pennsylvania's Cumberland Valley Railroad. Despite the publication of promotional materials proclaiming what an asset such a line could be, Harold A. Williams in his centennial history of the Western Maryland explained that financial difficulties impeded construction and delayed the railroad's formal opening until 1859.

Though it then ran only from the outskirts of Baltimore to Westminster, Maryland, the WM first became part of Pennsylvania's railroad history in 1863, when its trains moved troops and supplies toward Gettysburg (just nineteen miles from Westminster), and survivors, prisoners, and victims' bodies out of the area after the Civil War's most pivotal battle. In fact, the federal government actually took military possession of the Western Maryland for six days, making it part of the network of railroads that gave the Union a considerable advantage over the Confederacy. During that time, its cars moved neither passengers nor freight not in the service of the army. The government's takeover was actually very welcome because federal reimbursement for the railroad's services made up for poor sales of the railroad's stock and loss of business that had been caused by threats of Confederate raids ever since the war began.

The WM also transported a number of notable people associated with the Battle of Gettysburg, including the mortal remains of Maj. Gen. John F. Reynolds, who had been killed in action, and President Abraham Lincoln when he visited Gettysburg several months later. Lincoln actually traveled via three contemporary railroads to reach Gettysburg from Washington, including the Northern Central Railway, the Hanover Branch Rail Road, and the Gettysburg Railroad. The latter two lines were later incorporated into the Western Maryland system.

After the war, the Western Maryland continued the construction work that took its tracks steadily west. Its trains finally crossed into Pennsylvania when the railroad purchased land just north of the Mason-Dixon Line in order to follow the route that would best address the topographical challenge of the Blue Ridge Mountains. On this piece of real estate the Western Maryland built a park called Pen-Mar and its own railroad hotel, the Blue Mountain House, in 1883. Sometimes called the "Coney Island of the Mountains," the Pen-Mar amusement park successfully developed passenger and excursion business for the Western Maryland, which up to that time had carried mainly freight. Most of the guests hailed from Baltimore, not Pennsylvania. Well after the Blue Mountain House was destroyed by fire in 1913 and Pen-Mar closed in 1943, they were still reminiscing about the hotel's celebrated chicken dinners, the comfortable rocking chairs on its porch, and the fine buffet-parlor-observation cars that delivered them to the park.

WM saw further expansion around 1902 when George Jay Gould proposed that it become part of the transcontinental railroad empire that he was trying to create by stringing together existing railroads to link the Midwest with Baltimore and create a serious competitor to the Pennsy. Gould's efforts failed, and the Western Maryland went into receivership in 1908, but not before a number of important physical improvements had been made, including an extension to Cumberland, Maryland.

By 1912, the Western Maryland had extended its tracks to Connellsville, where the Pittsburgh & Lake Erie Railroad plus several other lines connected it to Pittsburgh and the Great Lakes. In 1915, the Western Maryland initiated luxury passenger service between Baltimore and Chicago through Pennsylvania.

Much of the Western Maryland's western main line paralleled a route of the Baltimore & Ohio (B&O) Railroad, and after the CSX Corporation acquired both lines, CSX chose to keep in operation the B&O line (which had fewer tunnels), abandoning much of the Western Maryland's route in 1975 and finally closing it in 1983. Today, western parts of the WM's route now accommodate the Western Maryland Scenic Railroad, a tourist line operating between Cumberland and Frostburg, Maryland. Other parts have been converted into bike trails. The Western Maryland Railway Historical Society was founded in 1967 to preserve the history and artifacts of this line in its museum in Union Bridge, Maryland.

Rail Stories of the Region

Philadelphia or Baltimore?

In a perfect Pennsylvania, the Susquehanna River that bisects the Commonwealth should have been a natural transportation route, but the Susquehanna flows rapidly over huge boulders and around tiny islands, with treacherous freshets in the spring and low water in the summer. Naming it the river that's "a mile wide and a foot deep," early settlers found much of the Susquehanna difficult to cross, challenging to navigate, and more of a hindrance than an aid to transportation. Those living in the valleys on its eastern shore generally sold their farm surpluses and purchased manufactured goods in Philadelphia. For those who settled towns west of the river, such as York, it was easier to travel south than east.

The Conewago Canal, constructed in 1797, represented one of the earliest attempts to link those living west of the Susquehanna with Philadelphia. It allowed canal boats, or "arks" as they were called, to avoid the treacherous Conewago Falls and arrive safely at Columbia, where goods could be sent to the city via turnpike.

William Penn was among the first to envision a canal link between the Susquehanna and Philadelphia via the Schuylkill River. Work began on what would become the Union Canal, linking Middletown on the Susquehanna with Reading on the Schuylkill, in the 1790s, but the canal was not completed until 1828, after the Commonwealth contributed financial aid. Although the Union Canal remained in operation until 1884, the locks on this early system had been designed too narrow for the passenger and freight vessels that would be widely used during the nineteenth century. The Chesapeake & Delaware (C&D) Canal, which was completed in 1829 and bisected the state of Delaware, was actually more successful in bringing trade from the lower Susquehanna Valley to Philadelphia via the Chesapeake Bay.

Entrepreneurs in the growing city of Baltimore attempted to maintain or increase their share of Susquehanna Valley trade with a canal the length of the lower Susquehanna that would connect with Havre de Grace, Maryland. Philadelphia politicians objected on the grounds that traffic on the expensive State Works system would be diverted to a "foreign" city. Only after the C&D opened did Philadelphians realize that the two canals would effectively form an all-water route between Columbia and Philadelphia. The Susquehanna & Tidewater Canal opened in 1840. It was later acquired by the Philadelphia & Reading Railroad, which continued to operate it until 1894.

As railroads gained favor over canals in public opinion, Maryland's legislature incorporated the Baltimore & Susquehanna Rail Road in 1828, another attempt to achieve the same result. Construction began in 1829, and by 1832, carriages were running between Baltimore and Owings Mills, Maryland, over what would eventually become part of the Western Maryland Railway.

Many residents of the lower Susquehanna Valley, particularly those on the western shore, were ready to welcome and assist this project. In 1831, a number of Adams County residents met at the county courthouse, where they resolved to petition the Commonwealth's legislature for a railroad running from Gettysburg to the Maryland state line, where it would intercept the Baltimore & Susquehanna. At around the same time, according to their report to the Pennsylvania legislature, residents of York, who also wanted to build tracks to the state line, encountered opposition from Philadelphians. At a meeting reported in the January 1832 issue of *Hazard's Register of Pennsylvania*, the Philadelphians contended that Maryland businessmen were really behind this project and insisted that "under no circumstances whatever, should it be authorized until the line of communication between the eastern and western parts

The scene at Columbia in 1842 as depicted in *History of the Pennsylvania Railroad Company*. The straight tracks at the left are those of the Philadelphia & Columbia Railroad, and the curved tracks belong to the Baltimore & Susquehanna Rail Road.

of the state [i.e., the State Works] had been completed and its practical effects have been fully developed."

Nevertheless, legislation was passed creating the York & Maryland Line Railroad, which in 1837 was granted the right to use the Wrightsville, York & Gettysburg Railroad to connect York with the Susquehanna River. By 1838, this second system was being operated in conjunction with the Baltimore & Susquehanna Rail Road. However, Baltimore's businessmen were no longer satisfied with the flour and other food products of the lower Susquehanna Valley, since the coal being mined a little farther north promised to be far more profitable. Little by little, the Baltimore & Susquehanna constructed its tracks up the Susquehanna Valley to Sunbury, but this effort overextended the railroad, parts of which were later absorbed by the Northern Central Railway and the Western Maryland Railway.

In the meantime, many little railroads that would eventually become absorbed in larger systems sprang up in this region to address the pressing concern of local residents that the railroad revolution would leave their towns behind.

A train passing through peaceful Lancaster County, from the *Pictorial Sketch-book of Pennsylvania*, published in 1852.

The Cumberland Valley Railroad

Residents of the Cumberland Valley wanted a railroad to transport to market the flour, iron, and whiskey produced in Cumberland, Franklin, and Perry Counties. In 1828, the state board of canal commissioners authorized a survey for a railroad connecting Chambersburg with the Susquehanna River as a component of the State Works. Engineer William R. Hopkins proposed a route from Harrisburg to Chambersburg, and the Cumberland Valley Railroad (CV) was chartered in 1831, its construction funded by local citizens and Philadelphia capitalists. The railroad opened in 1837, though a bridge spanning the Susquehanna was not completed until 1839.

In 1846, I. Daniel Rupp in his *History and Topography of Dauphin, Cumberland, Franklin, Bedford, Adams, and Perry Counties, Pennsylvania* listed the railroad under "Public Improvements," writing: "The Cumberland Valley Railroad passes through the center of a finely cultivated part of the country." He observed that the railroad extended for fifty-one miles west of Harrisburg, where it connected with the Franklin Railroad, providing a link with Hagerstown, Maryland. This second railroad had been organized about a year after the Cumberland Valley was incorporated, but problems accommodating steam locomotives made it less than successful until the Cumberland Valley took it over and made repairs in 1859, the same year the Cumberland Valley itself came under the control of the Pennsylvania Railroad. The CV was finally merged with the Pennsy in 1919.

The Harrisburg & Lancaster Railroad

The Portsmouth & Lancaster Rail-road was chartered in 1832 to link Portsmouth (now Middletown) to Lancaster, a city that was served by the Commonwealth's railroad. The original plan may have been to cross the river at Middletown and continue to Chambersburg, but both the railroad's charter and name were changed the following year to the Harrisburg, Portsmouth, Mountjoy & Lancaster Rail-road, indicating that this line was by then intended to join Harrisburg and Lancaster, two growing inland cities surrounded by prosperous farmland and with promising transportation connections of their own. Its original board included two prominent Lancaster citizens: future president of the United States James Buchanan and Simon Cameron, Abraham Lincoln's future secretary of war.

Despite all the streams and valleys that such a route necessarily had to traverse, this line was put into service in 1838 and connected with the Cumberland Valley Railroad in 1839. The railroad attracted many loyal customers, and according to the history of the Pennsy by George Burgess and Miles C. Kennedy, "By the time the Pennsylvania came to negotiate for operating rights, in 1848, the Harrisburg & Lancaster was able to dictate profitable terms."

The Reading & Columbia Railroad

The Reading & Columbia Railroad was the brainchild of Joseph Konigmacher, who owned the Ephrata Mountain Springs Hotel and wanted a railroad to bring visitors to his establishment and to develop communities in northern Lancaster County, such as Manheim and Lititz, perhaps even stretching into Berks County and Pennsylvania's coal regions. The Reading & Columbia Railroad was created in 1857 by a charter that also enabled it to purchase the bridge over the Susquehanna at Columbia. Construction began in 1861 despite the shortage of manpower and material caused by the Civil War.

The Reading & Columbia suddenly captured national attention the following year when the Confederacy's ironclad vessels first appeared. These shallow-draft, armored, steam-driven craft were designed for coastal waters where they could disrupt shipping for the Union, or even fire upon and destroy railroads located too close to the shoreline. Union military leaders thought the Reading & Columbia could form the nucleus of a route between New York and Washington located more securely inland.

After the Union was able to defend its coasts with its own ironclads, hopes for a government subsidy to complete the Reading & Columbia faded, and the line was prevented from acquiring the Columbia bridge, which had been burned by the citizens of Columbia to prevent Robert E. Lee's soldiers from entering Lancaster County. Nevertheless, trains began running between Columbia and Ephrata in June 1863, just a few days before the Battle of Gettysburg.

Perhaps the major stockholders feared that the Civil War would depress returns, for they offered their shares to the Philadelphia & Reading Railroad in 1864. The Reading & Columbia Railroad became its Reading & Columbia Division, which eventually included a number of other local lines in the Susquehanna Valley. The division was officially merged with the Reading system in 1945, and continued to serve industries located along its route.

Railroads and the Civil War

In a 1953 book titled *Victory Rode the Rails,* George Edgar Turner provided a comprehensive picture of the role played in the Civil War by railroads. "Great battles had been won or lost by virtue of rail transportation or the lack of it," Turner wrote. "The order of many campaigns had been determined by the courses followed by the railroads. Time and again major strategy had hinged on the question of available rail transportation."

Southern railroads had been constructed for the local convenience of sending cotton from farms to port cities, while in the North, competition for the trade of entire large regions had led to the development of trans-Allegheny railroads. Railroad expertise generally resided in the North in terms of men who knew how to build and repair locomotives and rolling stock. The Union's War Department was also able to call upon men with management experience on its larger rail systems, in particular Thomas A. Scott and Herman Haupt of the Pennsylvania Railroad.

The Historical Lincoln and Trains

Thomas A. Scott, president of the Pennsylvania Railroad, anxiously reconnected Harrisburg's telegraph lines and waited for an important message from Washington, D.C. It finally arrived in cipher: "Plums delivered nuts safely." Scott knew it meant that president-elect Abraham Lincoln had reached Washington secretly, foiling the assassins who were purportedly waiting for him in Baltimore.

What came to be known as the Baltimore Plot is one of three stories that tie Lincoln to this region of Pennsylvania and its trains. Always less familiar than Lincoln's train ride into Gettysburg to deliver the eponymous address, the Baltimore Plot is now fading from America's collective memory, but at the turn of the century it was covered in a number of Civil War histories. It was even part of the Pennsylvania public school curriculum, thanks to Martin G. Brumbaugh and Joseph Solomon Walton, who included it in their 1897 book, *Stories of Pennsylvania or School Readings from Pennsylvania History.*

Lincoln spent almost three weeks traveling by rail from his home in Springfield, Illinois, to his inauguration on a route that would take him through major cities in northern states. In Philadelphia, on February 21, 1861, Lincoln was warned that he had better not pass through Baltimore because rumors abounded that his enemies in that city had vowed he would never take office. In Baltimore, railroad cars were drawn slowly through the streets by horses, so the opportunity to board or sabotage a moving train was greatly increased. Lincoln, however, refused to change his plans, perhaps fearing that his reputation would be damaged if he sneaked into the nation's capital like a coward. He proceeded by train to Harrisburg, making remarks to supporters at all PRR stations along the way. He addressed the Commonwealth's House of Representatives when he reached Pennsylvania's capital.

Later that day, concerned friends, including Thomas A. Scott and Pennsylvania's governor Andrew G. Curtin, finally persuaded Lincoln to alter his route and his timing. Scott cleared the tracks for a special train from Harrisburg to Philadelphia. The engineer (who was later interviewed by Brumbaugh) recalled his sudden orders to take coach number 29 and a locomotive one mile east of the Harrisburg station, where Lincoln arrived alone. While the train sped back to Philadelphia, making no stops and taking on water in the most secluded places, Scott cut the telegraph wires connecting Harrisburg with other cities so that word about Lincoln's whereabouts would not leak out prematurely.

In Philadelphia, Lincoln simply caught a scheduled express train bound for Washington, which quietly passed through Baltimore overnight, and by morning, the president-elect was safely in the nation's capital. Mary Lincoln is said to have wept the entire night she spent alone in Harrisburg.

According to the centennial history of the Western Maryland Railway by Harold A. Williams, just as the train carrying President Lincoln to Gettysburg in 1863 was approaching Hanover Junction, Lincoln announced, "People will expect me to say something to them tomorrow, and I must

Lincoln funeral train. Lincoln's body was transported to his final resting place on a special funeral train. RAILROAD MUSEUM OF PENNSYLVANIA

give the matter some thought." Though Lincoln scholars tend to agree that the Gettysburg Address was written in Washington before Lincoln left, a legend has always persisted that Lincoln at least polished it on the train on the way to Gettysburg. If he did so between Hanover Junction and Gettysburg, then the Western Maryland Railway can claim the honor of being the scene of the final draft of the Gettysburg Address.

Lincoln and a number of dignitaries left Washington on November 18 by way of the Baltimore & Ohio Railroad on a special train decorated with flags and bunting. John W. Garrett, president of the B&O, greeted Lincoln and his entourage at Camden Station in Baltimore. Lincoln took the Northern Central Railway to Hanover Junction, and from there he reached Gettysburg via the Hanover Branch Rail Road and the Gettysburg Railroad, both of which later became parts of the Western Maryland Railway.

Lincoln entered Pennsylvania by rail one last time, in 1865, when his funeral train transported his remains back to Springfield, Illinois. After Lincoln had lain in state at the Capitol, his casket was transported for viewing in Harrisburg and then at Independence Hall in Philadelphia, the first leg on another lengthy rail journey, which ended at Oak Ridge Cemetery.

Local Chapters of the National Railway Historical Society

Besides the artifacts it maintains at the Harrisburg Transportation Center, the Harrisburg Chapter of the National Railway Historical Society publishes the *Harrisburg Rail Review.* Every March the chapter mounts the Harrisburg Railroad Show & Collectors Market with sales tables and operating layouts, as well as modeling workshops. It sponsors picnics, rail excursions, and educational entertainment at regular meetings.

In 2000, the Lancaster Chapter officially dedicated its new home, the Christiana Freight Station, originally a Pennsy freight station. Lancaster Chapter members brought the "J" tower to the Strasburg Rail Road, which they restored and sometimes open to the public for tours. They also restored the clock at the Lancaster train station. They own an FP7 diesel locomotive that once ran on the Reading system and sometimes operate it for excursions. They restored a GG1 called Old Rivets and donated it to the Railroad Museum of Pennsylvania in 2000. The chapter's publication is called the *Lancaster Dispatcher.* The chapter sponsors picnics, excursions, and other special events.

The Pottstown & Reading Chapter holds regular meetings with educational entertainment and organizes banquets for its members. Its publication is called the *Colebrookdale Local.*

The Cumberland Valley Chapter, which publishes the *Pioneer,* sponsors trips and rail excursions. Its members are repainting a caboose in Chambersburg and creating an oral history of railroading in the Chambersburg area, focusing on the Cumberland Valley Railroad.

The Region's Railroad Giants

John Mifflin Hood (1843–1906)

When he became president of the Western Maryland Railway in 1874, John Mifflin Hood presided over ninety miles of rusting single tracks stretching from the outskirts of Baltimore (not the city itself) to Williamsport on the Potomac. Hood served as president and general manager until 1902, and after twenty-eight years of buying and leasing other railroads and laying new track, he left the WM with 270 miles of new track that made it a vital link between Maryland's Baltimore & Ohio Railroad and the Reading system at Shippensburg, as well as the conduit for Cumberland coal to eastern Pennsylvania.

John Mifflin Hood was born in Maryland. He was working as a railroad engineer at the age of sixteen. After several months' employment as an engineer in Brazil, he returned to Baltimore in 1862. Because Maryland did not secede, Hood had to cross Union lines to offer his services to the Confederacy. He fought at Gettysburg and was a lieutenant in the Second Regiment of Engineers of the Confederacy at the time of the surrender at Appomattox.

Strong Southern sympathies on the part of many Marylanders meant that Hood's association with the Confederate army did not prevent him from finding positions with a number of Maryland railroads after the war. He gained considerable experience in central Maryland and the lower Susquehanna Valley with the Port Deposit branch of the Philadelphia & Baltimore Railroad and the Cecil County line of the Philadelphia & Baltimore Central Railroad.

His development and improvement of the Western Maryland Railway was his crowning achievement. Besides expanding the line, he also ensured that it actually entered the city of Baltimore. In 1876, the Hillen Station was opened as the Western Maryland Railway's Baltimore terminal and company headquarters.

His association with the WM ended only when the city of Baltimore sold its interest in the railway to the Fuller Syndicate, which was associated with the Gould family. Hood then became president of the United Railways & Electric Co. of Baltimore. In 1911, after his death, the grateful citizens of Baltimore erected a statue to honor his memory.

Sampling the Region's Railroad History

The Strasburg Rail Road

Even on a chilly, drizzling day in March, hordes of passengers are clustered around the Strasburg Rail Road Station buying tickets for a ride on what a sign calls "The Strasburg Rail Road to Paradise." The steam locomotive pulls slowly and majestically up to the station, and while it is switched from one end of the train to the other, parents guide their children into the restored cars, where anthracite coal is pleasantly sizzling in potbellied stoves.

The train travels through the heart of Pennsylvania Dutch Country, past unelectrified brick and stone farmhouses and dirt and gravel roads, through a landscape that hasn't changed much since a railroad was first

Steam power at the Strasburg Railroad in scenic Pennsylvania Dutch Country. SCHEFFEY ADVERTISING INC.

constructed through these fields in the nineteenth century. The conductor speaks mainly about Amish life while the train passes plainly attired farmers who are so accustomed to the hourly trips of the belching locomotive that they barely look up from the work of plowing fields with genuine horsepower.

The train proceeds only about four miles to the town of Paradise, where it halts behind a lumberyard while the locomotive is switched again. Here the tracks of the Strasburg Rail Road join the route originally established by the Philadelphia & Columbia Railroad, and passengers can sometimes spot an Amtrak train on its way to Philadelphia or Harrisburg.

As a tourist line, the Strasburg Rail Road has played a major role in the more recent development of Strasburg, but this town was important in Pennsylvania's transportation history before railroads existed. Strasburg is located on a plateau on an old colonial road linking Philadelphia with the Susquehanna River. Since it is roughly midway between these points, it became a town of inns and taverns during the eighteenth century, when this trip generally took two days. Some of the structures that once served drovers and travelers have been carefully restored and are identified with plaques.

Strasburg sensed disaster when the Philadelphia & Columbia Railroad proposed a route that would miss the town by about four miles. Concerned citizens and their state representative petitioned the Pennsylvania House of Representatives in 1831 for authority to construct a railroad that would intersect the Philadelphia & Columbia Railroad at Leaman Place (then the site of a hotel; also spelled Leman or Lemon).

In a history of the Strasburg Rail Road published in the *Journal of the Lancaster County Historical Society,* Lester James Kiscaden speculated that the railroad was not completed immediately after its charter was granted in 1835, although its roadbed might have been graded around that time. In Kiscaden's opinion, the panic of 1837 impeded construction until a second Strasburg Rail Road was incorporated in 1851.

Trains actually ran on the Strasburg Rail Road during the 1850s, but the railroad never made much money, so it was sold at auction in 1861. A number of other owners operated the railroad until the middle of the twentieth century, mainly hauling freight. A trolley linking Strasburg with Lancaster drew its passenger business, while the speed of the trains operating on the Pennsy's main line eliminated the need for travelers to ever experience Strasburg.

In 1957, after a series of storms severely damaged the line, its owners petitioned for abandonment. Henry K. Long, a Lancaster industrialist, saved the railroad by organizing fellow rail fans to purchase and restore it.

After going to considerable trouble to locate and clear tracks that had been buried in mud, the new owners put the Strasburg Rail Road back into passenger business in 1959 with a locomotive and a Reading passenger car. Business soared after 1960, when the owners purchased a steam locomotive.

The Strasburg Rail Road now has a fleet of steam locomotives and many restored passenger cars that enable it to operate year-round. The railroad even conducts business on the side with film and television producers looking for an old-fashioned steam train that operates in a place unspoiled by modern highways or architecture.

Few visitors to Strasburg realize that the structures and vehicles that make up the modern Strasburg Rail Road are a conglomeration of artifacts from other railroads and sites that may be nothing like those that were operating in Strasburg during the nineteenth century. The Strasburg railroad station was originally built in East Petersburg in 1882 for the Philadelphia & Reading Railroad. The "J" switch tower west of the station was built in 1885 by the Cumberland Valley Railroad and preserved by the Lancaster Chapter of the National Railway Historical Society. The railroad's parlor car, the Marian, was rebuilt in 1988 from an open platform coach. And standing majestically alongside the operating cars is a business observation car built for the Philadelphia & Reading Railroad in 1916, with its staterooms, dining room, kitchen, and observation room open to visitors.

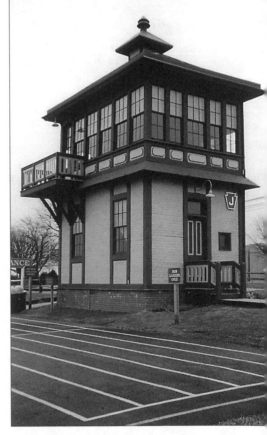

The success of the modern tourist Strasburg Rail Road quickly brought other rail-themed attractions to the area, making Strasburg a late-twentieth-century mecca for rail fans and a welcome change for visitors to Amish country.

The Lancaster Chapter of the National Railway Historical Society preserved this tower built in 1885 and relocated it in Strasburg.

Railroad Museum of Pennsylvania and Other Attractions

In the mid-1960s, shortly after the Strasburg Rail Road acquired its first steam engine, the Commonwealth was searching for a location for a new railroad museum that would be close to an operating railroad. There were popular railroad museums in Europe, and Pennsylvania was at that time celebrating its industrial heritage with museums dedicated to the history of lumbering, coal mining, and agriculture. Altoona wanted the museum, and Williamsport, Honesdale, and Mount Union had also been considered, but the Pennsylvania Historical and Museum Commission decided on Strasburg, probably because the town was easily accessible from major cities and already a tourist destination, partially due to the success of the Strasburg Rail Road.

The collection at the Railroad Museum of Pennsylvania grew from an exhibition organized by the Pennsylvania Railroad at the New York World's Fair in 1939–40. When the fair was over, the artifacts eventually made their way to a PRR engine house in Northumberland that was becoming an informal repository of historic trains.

Before the rolling stock could be moved to Strasburg, the little town needed a proper place to display it. Pennsylvania Historical and Museum Commission administrators studied other railroad museums and finally approved plans for the first building in North America designed specifically as a railroad museum, which would interpret not only the history of the Pennsy, but also the history of all railroads in Pennsylvania. Ground was broken in 1972, and the museum opened in 1975, attracting more than 300,000 visitors in its first year of operation.

Although Pennsy equipment tends to dominate the vast main hall of this museum, there are also artifacts from other lines that operated in Pennsylvania, including the Western Maryland Railway, the Lehigh Valley Railroad, the Delaware & Hudson Railroad, the Philadelphia & Reading Railroad, and the Cumberland Valley Railroad. The large array of locomotives interests rail connoisseurs, but everyone enjoys peering into the windows of the cars that offer a glimpse into railroad social life, such as the business car built for Carl Gray, president of the Western Maryland, with its elegant dining and observation area. The Lotos Club Pullman car, named after a club in New York, is equally luxurious. An old Pennsy passenger coach brings back memories of scratchy plush seats and "guillotine" windows that were part of a ride on the Paoli Local well into the 1970s.

The Railroad Museum of Pennsylvania also contains artifacts other than trains. The statue of Alexander Cassatt salvaged from the Pennsyl-

George M. Hart Locomotive and Rolling Stock Hall in the Railroad Museum of Pennsylvania. DAVID DUNN

vania Station in New York is one of the first exhibits that visitors see when they enter the museum's main hall, while a collection of Grif Teller oil paintings and other works of art has been installed in the second-floor gallery.

Since it would be difficult to offer much in the way of railroad education in the drafty and echoing main hall, docents provide a personal touch at the museum's Railway Education Center, where they use models to illustrate railroad technology. One working model of an early steam engine actually runs on the steam produced when paraffin is burned as fuel in its tiny engine.

Fans of model railroads can also visit Strasburg's Choo Choo Barn, which is located in a strip mall with a railroad theme. The Choo Choo Barn has seventeen hundred square feet of model buildings and figurines depicting daily life in the surrounding Amish country, including an Amish barn raising and the Memorial Day Parade in Strasburg. This layout grew out of one originally housed in the basement of founder George Groff, who transformed it into a business in 1961 (around the time the Strasburg Rail Road started using steam). Since 1979, Groff's son and daughter-in-law have been running the family business.

Model railroad enthusiasts can visit the National Toy Train Museum, which is housed in a building designed like a railway depot. This site also serves as the headquarters for the Train Collectors Association, which was founded in 1954 and specializes in the history of tinplate toy trains.

Model Railroading Elsewhere in Dutch Country

Toy makers marketed the first toy trains at about the same time that real railroads were transforming the world of the nineteenth century. German manufacturers made tin trains for wealthy customers and lead or wood toy trains for everyone else. British makers constructed tiny brass locomotives that were propelled by the steam created by burning fuel and left a trail of water behind on the floor or carpet.

During the late nineteenth century, manufacturers expanded their offerings from toy trains to model railroad systems consisting of different types of cars, railroad buildings, tracks that could be configured in a variety of ways, and figures to represent passengers and railroad personnel. Consumers could purchase the basic components and then spend a lifetime and small fortune endlessly expanding their systems.

By the turn of the century, Americans were operating their model railroads with electric power, rather than having their cars hauled by steam or clockwork locomotives. In 1902, Joshua Lionel Cowen published the first catalog for the Lionel Company, which he founded in New York. As the twentieth century progressed, it became the trend for the auxiliary pieces of the display to be powered to "do" something: Lights would flash on and off, doors would open and close, or figures would perform some task, such as loading coal, that happened on or around a real railroad.

During the 1930s, when railroads began to experience financial difficulties, model railroading may have been one more way for Americans to preserve their railroad heritage. Hobbyists formed organizations like the National Model Railroad Association to promote their hobby and began publishing information. Today, there are local clubs throughout Pennsylvania whose members may maintain a layout that they exhibit at shows or conventions. Museums and other institutions also acquire layouts, which sometimes are set up for viewing only on holidays or special occasions. This book limits coverage of Pennsylvania's model railroad sites to those that are unique and outstanding, as well as open to the public on a regular basis.

In the 1930s, a group of model railroaders began building locomotives and cars from kits that they set up in the basement of a men's store on Reading's Penn Street. They subsequently moved to a warehouse and then to a basement and garage. At Christmastime, they organized special

The steam engine for the Laurel Run Railroad.

displays at a volunteer fire company. By 1945, they had fifteen locomotives, sixty freight cars, and twenty-five passenger cars that drew hundreds of visitors each month. They incorporated in 1948 as the Reading Society of Model Engineers, and today they host several open houses each year, inviting the public to tour their property outside Reading on the appropriately named Ironhorse Lane.

The Reading Society of Model Engineers owns an entire building filled with model railroad layouts, but their most fascinating models operate on the grounds outside. The Laurel Run Railroad is a miniature railroad, or cross between a model railroad and a tourist line. Its rails are fifteen inches apart, and its locomotives and other cars are proportionately sized. Passengers sit on seats mounted on, not in, its miniature boxcars, and on any given ride, most of the passengers are not children.

Society members laid the tracks that run through a pleasant copse and over a miniature trestle bridge spanning a brook. They also built or adapted the rolling stock, which includes a steam engine and a replica of a Reading Company diesel engine that runs on a car motor fueled by gasoline. They may have taken their name Laurel Run from Franklin B. Gowen's Laurel Run Improvement Company (whose name was later changed to the Philadelphia & Reading Coal & Iron Company), which he employed to get the Philadelphia & Reading Railroad into the coal-mining business.

The Reading Society of Model Engineers also operates what members call their light rail division. The light rail engineers are building a 7 1/4-inch gauge railroad, as well as a 4 3/4-inch gauge railroad. One of the Laurel Run's other engineers explained, "The difference between them and us is that they can take their stuff home with them."

The model engineers did move the Laurel Run trains once, however, when they transported both cars and tracks into the city of Reading for the grand opening of the Reading Station Outlet Center.

An early member of the Reading Society of Model Engineers, Laurence Gieringer held a deep interest in model railroading, inspired by the scenery he witnessed during childhood rambles with his brother in and around the city of Reading. The two started building models at a small workbench in their cellar. After many years of working together, Paul Gieringer became a priest but encouraged Laurence to continue with his hobby.

At Christmastime in 1935, the *Reading Eagle* reported on the miniatures that Gieringer set up for the enjoyment of his own children. Gieringer began using a local fire company to house the display, and by 1938, Gieringer's miniatures were being featured in magazines and newsreels, where they were called the World's Largest Miniature Village. After a brief stay near Hamburg, the village was relocated to its current home in Shartlesville and officially named Roadside America.

Even smaller, but still rideable. Engineers demonstrate the "light rail" equipment at the Laurel Run Railroad.

A vintage postcard image shows Roadside America's creator, Laurence Gieringer, at work in the western village. ROADSIDE AMERICA, INC.

Signs proclaiming "You have to see it!" guide visitors to Roadside America, where models recreate scenes of American life from the eighteenth to twentieth centuries. A constant hum of moving model trains permeates the building, but the trains are almost incidental to the landscaping and the tiny buildings and figures, some of which can be manually operated by buttons on a partition that separates tourists from the layout. Roadside America has rivers, canals, and even a waterfall cascading from a mountain that rises up the side of one wall. Cable cars climb to the summit of this peak, where tiny skiers and skaters are perpetually enjoying winter weather.

From time to time a loudspeaker announcement advises guests to proceed to the rear of the exhibit to observe the "night scene." The ceiling lights dim while lights inside the model buildings glow brighter. On the opposite wall, the sun sets behind the Statue of Liberty, whose crown and torch light up while a spotlight illuminates an American flag and visitors hear the voice of Kate Smith singing "God Bless America." At the end of this intensely patriotic production, which no longer seems so corny after September 11, 2001, the red light of dawn heralds a new day for the enduring little citizens of Roadside America, who have remained in place since their creator's death in 1963.

Railroad Artifacts of Lancaster

The very first train to run from Columbia to Philadelphia on the old
State Works came through the city of Lancaster, which in the early nineteenth century was Pennsylvania's largest inland city, located in one of
the Commonwealth's most fertile belts of agricultural land. Imagine the
furor of Lancaster's citizens when the original route for this line was
intended to bypass Lancaster. It's possible that plans were abruptly
changed not only due to local outcry, but also because, in 1828, organiz-
ers of the Baltimore & Susquehanna Rail Road, then in the planning
stages, were considering York Haven as a destination, which threatened
to pull Lancaster into Baltimore's economic sphere.

By 1830, the *Lancaster Journal* was reporting on the remarkable railroad bridge being built over the Big Conestoga Creek, whose sixty-foot
piers were purported to be the highest in the world constructed of rubble
masonry. A second bridge, spanning the Little Conestoga, rose about
forty feet above the water and stretched one thousand feet in length. The
newspaper article noted "these bridges are becoming objects of great
curiosity and are now much visited."

About this time, the Pennsylvania Railroad was helping Lancaster
become an industrial city, as well as an agricultural entrepôt. John Brandt
Sr. operated the Lancaster Locomotive Works from 1853 to 1857, when
the facilities were acquired by James A. Norris and later his brother

In his 1899 *History of the Pennsylvania Railroad Company*, William Bender Wilson
included a drawing of Lancaster, circa 1842, with a train moving through town on
what would then have been the Philadelphia & Columbia Railroad.

Also serving as headquarters for the local chamber of commerce, Manheim's train station houses a small transportation museum.

Edward, who operated the Lancaster Locomotive and Machine Works from 1863 to 1868 in buildings located along East Fulton Street between North Ann and North Plum Streets, adjacent to the Pennsy's tracks. Here they made locomotives for a number of American railroads, including the Reading & Columbia Railroad. Some of the old buildings remain and have been incorporated into a complex of industrial buildings that can still be found near the Amtrak station in Lancaster.

Lancaster will lose another artifact of its railroad heritage when its old stockyard, also located near the Amtrak station, is torn down. The Lancaster Union Stockyard opened in 1895 on what was then the edge of town, a more formal successor to the animal pens that had long been springing up along the railroad tracks. By 1925, it had become the largest stockyard on the East Coast, where hundreds of thousands of animals were sold each year. Railroad officials operated the stockyard until 1972, when it was purchased by businessmen who formed Lancaster Stockyards Incorporated.

In today's high-tech world, farmers no longer have to physically transport livestock to stockyards for sale. The empty, collapsing pens and stalls are beginning to attract litter, despite signs warning against trespassers, while they await rezoning and development geared to revitalize the rail station neighborhood.

Outside Lancaster, the Manheim Historical Society interprets the history of trolleys and trains in the town's restored train station. Manheim was a stop on the old Reading & Columbia Railroad, and this particular station, completed in 1881, is thought to have been designed by Frank Furness at a time when the line had become part of the Reading system. Passenger service to Manheim ceased in 1950, and the station was abandoned in 1976. The society and concerned citizens acquired it and restored it with the help of grants and private donations. The society also owns a caboose, two boxcars, and an engine and houses an operable 1930s trolley car—part of the Railroad Museum of Pennsylvania collection.

The Railroad House of Marietta

There seems to be a trend in modern America to adapt old railroad stations for reuse as restaurants. They are well suited for the job because their dominant architectural feature, a passenger waiting room, tends to be a large, open interior space often finely ornamented with marble, terra-

cotta, or stained glass. This book will visit only the particularly beautiful, successful, or unique railroad stations that now function as restaurants. In Marietta, the Railroad House is unique because before it became a railroad station, the little brick building was a place to eat.

Marietta got its start as two separate communities established in 1803 and 1804 side by side on the eastern shore of the Susquehanna, named by their respective founders David Cook and James Anderson for their wives, Mary and Henrietta. The tavern that became the Railroad House is supposed to have been built between 1820 and 1823, a time when the town's growth might have been spurred by operations on the Conewago Canal linking York Haven and Columbia.

First a tavern, then a train station, now a restaurant and bed and breakfast: the Railroad House in Marietta.

The Railroad House acquired its name during the time that Pennsy passengers boarded trains from it. In 1860, the Pennsylvania Railroad built a new station across the street; the Railroad House continued to function as a hotel until the 1930s, when passenger railroad business started dropping off nationwide. It then changed hands a number of times and housed various local businesses. Since 1989, it has been the property of a couple who operate it as a Victorian restaurant and bed and breakfast.

Harrisburg's Railroad Station

Which American railroad station first sold food to travelers? In his 1899 history of the Pennsylvania Railroad, William Bender Wilson speculated that the railroad station in Harrisburg was "the ancestor of all the railroad station restaurants in America." The first station to be constructed in the Commonwealth's capital was built by the Harrisburg, Portsmouth, Mountjoy, & Lancaster Rail-road in 1837 on the site of the present station. It was little more than a two-story house beside the tracks with a bell mounted near its chimney that an attendant would ring when he heard the engine whistle of an approaching train. According to Wilson, a cake and pie stand on the outdoor platform was the very first attempt to satisfy hungry passengers waiting for their trains.

Harrisburg's second station, built in 1857, was much larger and Italianate in style, with a dining saloon that could seat up to three hundred.

An image of the first train station in Harrisburg, from *History of the Pennsylvania Railroad Company*. In the picture, a traveler is making a purchase at an outdoor cake and pie stand, identified by the author as the very first train station restaurant.

The third and current station to occupy the same site was completed in 1887, a more modest brick structure now known as the Harrisburg Transportation Center. Some of the adjacent train sheds were preserved and are now examples of the trussed roof design pioneered by Albert Fink in 1854.

Thanks to the local chapter of the National Railway Historical Society, this station is equipped with an example of the Pennsylvania Railroad's GG1 locomotives. In 1938, this particular GG1 pulled the first electric train to arrive at the Harrisburg station, making Number 4859 a tribute to the electrification of the Paoli-to-Harrisburg portion of the Pennsylvania Railroad main line. The historic locomotive was retired in 1979, acquired by the National Railway Historical Society in 1982, and restored in Strasburg. It is part of the Railroad Museum of Pennsylvania collection. Often obscured by the Amtrak passenger coaches parked beside it, the GG1 can be hard to find. The Harrisburg Chapter of the National Railway Historical Soceity also owns the wooden 1920 Pennsylvania Railroad caboose located near the GG1 and the PRR 1929 "Harris" switch tower just north of the Harrisburg station, which its members are restoring.

The first Pennsylvania Railroad train to cross the Rockville Bridge. RAILROAD MUSEUM OF PENNSYLVANIA

When the Pennsylvania Railroad printed a catalog of its summer excursion routes in 1903, it included a photo of the railroad's new bridge in Rockville.

Rockville Bridge and Other Harrisburg Railroad Artifacts

About five miles north of Harrisburg, Amtrak trains still cross Rockville Bridge, completed in 1902 as part of Alexander J. Cassatt's general improvement plan to increase the capacity of the Pennsylvania Railroad system. Like the train station in Harrisburg, it too is the third structure of its kind on the same general site, which was chosen because the river is shallow here, making construction relatively easy. Rockville Bridge, which is constructed of Pennsylvania sandstone and concrete, replaced an iron-truss double-track bridge built in 1877, which in turn replaced the initial single-track wooden bridge completed in 1849. Rockville Bridge is 3,820 feet long, making it the longest stone-and-concrete arch railroad bridge in the world and the crowning achievement of William H. Brown, chief engineer of the PRR for thirty-six years. After it withstood the devastation of Hurricane Agnes in 1972, it was listed on the National Register of Historic Places in 1975 and became a National Historic Civil Engineering Landmark in 1979.

Other railroad bridges and their remains are located in downtown Harrisburg. The city's northernmost railroad bridge was built by the Cumberland Valley Railroad and is being considered for a light rail commuter line. The southernmost bridge was built in 1920 as part of the Reading system and is now used by Norfolk Southern Corporation. Next to it, several stone piers remain that would have supported a bridge for the South Pennsylvania Railroad, but that line was never completed.

Just south of the Rockville Bridge on the Susquehanna's western shore stand the remains of Enola Yard, a freight classification yard constructed between 1903 and 1906. For a while it was the largest yard in the world. It had two turntables and could hold up to twelve thousand standing cars,

Another railroad bridge in Harrisburg, this one built by the Philadelphia & Reading Railroad in 1920, is visible from the Capital Area Greenbelt.

Today's freight action in the vicinity of the Enola Yard on the west shore of the Susquehanna River above Harrisburg.

but during World War II, many more than that passed through Enola every day. Traffic declined in the late 1950s after the Pennsy opened Conway Yard outside of Pittsburgh and Conrail downgraded Enola Yard.

In 2001, the National Civil War Museum opened in Harrisburg's Reservoir Park. Harrisburg is not particularly famous for its role in the Civil War, but the city was the location of Camp Curtin, an important training and receiving center for volunteers and recruits located at the junction of several railroads. Despite the importance attributed by military historians to the Union's railroads in the Civil War, there is relatively little emphasis on railroads in this museum. However, one display demonstrates how closely tied were the lives and activities of all people of this era to railroads. "Lee's Last Battle Map" is actually a railroad map published by the Richmond & Danville Railroad that Lee had used after withdrawing from Petersburg in his attempt to join Gen. Joseph Johnston at Danville, Virginia.

The Historic Gettysburg Train Station

In December 1858, the town of Gettysburg witnessed one of the largest celebrations of its history when some eight thousand residents and visitors gathered to watch the first train roll up to the new Gettysburg train station. Gettysburg, which had long been the crossroads of several strategic roads, might have had rail service sooner, but an effort begun in 1835 to connect Wrightsville with the Baltimore & Ohio Railroad line via Gettysburg was abandoned for lack of financial support.

In 1850, several Gettysburg businessmen formed the Gettysburg Railroad Company, which was officially chartered in 1851. They built an engine house, turntable, and freight station on the north side of the railroad tracks and located their passenger station conveniently near what was then the McClellan House, now Best Western's Gettysburg Hotel. Like the 1857 station in Harrisburg, the Gettysburg train station was Italianate in style with a cupola for its bell.

No one realized that within a few short years Gettysburg's railroad capabilities would be severely tested in the wake of the Battle of Gettysburg. Commercial warehouses located along the train tracks became the first field hospitals, while army surgeons also commandeered the train station ticket office and passenger platform. In July 1863, countless people visited the Gettysburg train station, including wounded soldiers heading for other hospitals or home and civilians coming to learn the fate of their loved ones or to claim their remains.

The Gettysburg train station is also where Abraham Lincoln first alighted when he arrived to deliver the Gettysburg Address. In the nearby town square of modern Gettysburg, there's a statue of Lincoln pointing to the window of the room where he stayed. Many other American presidents and dignitaries would follow Lincoln to Gettysburg, arriving at its train station when they came to the town for various commemorative events.

The Gettysburg Railroad was merged into a number of other small railroads before it became part of the Western Maryland Railway system, which petitioned the Commonwealth to discontinue passenger service to Gettysburg at the end of 1942, following a steady decline in passenger receipts. After CSX Corporation donated the train station to Gettysburg in the 1990s, a local organization, Main Street Gettysburg, began raising funds for the station's restoration. Among other promotional materials, the group videotaped a public service announcement in which an actor dressed as Lincoln explained the extent of damage to the station from water and the vibration of freight trains that still use the adjacent tracks.

Federal money for the station's restoration was available, but only if the local community could raise $200,000. The amount decreased to $100,000 thanks to a challenge grant from the LeVan Family Foundation, created by David and Jennifer LeVan, who had noticed a plea for help posted in the train station window. In 2001, plans were in place to restore the station to its 1886 appearance and make it an orientation site for tourists arriving in Gettysburg.

Reliving Lincoln's Ride

Tourists interested in Lincoln visit Gettysburg's Lincoln Train Museum, just opposite the National Park Service Visitors Center parking lot. The building roughly resembles a nineteenth-century train station and is filled with toy trains, including a Civil War layout that occupies visitors waiting to board the Lincoln Train.

Guests enter a long, narrow auditorium that is furnished like a passenger railroad car. On a screen at the front of the car, they view a moving picture of train tracks, showing them what an engineer would witness from the front of the train. They hear the conversation of those traveling on the train that took Lincoln to Gettysburg.

Just when the tourists think they know what the Lincoln Train ride is all about, the entire room begins to move, imitating the shaking vibration of a train in motion. Even the lantern suspended from the ceiling swings realistically back and forth.

The Lincoln Train ride is pretty tame compared to what tourists can find in today's theme parks, but it might have been the ancestor of these other simulations, giving it a place in the history of American amusement as well as in the rail-themed attractions of Gettysburg.

The Northern Central Railway and the Liberty Limited

The original Northern Central Railway Company (NCR) was created in 1854 by Articles of Union combining the insolvent Baltimore & Susquehanna Rail Road with the York & Maryland Line Railroad, the York & Cumberland Railroad, and the Susquehanna Railroad. According to George M. Burgess and Miles C. Kennedy in their history of the Pennsylvania Railroad, "The consolidation of 1854 had not produced a strong enterprise, either financially or physically." In 1860, the state of Maryland took legal action to foreclose a mortgage it held on the Northern Central Railway. J. Edgar Thomson, president of the Pennsylvania Railroad, took a chance and purchased considerable stock in the company, which he transferred to the PRR in 1861, the same year that NCR installed a board of directors friendly to the Pennsy. By 1900, the Pennsylvania Railroad owned a majority of the company's stock.

The line was abandoned after Hurricane Agnes did her damage in 1972. York County eventually purchased it and leased it to a new corporation that called itself the Northern Central Railway, Inc.

From June 1996 until the fall of 2001, a tourist train called the Liberty Limited ran about half the distance between New Freedom and York, Pennsylvania, along the Codorus Valley, through tiny towns and past brick farmhouses and green hillsides. Passengers were entertained by professional actors inviting their participation in solving murder mysteries, or by a trio of musicians called the Bluegrass Brakemen. On dinner trains they dined on tables set with linens, fresh flowers, and placecards. Passengers could also experience the view from the observation deck of the Liberty Limited's dome dining car and even peek into the dining car kitchen.

Unfortunately, the president of the modern Northern Central Railway announced that the business would cease operations and auciton its assets in September 2001. An editiorial in the *York Daily Record* lamented the railroad's demise, saying that it should have been a major atrraction and moneymaker for the area. Perhaps some other entrepreneur will someday put the trains back on these historic tracks.

The Region's Other Tourist Railroads

Wanamaker, Kempton & Southern, Inc. (WK&S), operates the Hawk Mountain Line, one of the many other tourist railroads of this region. Taking its name from a nearby nature preserve favored by bird-watchers, the railroad employs both steam and diesel locomotives on the weekends

The Hawk Mountain Line being prepared for steam operation in Kempton near the popular nature preserve of Hawk Mountain.

to pull its passenger coaches along Ontelaunee Creek (also known as Maiden Creek) from its terminal in Kempton. There are several special themed rides during the year, some with entertainment.

This railroad was originally built in 1874 as the Berks County Railroad, a link between the Philadelphia & Reading Railroad and the Lehigh Valley Railroad. Though it officially became the Schuylkill & Lehigh branch of the Reading system, it was long known as the "Berksy" by its regular passengers. Wanamaker, Kempton & Southern, Inc., which was formed after the Reading Company abandoned the line in the 1960s, added the current buildings from other Reading stations.

For the past several years, residents of this general area have been involved in controversy over whether to capitalize on the attraction of Hawk Mountain and develop restaurants and hotels to encourage visitors to stay longer. If the promoters of development win this argument, this tourist railroad could become one of a number of things to see and do around the town of Kempton.

The Gettysburg Scenic Railway operates out of an 1884 station about a block from the historic Gettysburg train station. Because its twenty-two-mile round-trip passes through part of Gettysburg National Military Park, it is very popular with visitors. Early in 2001, the Gettysburg Scenic Railway became a part of the Gettysburg & Northern Railroad, a wholly owned subsidiary of Pioneer Railcorp. The Gettysburg Scenic Railroad is the first tourist line to be acquired by this short-line holding company that owns sixteen other railroads nationwide, all hauling freight. According to a press announcement, the purchase "represents an opportunity the Company intends to vigorously pursue."

The Middletown & Hummelstown Railroad is located near Hershey, another popular destination for tourists. Its eleven-mile-round-trip ride runs along the old Union Canal, with a dramatic moment coming as the train crosses a bridge spanning Swatara Creek. Visitors can board in Middletown at the freight station or at Indian Echo Caverns. Independent since 1976, this line was originally incorporated in 1888 and became part of the Reading system in 1890, where it served local industries for most of the twentieth century. The Middletown & Hummelstown Railroad employs diesel locomotives pulling commuter coaches that were used by the Delaware, Lackawanna & Western Railroad from the 1920s to the 1980s. It offers a number of themed excursions, including Civil War living history presentations and a train robbery.

The Historic Stewartstown Railroad Company operates excursions on the "Famous Farmer's Railroad" on the Deer Creek Valley route. This seven-mile branch railroad was chartered in 1884 to connect with the Northern Central Railway in New Freedom, thanks to Stewartstown's merchants and farmers, particularly Anthony Stewart, who needed to get their crops to market in York and Baltimore. At one time, its freight trains made four round-trips each day; today, tourist trains operate mainly on a limited schedule. Passengers board at a depot built in 1914, and the train travels over an iron bridge built in 1870.

The Region's Rail Trails

On weekends, when the state government workers are home, few people use the Capital Area Greenbelt, unless it happens to be the date of the annual bike tour or some other riverfront event. The Capital Area Greenbelt Association (CAGA) manages this recreational facility, which will become a twenty-mile trail surrounding the city of Harrisburg, linking its parks and other open spaces. Hikers in particularly good condition can walk clear from the riverfront to the new National Civil War Museum, located atop a hill in Harrisburg's Reservoir Park.

The idea for this kind of linear park in the Commonwealth's capital dates from the turn of the last century. The project was revived in 1990 when CAGA was organized. Probably few of the users realize it, but the greenbelt does incorporate a segment of rail line that once ran between Harrisburg and Steelton; it was abandoned in 1982.

The most attractive and interesting portion of the greenbelt stretches along the Susquehanna River. Near the state capitol, where the trail passes the home of John Harris, founder of Harrisburg, users get a view of the various downtown bridges spanning the Susquehanna.

The Heritage Rail Trail County Park stretches from the historic district of York south to the Mason-Dixon Line, where it joins the NCR Trail (named after the Northern Central Railway) in Maryland. Originally part of the Baltimore & Susquehanna Rail Road, this route was subsequently in the hands of the Northern Central Railway, the Pennsylvania Railroad, and the Penn Central Railroad. After the corridor was greatly damaged by Hurricane Agnes in 1972, it was rebuilt by the Commonwealth for freight in 1985, but little business materialized. York County purchased it in 1990 and completed the trail in 1999.

In a few short years, it has become extremely popular with bicyclists, who flock to the parking areas at its access points and literally spend the

Families enjoying the Heritage Rail Trail at New Freedom.

day on the trail, which is well maintained by the York County Department of Parks and Recreation and patrolled by York County park rangers. Much of the trail runs through shady woods along the pleasant Codorus Creek. Here and there, trail users find benches and picnic tables.

The trail passes through the Howard Tunnel, which its promotional literature bills as "the oldest operational tunnel in the nation." This claim may or may not be true. Completed in 1838, the Howard Tunnel is just slightly older than the Black Rock Tunnel in Phoenixville, but which tunnel was officially placed in operation first is not clear. In any case, since the trail proceeds through the tunnel, it offers hikers and rail fans a great opportunity to see an early railroad engineering feature.

Trail users also pass through Glen Rock, Seven Valleys, and the town named Railroad, whose growth was prompted and promoted by the railroad's existence. The owners of restaurants, taverns, and grocery stores in these towns are now noticing an increase in their business, thanks to the trail users. One homeowner who set up a snow cone stand on his property adjoining the trail probably won't be the only entrepreneur to capitalize on these new customers. In the spring of 2001, a new organization, the Hanover Junction Northern Central Railroad Historical and Preservation Society, was formed to manage a new museum in the refurbished Hanover Junction train station, which lies along this trail, and to promote the history of the railroad between York and Baltimore.

The Thun Trail in Berks County got its start when the Schuylkill River Greenway Association purchased ten miles of right-of-way from Conrail in two five-mile segments located between Reading and Stowe. Named after the organization's founder, Ferdinand K. Thun (pronounced "tune"), the trail is planned to link scenic and historic sites in the vicinity of Reading and become part of the Schuylkill River Heritage Corridor. In the spring of 2001, the unfinished Thun Trail was still a pretty well kept secret. Signs on two concrete arch bridges visible from Route 422 proclaim its existence, but even a map obtained from the organization failed to clearly explain how to get to this old stretch of the Pennsylvania Railroad's Schuylkill branch. Near the town of Gibraltar, there were several access points marked "bike trail," but nothing particularly identifying the Thun Trail. Mountain bikers, who are the most frequent users of this completed portion, can access a number of biking websites for further information.

The region's other rail trails include the Cumberland Valley Rail Trail, the Cumberland County Biker/Hiker Trail, the Letort Spring Run Nature Trail, the Stony Valley Railroad Grade Trail, the Conewago Trail, the Ephrata Railroad Linear Park Trail, the Lancaster Junction Trail, the Swatara State Park Trail, and the Little Buffalo State Park Trail.

Valleys of the Schuylkill and Susquehanna

Great Railways of the Region

The Reading

The Pennsylvania Office of Travel and Tourism calls this largely agricultural region the Valleys of the Susquehanna, but its railroad history is more closely associated with another river and another industry. Some of Pennsylvania's best fields of anthracite coal lie in Schuylkill County and the counties surrounding it. The entity commonly known as Pennsylvania's Reading Railroad got its start in the Schuylkill River valley to serve the mining industry, but eventually it extended its tracks to most of the counties in this region. For the purposes of studying Pennsylvania's most famous anthracite railroad, Schuylkill County will be included in this region, which in this book shares Berks County with the Hershey, Gettysburg, and Dutch Country region.

According to a report of the Coal Mining Association published in *Hazard's Register of Pennsylvania* in 1833, "The year 1825 may be considered as the era from which we may date the fair introduction of anthracite coal," meaning by that time it was generally acknowledged that the anthracite coal discovered in Schuylkill and Lehigh Counties would become a superior alternative to the use of wood as fuel. As early as 1813, independent miners started floating coal downstream to Philadelphia on the Schuylkill River on boats they called "arks," and by 1828, two canals stretched toward the coal fields: the Union Canal linking Reading on the Schuylkill River with Middletown on the Susquehanna River, and the Schuylkill Canal (completed by the Schuylkill Navigation Company in 1825 and sometimes known simply as the Schuylkill Navigation) linking Port Clinton with Philadelphia.

Although the Union-Schuylkill canal system would continue to function for many years, it shared the drawbacks of all canals. A number of accounts written between 1815 and 1830 refer to particular problems with the Schuylkill Canal, including frequent breaks in its banks that required expensive repairs and rebuilding. Surely, there was a better way to get anthracite coal to potential customers.

In his two-volume work titled *The Reading Railroad: History of a Coal Age Empire,* James L. Holton traces the origin of this railroad to the Little Schuylkill Navigation, Railroad, & Coal Company founded in 1826 by Isaac Hiester and Friedrich List, both of Reading. Although this enterprise was originally organized to build a feeder canal linking a coal field to the

This illustration for the 1852 *Pictorial Sketch-book of Pennsylvania* by Eli Bowen depicts the Schuylkill corridor where train tracks ran parallel to the canal.

Schuylkill Canal, its charter allowed for either a canal or a railroad. Holton contends that the founders signaled that they had bigger plans when they had the charter amended in 1829 to extend operations from Port Clinton (the terminus of the Schuylkill Canal) to Reading, secured the support of Philadelphia's wealthy merchant and investor Stephen Girard, and hired engineer Moncure Robinson. Holton writes, "Instead of providing a service in getting coal from the mines to the canal, it meant the railway intended to compete with the [Schuylkill] canal in reaching the anthracite market." Their Little Schuylkill Railroad, following the Little Schuylkill River from Port Clinton to Tamaqua, was in operation by 1831.

In 1833, the Commonwealth granted a charter to a second entity, the Philadelphia & Reading Railroad Company. In his 1927 book, *The Anthracite Railroads: A Study in American Railroad Enterprise,* Jules Irwin Bogen noted that its investors were friendly toward the Little Schuylkill operation; in fact, they "apparently planned to operate the two lines, when built, as a single through route." Their line would connect with the Philadelphia, Germantown & Norristown Railroad, as well as with the Philadelphia & Columbia Railroad (the old State Works, later part of the Pennsylvania Railroad), eventually making it not only an important anthracite railroad that greatly aided development in the lower coal region of Pennsylvania, but also a major passenger carrier and a rival to the Pennsy for Philadelphia area commuter traffic.

Moncure Robinson surveyed the Schuylkill River valley from Port Clinton to Reading and from Reading to Philadelphia beginning in 1835. The railroad he designed was an engineering marvel for its time; its roadbed was graded in a way that allowed any number of loaded cars to be hauled to Philadelphia and returned empty by the same locomotive.

The project was the largest private railroad enterprise actually under way in the Commonwealth at the time, and the panic of 1837 brought both challenge and opportunity. To secure needed capital, its determined managers sought aid from the banking firm of McCalmont Brothers & Company in England; the Little Schuylkill Railroad had already received aid from the British banking firm of Gowan and Marx. The same panic probably caused the Little Schuylkill managers to relinquish their rights to build between Port Clinton and Reading to the Philadelphia & Reading Railroad, which got the rights extended to Mount Carbon the following year, 1838.

The industrial city of Reading as it appeared in 1852 in the *Pictorial Sketch-book of Pennsylvania* by Eli Bowen. In the foreground, a train approaches the city.

In 1842, the Reading ran its first train the full ninety-four miles from Mount Carbon in the heart of coal country to Philadelphia. Ten years later, Eli Bowen described the effect of the railroad on the city of Reading in his book, *The Pictorial Sketch-book of Pennsylvania:* "[Reading's] accessibility, by canal, to the Susquehanna; and by both railroad and canal to Philadelphia and Pottsville, [gives] it a commanding interior position, which must ultimately be used to its great and permanent benefit."

Moncure Robinson chose the estate of Joseph Ball on the Delaware to locate the first five piers and intermediate basins of the Philadelphia & Reading's Philadelphia terminal for receiving and shipping cargo. The place was already known as Richmond Hall, which would have appealed to Robinson, a native Virginian born in Richmond. The railroad opened a connecting line across the Schuylkill with the Falls Bridge, and by the early twentieth century, Port Richmond was more than a mile long, covered 140 acres, and was the largest such operation in the world under the management of one company.

The third quarter of the nineteenth century was very profitable for the expanding company. The Philadelphia & Reading acquired or leased many lateral or formerly independent "feeder" lines. It financed construction of the Lebanon Valley Railroad from Reading to Harrisburg, offering Pennsylvanians a different route between Philadelphia and the capital, while also siphoning off some of the Pennsy's Cumberland Valley traffic. In 1870, its old competitor, the Schuylkill Navigation Company, leased its canal to the Philadelphia & Reading, which gradually abandoned it and allowed it to decay.

It does not appear that the early investors and managers of the Philadelphia & Reading Railroad intended to mine as well as transport coal, but Franklin B. Gowen, who was elected president of the company in 1870, decided that the railroad should purchase the coal lands it served, freeing it from dangerous competition from other railroads. In 1871, Gowen created an entity called the Philadelphia & Reading Coal & Iron Company to hold his real estate acquisitions. In his book on anthracite railroads, Jules Irwin Bogen comments, "By buying its coal land estate of 100,000 acres, the Reading assured itself of a regular source of traffic. It did not, however, obtain assurance that this traffic would be profitable." Gowen's ambitious plans drove the Philadelphia & Reading into receivership in 1880 and lost the railroad its European investors two years later.

Gowen also had the misfortune of making enemies of the powerful John D. Rockefeller and the future president of the Pennsylvania Railroad, Alexander J. Cassatt. At Gowen's urging, William H. Vanderbilt acquired a substantial interest in the Philadelphia & Reading, bringing Gowen into the syndicate that was then planning construction of the South Pennsylvania Railroad, which was intended to compete with the Pennsy. Gowen also joined several oil well operators in northwestern Pennsylvania in their plans to construct a pipeline from Bradford to Williamsport, where oil could be transported via the Reading system, which would have freed the oilmen from the monopoly of Rockefeller's Standard Oil Company.

While the railroad was on the verge of a second bankruptcy, Gowen resigned in 1883 and J. P. Morgan, the famous banker and financier, made peace between the Reading and the Pennsy and organized a trust of bankers that would direct the affairs of the company for five years. Morgan stepped in a second time to reorganize the company during a receivership that lasted from 1893 to 1897, incurred by an ambitious expansion program of another one of the Reading's more colorful presidents, A. A. McLeod, who had leased the Lehigh Valley Railroad and opened the railroad's elaborate new terminal and headquarters in Philadelphia. Both the Philadelphia & Reading Railroad and the Philadelphia & Reading Coal & Iron Company were absorbed by a holding com-

A museum in Leesport, dedicated to the history of the Reading system, is operated by the Reading Company Technical and Historical Society.

The Reading Anthracite Company recently restored the historic corporate headquarters in Pottsville of its ancestor, the Philadelphia & Reading Coal & Iron Company.

pany, the Reading Company. In 1896, the Reading Company formed the Philadelphia & Reading Railway Company to conduct its railroad operations. After further mergers and corporate streamlining, the Reading Company in 1923 became the operationg company.

After some modest expansion in the early years of the twentieth century, including the construction of one of the largest locomotive shops of the day in the city of Reading and a concrete bridge spanning the Susquehanna at Harrisburg, business for the Reading Company slowly declined. Starting around 1930, gas and petroleum, as well as other forms of energy, largely replaced coal in both industrial and domestic use, while highway construction and road improvement made automobiles the preferred means of travel for those residing in this region. The Reading Company made a notable attempt to increase its passenger miles by marketing nostalgia with its "Iron Horse Rambles" through the still scenic coal regions on weekends from 1959 to 1964, but its losses continued to grow.

The Reading Company declared bankruptcy in 1971 but continued to run while the Regional Rail Reorganization Act of 1973 attempted to sort out the difficulties of northeastern railroads. Its commuter lines in and around Philadelphia became part of SEPTA. In 1976, its remaining viable freight lines became part of Conrail, which later sold the Port Richmond freight station.

That same year, the Reading Company Technical and Historical Society was established to preserve its history. The organization now numbers more than a thousand members in many parts of the United States. On any given day, visitors can hear its members and volunteers hammering away at the rolling stock they are preserving and refurbishing at their train yard in Leesport, but the society officially receives visitors only on

Saturday and Sunday afternoons in the summer. The society maintains Reading locomotives, passenger cars, freight cars, and cabooses, including the last caboose built at the Reading shops complex. From time to time, it uses its artifacts for special excursions, but the society does not do regular tours. In addition to the artifacts, the society also salvaged the files of the railroad's mechanical department, giving it an extensive collection of photos, maps, and blueprints.

Another repository of Reading Railroad information is housed in Pottsville at the headquarters of the Reading Anthracite Company, a privately held and locally owned business created in 1961 when the Philadelphia & Reading Corporation, the modern successor to the Philadelphia & Reading Coal & Iron Company, divested itself of its coal interests. This firm is currently mining coal in the area around Minersville and also working to keep the memory of the Reading Railroad alive. The Anthracite Railroads Historical Society in Lansdale, Pennsylvania, also retains information on this railroad.

Rail Stories of the Region

The Danville & Pottsville Rail Road

In the summer of 1829, the *Miners' Journal* reported from Pottsville, "A new era of things is rapidly approaching at this place, which is of vital importance to the citizens, generally—we mean the extension of rail roads throughout the coal district." At about the same time that the founders of the Reading system were planning to link Schuylkill County's coal fields by rail to Philadelphia, a project equally ambitious was born at the courthouse in Sunbury. Sometimes called the Central Rail Road, the Danville & Pottsville Rail Road was intended to run from the Schuylkill County coal region through the coal fields located farther north at Shamokin and Mahanoy Mountain, to the Susquehanna River at Danville and the town called Sunbury, which was strategically located at the confluence of the Susquehanna's northern and western branches.

Hazard's Register of Pennsylvania attributed the idea for this project to General Daniel Montgomery, one of Pennsylvania's canal commissioners and a resident of Danville, who died before much construction was under way. The concept was eagerly adopted by residents of Northumberland and Columbia Counties, and Stephen Girard became its advocate and largest shareholder.

Two years earlier, in the summer of 1828, Montgomery had secured the services of Moncure Robinson and instructed him to survey the topography between Sunbury, Danville, and Pottsville to determine whether such a project was even possible. In two separate reports, Robinson declared there was a route over which a double-track railroad could be built for locomotive power, but it would require a tunnel eight hundred feet long and no less than nine inclined planes.

"In the summer of 1832, the formation of the Eastern division of the road was commenced in conformity to the desire of Mr. Girard [who had died in 1831]," *Hazard's Register of Pennsylvania* reported in December of 1835. Stephen Girard had also imported English iron to plate the rails and established sawmills and other industrial businesses in Girardville, the town named in his honor. By 1834, a ten-mile railroad stretched from the Mount Carbon Railroad (a feeder connecting with the Schuylkill Canal) to the pioneer town of Girardville. These ten miles accounted for about a third of the entire project "not in length, but in expense and labor," *Hazard's Register of Pennsylvania* reported that year. The tunnel had been constructed and so had a number of inclined planes, most notably the Mahanoy Plane, which was 1,625 feet long and 350 feet high.

Construction of the western portion of the railroad started in the summer of 1834. This twenty miles of track was supposed to connect the Shamokin coal field with one of the State Works canals on the Susquehanna at Sunbury to give miners yet another route for shipping coal, and to haul the produce of farmers in the upper valleys of the Susquehanna in the opposite direction. In 1835, *Hazard's Register of Pennsylvania* confidently reported, "Thus a rapid and reciprocal trade, of the most advantageous nature, will be prosecuted, by a route seventy miles nearer than the Schuylkill Canal."

Such great expectations were never realized, and thus the region's other big idea never attained the success of the Reading system. By 1835, the tracks of the Danville & Pottsville Rail Road ran from Sunbury to Shamokin, but the eastern and western portions of this enterprise would never be connected. Sale of the railroad's bonds dropped off after the deaths of Girard and Montgomery. The railroad also lost the services of Moncure Robinson, who went to work for the Philadelphia & Reading Railroad, even suggesting that work on the Danville & Pottsville Rail Road be halted because little was being done in Sunbury to construct a means for getting coal from the trains into the canal. More unfortunate still, the western tracks had been constructed in a way that caused frequent locomotive derailments, making it necessary for the railroad to return to horsepower. This dampened the hopes of investors for profitability throughout the nineteenth century, and the line changed hands several times before its western portion was acquired by the Pennsylvania Railroad and its eastern section, which included the inclined planes, was absorbed into the Reading system.

According to James L. Holton's history of the Reading, the most dramatic feature of the Danville & Pottsville Rail Road and its most enduring artifact was the Mahanoy Plane. This engineering feature long served as a model for other railroad engineers and became a regional landmark and tourist attraction, remaining part of Girardville's landscape well into the twentieth century.

The Molly Maguires

The role Franklin B. Gowen played in ridding Pennsylvania's southern coal fields of what was believed to be a secret terrorist organization popularly called the Molly Maguires made him a hero to his genteel contemporaries, but a villian to modern historians with pro-labor sensibilities. By 1874, under his leadership, the Philadelphia & Reading Railroad had acquired coal lands estimated at 100,000 acres served by nearly a hundred collieries. In 1873, he had met in New York with the presidents of several Pennsylvania coal and railroad concerns to agree on quotes and set the rate for coal shipment at five dollars per ton, an arrangement sometimes called America's first cartel or incidence of price fixing. While Gowen was not antilabor per se, empty freight cars were not welcome in this scenario, so Gowen used contract labor to break a miners' strike mounted by the Workingman's Benevolent Association in 1875.

The miners, mainly Irishmen in this region, found themselves back at their dangerous and filthy work despite their grievances. Back in Ireland, they had had to contend with landlords and rent agents, so being pressured into renting company-owned housing and purchasing their goods at a company store may have seemed familiarly galling. Though some historians have expressed doubt that an organization called the Molly Maguires formally existed, most concede that certain Irish miners joined a secret association that took its name from an Irish widow who had once led an anti-landlord movement and operated through a legal fraternal association called the Ancient Order of Hibernians.

The violence that plagued this part of Pennsylvania since the 1860s was certainly real. Mine owners, supervisors, and any other authority figures considered a threat were intimidated, beaten, and even murdered by unidentifiable perpetrators who seemed to come from nowhere. It was thought that the Molly Maguires would meet secretly, identify a victim, and then appoint members from a distant part of the county to steal into town and execute the sentence they had summarily passed, while the obvious local suspects all made sure they had alibis for the evening.

Sometime in 1873, Franklin B. Gowen met with Allan Pinkerton, head of a national detective agency, and arranged for an Irish native, James McParlan, to infiltrate the Molly Maguires. McParlan was able to win the trust of John Kehoe, sometimes called the King of the Mollies, whose day job was owner of the Hibernian House Tavern in Girardville.

In 1876, Franklin B. Gowen took over the prosecution as counsel for the Commonwealth of Pennsylvania at what were called the Molly trials. James McParlan was the star witness, but Gowen went down in history with an address to the jury that obtained a conviction.

By 1879, nineteen Mollies had been hanged for murder and fourteen others were imprisoned. To this day, controversy remains as to whether the men executed were actually responsible for the crimes for which they were convicted and whether the evidence used against them would stand up in court today.

Gowen's association with the Mollies made contemporaries wonder whether his apparent suicide in 1889 was really a murder in retribution for the role he had played in breaking up this organization. Since then, certain members of the pro-Molly school of historians have attributed the suicide to Gowen's sense of guilt.

The Schuylkill Valley Metro

It may soon be possible to once again travel the Schuylkill corridor by train. Since 1998, SEPTA and the Berks Area Reading Transportation Authority (BARTA) have been seeking permission first from Conrail and then from Norfolk Southern Corporation to run passenger trains on what is now used as a major freight corridor from Norristown to Reading.

In the years since the collapse of the Reading system and the elimination of passenger service on this route, the Schuylkill corridor has become one of the fastest growing areas in Pennsylvania. Besides redevelopment projects in the old industrial towns, new office complexes have been attracting "new economy" businesses. One unfortunate result has been severe daily congestion on highways such as the Schuylkill Expressway and Route 422.

The Delaware Valley Regional Planning Commission approved a plan for rail transit in the Schuylkill corridor in December 2000, but the city of Philadelphia dissented. Philadelphia would support the massive project, alternately called the Schuylkill Valley Metro or MetroRail, only if it was expanded to include Philadelphia destinations such as the Philadelphia Museum of Art and the Philadelphia Zoo.

At first Norfolk Southern Corporation also objected, protesting that confusion would arise from attempts to accommodate both passengers and freight on the same rails. Then an article by Jere Downs in the December 24 edition of the *Philadelphia Inquirer* abruptly announced that Norfolk Southern proposed to give SEPTA its railroad running from Norristown to Reading if SEPTA would provide it with a new freight line built on an abandoned NS railbed running through Lancaster and Chester Counties to Creswell, Pennsylvania, where another freight line would connect it with Harrisburg.

The railroad in question had been constructed by the Pennsy as its Atglen and Susquehanna branch in 1906 and is sometimes called the Enola branch or the "Low Grade." Its history was chronicled in an article for the *Journal of the Lancaster County Historical Society* by Frederic H. Abendschein. It was a double-track freight-only line bypassing the Pennsy's passenger main line through Lancaster over a route that purposely avoided steep grades. Although Alexander J. Cassatt was president while the line was being built, it was probably conceived by J. Edgar Thomson as part of his larger plan for a low-grade route stretching all the way from the East Coast to the Midwest.

Conrail had begun removing its tracks in 1990 after having diverted its own freight operations to the Reading's old main line. The Low Grade might have become a rail trail, but its transformation was halted by the owners of property along its length who didn't want strangers hiking through their backyards.

Late in 2001, SEPTA filed a funding application with the Federal Transit Administration for the Schuylkill Valley Metro; in January 2002, SEPTA and BARTA received approval to begin preliminary engineering. The completed project may open a new era in Pennsylvania's transportation history: railroads serving the needs of commuters who have had it with traffic and road rage.

Local Chapters of the National Railway Historical Society

The Central Pennsylvania Chapter of the National Railway Historical Society is headquartered at the train station in White Deer, Pennsylvania, where it is developing a museum. The chapter publishes a newsletter called *The Susquehannock* and sponsors an annual train meet attended by browsers and vendors. It offers educational entertainment at its monthly

Tucked away in White Deer on the bank of the Susquehanna are the train station and rolling stock of the Central Pennsylvania Chapter of the National Railway Historical Society.

meetings and organizes excursions. The chapter owns railroad cars and one and a half miles of railroad between New Columbia and White Deer, formerly part of the Reading system.

The Region's Railroad Giants

Moncure Robinson (1802–1891)

This master engineer, born in Richmond, Virginia, graduated from William and Mary College at the age of sixteen. A visit to the Erie Canal, employment on the James River Canal in Virginia, and study of the public works of Europe firmly convinced him that railroads would prove superior to canals.

On his return to the United States, he worked on some coal feeder lines and made the surveys for the Allegheny Portage Railroad. According to a brief history of the Danville & Pottsville Rail Road published in *Hazard's Register of Pennsylvania* in 1835, when hopes were still high for this project, "The friends of the rail road owe much to their Chief Engineer, and they are not insensible to their obligations. Even the boys of Sunbury, at one of the illuminations for some success in the road, raised a bonfire in his honor, aloft upon an eminence, and in shouts of joy around it, called it Moncure Robinson. The road owes much of its success to his judicious selection of his engineer corps."

Robinson's work for the Philadelphia & Reading Railroad would be his crowning achievement and make him the world's foremost civil engineer. In the winding and narrow valley of the Schuylkill River, Robinson formulated the fundamental rules for determining grades and curvatures. So great was Robinson's reputation that in 1840 the czar of Russia tried to hire him to design and build the new railroad system for the Russian Empire. Robinson declined and went on to establish the Bay Line, a line of steamboats running between Baltimore and Norfolk. In his history of the Reading system, James L. Holton wrote that after 1842, there is no documentary evidence of any further connection of Robinson with the railroad that he had worked so hard to establish, noting that no historian has ever sufficiently explained what appears to be an abrupt breach.

An entry in the *Dictionary of National Biography* sums up what was remarkable about Robinson's achievements: "As were other engineers of his day, with the exception of those from West Point, he was untrained in the technique of the profession. These men worked out their technique in the school of experience, and for that reason their lives were characterized by a peculiar initiative and resourcefulness."

Franklin B. Gowen (1836–1889)

Those writing about the history of the Reading system have weighed in with some strong opinions on the life and work of Franklin B. Gowen, its most fascinating, but not most successful, president. According to Jules Irwin Bogen in his book on anthracite railroads, Gowen was "forceful, courageous and daring with a personal magnetism that proved well-nigh irresistible even when his arguments were obviously preposterous, his greatest weakness was an incorrigible optimism and an apparent unwillingness to conform his larger projects to the practical necessities of the moment." James L. Holton in his history of the Reading system wrote that "he was impatient, even bored, when details of real railroading practices came to his attention. It was corporate power and financial finagling that interested this complex man." Marvin W. Schlegel, who wrote a 1947 biography of Gowen, added, "In an age when business shuddered at the very thought of publicity, he gloried in it."

As a young man, Gowen had worked as a store clerk in Lancaster and as superintendent of a furnace in Shamokin, where he became aware of the vast potential of this coal region. He studied law and became district attorney of Schuylkill County. In 1864, he became counsel for the Reading and was elected president of this railroad in 1870.

He built a home, which he named Cresheim, on Stenton Avenue in the Mount Airy neighborhood where he had grown up. There was already a street that bore his father's name, and Gowen saw that the neighborhood was provided with a railroad station built by Frank Furness, which made it all the more desirable. Although Gowen's mansion was torn down in 1940 when his estate was subdivided, other late-nineteenth-century mansions still standing on East Gowen Avenue caused it to be named the "prettiest street in Philadelphia."

Gowen took an enormous risk for the Philadelphia & Reading Railroad when he began buying up coal lands. His faith that the American economy could only expand in the long run resulted in his borrowing vast amounts of cash to invest in property that could not possibly be made productive for decades. In a report to stockholders he stated that his objective was securing "a body of coal-land capable of supplying all the coal-tonnage that can possibly be transported over the road."

Such optimism resulted in the two bankruptcies that broke his spirit and clouded his reputation. According to his biographer, Marvin W. Schlegel, "When he failed in his last effort to reorganize the Reading in 1886 and surrendered to J. P. Morgan, that defeat, the first of his career, seemed to wipe out the memory of all his previous triumphs. Even though he never conceded that Morgan had beaten him, the victory-loving public looked on Gowen thereafter with the regretful gaze it reserves for an ex-champion trying to make a come-back."

According to contemporary newspaper accounts, on a December day in 1889, a chambermaid at Wormley's Hotel in Washington, D.C., reported that Gowen had apparently remained locked in his room for nearly an entire day. The hotel manager stood on a chair to peer over the transom and spotted Gowen's lifeless body beside the pistol with which he had shot himself in the head. In a 1905 work called *Old Time Notes of Pennsylvania*, Alexander K. McClure, who knew Gowen, wrote, "I was not greatly surprised one morning . . . to learn that in a moment of utter despair, with his own hand, he had sent the deadly bullet crashing into his own brain."

Gowen's obituaries predicted that he would be remembered. In 1927, when his book on anthracite railroads was published, Jules Irwin Bogen eulogized, "The Reading Railroad as it stands today is much the system he made it." Now that documents and artifacts are all that remain of the Reading system, Gowen's final epitaph may well be written on a rusty sign in quiet Gowen City near Shamokin, identifying Gowen merely as a capitalist and landowner.

John E. Wootten (1822–1898)

It was in 1876, while the Reading was in serious financial trouble and Franklin B. Gowen was desperate to save some cash, that John E. Wootten made a proposal that sounded almost too good to be true. Wootten had started his career as apprentice to Matthias Baldwin, later becoming foreman at one of the Reading's smaller shops. He took over running the main shops in Reading at the age of forty-five. What he proposed was an engine that burned culm, the waste that piled up around the breakers in the coal region. In other words, he planned to build an engine that eliminated the cost of fuel and ran essentially for free.

Gowen eagerly agreed, and Wootten got the Reading shops working on his plans. He designed a locomotive with a wider firebox above its driving wheels and the cab astride the boiler. By 1878, Wootten's experimental Engine Number 412 had been built and was ready for shipment to the Paris Industrial Exhibition, where its camelback design drew criticism for its ungainly appearance. Although the camelbacks did not exactly run for free, their use of smaller pieces of coal did save a great deal of money, while also cutting down on smoke emitted from the locomotive, which made them popular for passenger trains. The camelback became the standard for all anthracite railroads and an icon for the Reading.

Wootten retired from the Reading in 1886 as general manager. Perhaps it was too close an association with the controversial Franklin B. Gowen that prevented Wootten from having attained the title of president himself.

Sampling the Region's Railroad History

Reading Artifacts in Reading

Before the advent of railroads or even canals, Reading, Pennsylvania, was already an industrial town known for its hat-making and iron-manufacturing industries. By the 1920s, it was a leader in textiles and famous as the "Women's Stocking Capital of the World." Another important industry for Reading for more than a century was the construction and repair of locomotives and railroad cars for the Reading system.

A Philadelphia & Reading Railroad train nears the town of Reading, circa 1875, as depicted in *Philadelphia and Its Environs*.

In the late 1830s, when the Philadelphia & Reading Railroad's managers decided that their corporation would require repair shops at their northern terminus, Gus Nichols purchased an existing machine shop and reestablished it near Chestnut and Seventh Streets, where the company's trains ran through the town at grade level. The shops grew to occupy the west side of Seventh Street between Franklin and Chestnut Streets, and the job opportunities created by the Reading shops caused the population of the town to triple by midcentury.

By the turn of the century, the Reading's equipment needs made it necessary to construct a second complex that was completed by 1903, when it became one of the largest locomotive shops of its day, locally known as the North Sixth Street Plant. As passenger business dwindled during the twentieth century, so did business at the shops, which were closed in 1991.

Modern Reading's factory outlet centers, a concept that originated during the 1960s, have contributed greatly to the rebirth of this town after the loss of most of its major industries. In fact, the phrase "Outlet Capital of the World" is claimed as a registered trademark by the Reading and Berks County Visitors Bureau. Although Reading's best outlet centers are in the western and northern parts of town, the city's downtown area has also seen recent redevelopment and now sports more shops and restaurants than vacant real estate.

Motorists entering the town from any direction pass beneath numerous aging railroad viaducts, some of them still emblazoned with the name of the Reading. At certain intersections, visitors might face a long wait while a freight train travels north or south where Seventh Street used to be.

At Franklin Street at the boundary of the original shops complex, there's an abandoned platform and a boarded-up train station with a cornerstone that proclaims its date of construction as 1929. It sits amidst vacant lots where iron rails are still embedded in the concrete underfoot. An old brick building on nearby Chestnut Street has survived and now bears the name of the Reading Foundry & Supply Company.

Further north in Reading on Sixth Street, drivers pass beneath a Reading Company viaduct known as a skew bridge because it crosses the street diagonally. This brownstone bridge was erected in 1857 by construction engineer M. E. Lyons from a design by Richard B. Osborne. Its courses of stone are laid in ellipsoidal curves, and its arches have no keystones. For years, engineering schools sent their students to study it. Because

Reading's skew bridge, built in 1857, still spans Sixth Street.

Osborne was supposed to have carved his model out of soap and the Irish stonemasons were said to have been paid in whiskey, this viaduct has also long been known locally as the "Soap and Whiskey Bridge."

The town's first railroad station was built in 1836 at the corner of Seventh and Chestnut Streets in the midst of the shops neighborhood. As passenger service grew, a new station was constructed where the Reading's main line intersected with its Lebanon Valley and East Pennsylvania branches. This two-story brick structure about a half mile north was called the Outer Station from the time it was completed in 1874. The station itself stood within a triangle of railroad tracks and boarding platforms. The clock in its tower had dials facing all four cardinal directions, and its second floor housed the railroad's local business offices. By the late nineteenth century, it served over seventy passenger trains a day.

Near Reading's skew bridge, there's a drive leading to a vacant lot where the Outer Station used to be. The last trains left this station in 1969, and the station was destroyed by fire during the 1970s, but the city paid a sort of tribute to it when the Reading Station Outlet Center was opened a few blocks farther north on Sixth Street. It incorporates part of an old Reading Company building, and its modern architectural ornament includes a steam engine motif.

Between the site of the old Outer Station and the Reading Station Outlet Center, there was once a rail yard so vast that pedestrians crossed it on a suspension bridge that the locals called the Swinging Bridge. A portion of the Swinging Bridge was saved and has been reinstalled at a park at the southern end of Reading.

The Outer Station was one of a number of civic improvements made to Reading during the 1860s and 1870s that caused the neighborhood along the old Centre Turnpike to Sunbury to become a place for wealthy industrialists to build their mansions. Now a well-maintained neighborhood, the Centre Park Historic District has elegant examples of just about every architectural style popular during the late nineteenth and early twentieth centuries.

The Centre Park Historic District is home to the Historical Society of Berks County, which occupies a building completed in 1928. Its museum is not known for railroad artifacts per se, but images of trains are captured in many of the paintings and photographs on display, including a painting of the Outer Station train yard with its Swinging Bridge. The museum also includes the List alcove, which is dedicated to the memory of Friedrich List, whose bust identifies him as a railroad pioneer, as well as the original editor of the *Readinger Adler*, today the *Reading Eagle*.

Port Clinton

North of Reading, where considerable truck and automobile traffic moves along the Schuylkill corridor on busy Route 61, in the Schuylkill Gap at the border between Berks and Schuylkill Counties, lies a town called Port Clinton. Once the important terminus of the Schuylkill Canal, this town was named after DeWitt Clinton, founder of the Erie Canal. Today, the place is familiar mainly to hikers because the Appalachian Trail runs practically through it. Motorists rarely stop here, unless the local police pull them over for ignoring the speed limit postings of thirty-five miles per hour.

According to James L. Holton's history of the Reading system, Port Clinton is the historic location of "the oldest existing railroad-associated

This illustration of a Philadelphia & Reading Railroad train traveling north of Port Clinton appeared in *Philadelphia and Its Environs* in 1875. Contemporary writers noted that the scenery became more like wilderness in the northern portion of the Schuylkill corridor.

Is this the nation's "oldest railroad-associated structure"? The house was built for Moncure Robinson between 1830 and 1833 in Port Clinton.

structure in the United States." Among its other modest early-nineteenth-century buildings stands a two-story house built between 1830 and 1833 for the use of engineer Moncure Robinson. At one time housing the local post office as well as the office where Robinson and his assistants worked, the Moncure Robinson House has since been divided into apartments, with only a sign on its front porch attesting to its noble history.

Nineteenth-century guidebooks described Port Clinton as the gateway between rolling farm country and the more wild and rugged topography of the coal region. The Schuylkill River's course through the town is different today because the Reading Company literally shifted it in 1926 by cutting off an oxbow, eliminating the need for two bridges and a tunnel that would ill accommodate the heavier trains then coming into use.

Port Clinton's transportation history can be studied at the Transportation Museum, an independent, community-run establishment maintained by the Northern Berks and Southern Schuylkill Historical Association. This small, two-story structure, formerly a school, is now a repository for models, photographs, and documents.

Remains of the Marriage of Coal Mining and Railroad Transportation

Farther up the Schuylkill corridor, Route 61 winds through the town of Ashland, an excellent location for studying the relationship of Pennsylvania's mining and railroad industries. Since 1963, about forty thousand visitors per year have been learning about mining at Ashland's Pioneer Tunnel, named after the Pioneer Colliery on Mahanoy Mountain that was part of the Philadelphia & Reading Coal & Iron Company from 1911 to 1931, when its mining operations were shut down. The mine cars are running again in the retimbered tunnel, taking tourists to see just how cramped, dark, and intensely cold the mines were while they hear about a miner's life from a guide who very likely once held the job himself.

The site also has a specialized railroad powered by the Henry Clay, a narrow-gauge locomotive that is known colloquially as a "lokie." Such engines were used by the Philadelphia & Reading Coal & Iron Company to move loads of coal from strip mines after steam-powered shovels had chewed their way into coal veins. The Henry Clay now pulls passengers around the side of Mahanoy Mountain, where visitors can witness other artifacts of the region's mining industry, including a bootleg coal hole, an unofficial and often unsafe mine dug by miners in their spare time without the formality of obtaining deeds or creating corporations.

From the train, they can also see the phenomenon of steam rising from the ground in the nearby ghost town of Centralia. In 1962, a fire started in the mines beneath Centralia when something ignited in a trash dump located over a coal vein, and the flames quickly spread underground. For more than a decade, millions of dollars were spent on efforts to put the fire out. In 1984, Congress approved $42 million for the relocation of Centralia's residents and businesses. More than five hundred people moved, but a few hardy souls remained. Those intrigued enough to drive through what is left of Centralia will see isolated and shored-up structures that once were row homes. Some blocks have sidewalks, but no remaining buildings. Although there are several signs saying "We love Centralia!" soon only Centralia's cemeteries may stand as evidence that anyone ever lived on this desolate hilltop.

Just a stone's throw from the Pioneer Tunnel, tourists can visit the Museum of Anthracite Mining, operated by the Pennsylvania Historical and Museum Commission. Exhibits showing how coal is formed, processed, and brought to market add technical information to the visitors' experience and reiterate how closely interwoven were the businesses of mining and railroads in this region.

The Girard estate office in Girardville.

Girardville, Tamaqua, and Gowen City (Molly Maguire Country)

A great deal of fanfare was made in 1834 to mark the opening of the Danville & Pottsville Rail Road to Girardville. According to a report of the Committee of Inland Navigation published in *Hazard's Register of Pennsylvania* in February of that year, this meant that "the great coal region beyond the Broad Mountain (which until now was inaccessible) is connected with the improvements on the Schuylkill." Later that year, the same publication carried information on Moncure Robinson's Mahanoy Plane, which carried coal or passengers at a rate of four to six miles per hour up or down the mountain to or from the Mahanoy Creek in the valley below.

Located just east of Ashland, Girardville still bears the name of Stephen Girard, who once owned vast amounts of property in this area and provided the financial support for all the important transportation projects in his day, including the Danville & Pottsville Rail Road, the Little Schuylkill Railroad (which grew into the Reading system), and the Schuylkill Canal. When Stephen Girard died in 1831, he left cash and real estate worth more than $6 million to the city of Philadelphia, an estate that today is one of 110 trusts administered by the Board of Directors of City Trusts.

The Mahanoy Plane, which was demolished in the 1950s, is missing from modern Girardville, but the town still has a private residence popularly called the Girard Mansion on a hill overlooking a road that just skirts the town. This large but modest and unornamented dwelling was the home of William Boyd, the first supervisor of land in this area. At a corner nearby, a small brick building called the estate office is surrounded by a wrought-iron fence. Some Girard estate records are still stored here, where a local assistance program is also being administered.

Everywhere in Pennsylvania, old railroad stations are being reclaimed. This one in Tamaqua will be the site of the Schuylkill River Heritage Corridor Visitors Center.

Tamaqua was an important mining town, now known as the final resting place for a number of Molly Maguires, including John Kehoe. Its former Reading Company station is being renovated to serve as a visitors center for the Schuylkill River Heritage Corridor. The town has another office for the Reading, Blue Mountain & Northern Railroad, whose cars can be seen hauling coal throughout this general area. Just outside of town a sign leads visitors to the mouth of the New Kirk Tunnel, which is actually a coal mine owned by the Philadelphia & Reading Coal & Iron Company since 1875 (the height of the Molly Maguire era) that was expanded during the 1940s.

A sign in nearby Gowen City informs passersby that the town was founded in 1835 and named for Franklin B. Gowen. Whatever community occupied this hillside crossroads upon its founding must have borne some other name at the time, for Gowen was born in 1836. Gowen himself may have seen this area for the first time at the age of nineteen, while he was managing a furnace in nearby Shamokin for one of his older brothers.

After Gowen became president of the Philadelphia & Reading Railroad, and an independent colliery was named in his honor in 1869, this town began appearing on maps as Gowen City. However, few of the lots optimistically laid out for residences, churches, and schools were actually sold. Today, Gowen City consists of an abandoned and crumbling hotel that stands—at least for now—in striking contrast with its single street of pleasant and prosperous-looking homes overlooking a wide, cultivated valley.

Catawissa—Caboosenut Country

Catawissa may become a favorite destination for rail fans if Walter Gosciminski has his way. Located on the eastern shore of the northern branch of the Susquehanna River, this town was originally established in 1787. By the 1850s, it was served by a railroad that eventually became part of the Reading system after changing hands a number of times.

In 1979, Walt Gosciminski purchased the Catawissa train station and later a number of cabooses that he relocated on a lot between the station

A steam engine belonging to Walt Gosciminski at his complex in Catawissa.

and the railroad tracks that lie on the shore of the river. Now that he has fitted out a few of them as motel rooms, he plans to operate the train station as a bed and breakfast. The steam engine that he acquired, which is currently located among the cabooses, he intends to use for his own scenic tours. To this end, he also bought a bridge over the Susquehanna, where he has positioned yet another caboose, advertising his Catawissa enterprise to motorists.

The Railroad Heritage of Clinton and Centre Counties

The passenger car of the Bellefonte Historical Railroad arrives at the town's restored railroad station minus a locomotive. Since there are no wires overhead to indicate that the line is electrified, the passengers might be curious about what is moving this train, but they are mostly young adults and children too young to question why such a vehicle shouldn't move by itself. The conductor soon explains that this railroad's cars, made by the Budd Company of Philadelphia in the 1950s for commuter lines, have self-contained diesel engines beneath their floors.

The Bellefonte Historical Railroad operates excursions on self-propelled diesel cars from this restored station in Bellefonte.

The cars move uphill on a pleasant shaded route past a trout hatchery. The conductor identifies an imposing structure as Rockview State Correctional Institution, where Pennsylvania's convicted murderers are executed by lethal injection. The train passes a few industrial buildings and a shopping mall outside State College. The engineer walks to the opposite end of the car and takes the train downhill, back to Bellefonte.

Trains once traveled from Bellefonte to bituminous coal mines in Snow Shoe, Lock Haven on the Susquehanna, and Tyrone on the main line of the Pennsylvania Railroad. Although coal is still being mined around Snow Shoe, the tracks connecting this remote town with Bellefonte have long been abandoned. Norfolk Southern freight trains run frequently between Lock Haven and Tyrone, making it nearly impossible for a historical railroad to share the line. Around 1964, the last special train consisting of coaches, diners, and bar cars made a trip from Pittsburgh to Bellefonte for a Penn State–Pittsburgh football game.

When railroads were being studied and promoted in the early years of the nineteenth century, Bellefonte was already a small metropolis known for its industry and Big Spring, the source of Spring Creek and water power for the town's factories. An excellent calcium deposit provided the town with a second major industry. Several turnpikes connected it with the rest of the world, and in 1834, construction began on a canal that would run east to Lock Haven, where iron and other products could be shipped to Harrisburg via a State Works canal.

By 1859, the Bellefonte & Snow Shoe Railroad was hauling coal from the Snow Shoe region. On its tracks ran a steam locomotive that had been transported to Bellefonte on the canal. In 1857, the Tyrone & Lock Haven Railroad was incorporated, linking Bellefonte with Tyrone, a station on the PRR main line, and Lock Haven, on the Philadelphia & Erie Railroad.

Both railroads were merged into the Bald Eagle Valley Railroad, which was later leased to the Pennsy in 1864. Railroads opened a new era of growth and development in Bellefonte during the late nineteenth century, spurred also by the fact that Pennsylvania's Civil War governor, Andrew G. Curtin, came from Bellefonte.

Many of Bellefonte's nineteenth-century buildings are still standing, making the town a tourist attraction. The neat brick railroad station, where passengers board the Bellefonte Historical Railroad, doubles as an information center where tourists can pick up maps for walking tours. Just as nineteenth-century visitors would have proceeded from the train station to a convenient hotel, modern tourists can cross the street to the Bush House Hotel, completed in 1869. Not exactly a railroad hotel, the

Bush House was built by Daniel G. Bush, a salesman who became one of Bellefonte's key real estate developers. If visitors dine in the hotel's restaurant overlooking Spring Creek, they'll hear the freight trains running.

A drive through the Bald Eagle State Forest brings visitors to Lock Haven, which has an even older railroad hotel, the Fallon House. When it was completed in 1856, this establishment could claim to be the largest hotel in northern Pennsylvania. Lock Haven also retains many of its nineteenth-century and early-twentieth-century residences on Main Street. Although freight trains often stop downtown traffic, Lock Haven feels less like an old railroad town than Bellefonte. It also feels less like a river town now that its river view is blocked by a tall, grass-covered levee.

Knoebels Grove

Officially named Knoebels (the K is pronounced) Amusement Resort, this amusement park and picnic grove, located near Elysburg, is home to two popular miniature train rides that have been in operation for about forty years. The one called the Pioneer was installed around 1960 on narrow-gauge tracks that took passengers through what was then Pennsylvania woodland embellished to suggest the Old West. The little gas engine traveled past a covered wagon, an Indian village, and a coal mine disguised as a gold mine. Today, it winds its way among other attractions that have sprung up along its tracks. Knoebels also has the appropriately named Old Smokey, a miniature steam engine train ride with a locomotive that burns anthracite coal. It replaced an earlier miniature train ride installed in 1946 called the Nickel Plate. With these trains and some of its other attractions, Knoebels still manages to suggest a bygone era.

The Region's Rail Trails

Truly dedicated hikers will be interested in the Mid State Trail, one of the Commonwealth's most rugged and demanding hiking trails. Students from the hiking division of the Penn State Outing Club began working on this trail in 1969, and it was completed in 1986 with the cooperation of a number of other interested groups, including the Boy Scouts and Girl Scouts. The trail runs through some very isolated territory that has been incorporated into state forests and parks. It offers magnificent mountaintop views, but demands a great deal of climbing.

Hikers are spared one climb by the 250-foot Paddy Mountain Tunnel that was originally built to take trains to the lumbering village of Poe

Mills. Now a ghost town, Poe Mills was named for its sawmill on Poe Creek. In 1879, a railroad was built to Poe Mills; it eventually became part of the Pennsylvania Railroad system. Trains continued taking tourists on excursions to Poe Mills well into the early 1900s after the mills closed. Modern tourists can reach the rail trail from Poe Paddy State Park after crossing Penn's Creek on an old railroad bridge.

The region's other rail trails include the Lycoming Creek Bikeway, the Susquehanna Bikeway, and Penn's Creek Path.

Allegheny National Forest

Great Railways of the Region

The New York Central

The New York Central Railroad (NYC) was not the result of a grand scheme or ambitious plan on the part of an individual or group. Instead, it was a consolidation of smaller railroads, including the very first railroad to operate in the state of New York, whose managers came to see the wisdom of joining their lines together.

In a 1985 history, Aaron E. Klein tells the story of the Mohawk & Hudson Rail Road, the oldest of the tiny lines that would become the NYC. In the 1820s, George Featherstonaugh of Duanesburgh traveled to Albany, where he convinced the wealthy and politically powerful Stephen Van Rensselaer to support the concept of a railroad running seven miles between the Mohawk and Hudson Rivers, linking the cities of Albany and Schenectady. Opposition was expected from promoters and supporters of the Erie Canal, but it was also raised by certain citizens of Albany and by the Albany & Schenectady Turnpike Company. However, the New York legislature granted a charter in 1826, and opening day came in August 1831.

The Mohawk & Hudson was followed by the creation of other small passenger lines connecting the cities all along the Erie Canal, such as the Schenectady & Troy, the Rochester & Syracuse, and the Buffalo & Rochester. By the 1850s, it seemed logical to consolidate these individual operations, creating a single railroad that could stand up to competition from the New York & Erie Railroad, the Pennsylvania Railroad, and the Baltimore & Ohio Railroad. The legislature permitted the railroads to merge in 1853 as the New York Central Railroad, running between Albany and Buffalo. Key promoter of the merger, Erastus Corning, a manufacturer who had also served as mayor of Albany and president of the Utica & Schenectady Railroad, served as president of the new railroad until 1864.

In 1867, Cornelius Vanderbilt (known as the Commodore, thanks to his steamship fortune) took over the New York Central, and two years later, he consolidated it with two other railroads into the New York Central & Hudson River Railroad. For the first time, passengers could travel between New York City and Buffalo via a single line.

In 1873, the Commodore formally extended his railroad's reach to Chicago by taking over the Lake Shore & Michigan Southern Railway and later the Michigan Central Railroad, which had been serving as the NYC's link with that city since through service was established in 1849. His son William would add the New York, West Shore & Buffalo Railroad in 1885, and eventually would extend the company's reach to Boston and St. Louis.

As early as the 1830s, semibituminous coal had been discovered in several areas of Pennsylvania's Tioga and Lycoming Counties, prompting the NYC to extend its operations into Pennsylvania in order to gain ready access to its locomotive fuel. The NYC leased the Fall Brook Railway in 1899, merging it into the parent company in 1914. The earliest portion of this line had opened in 1840 as the Tioga Railroad, connecting the coal fields near Blossburg, Pennsylvania, with Corning, New York. It had become the Corning, Cowanesque & Antrim Railway after a merger with another railroad in 1873. An 1892 reorganization then combined it with three other railways, renaming it the Fall Brook Railway after Fall Brook Creek, a tributary of the Tioga River, which had significant deposits of coal. The New York Central had also promoted the creation of the Beech Creek Railroad, running from the Clearfield area to the Pennsylvania town of Jersey Shore near Williamsport, where it would connect with the Fall Brook Railway. The New York Central leased this line in 1890 and made it part of its Pennsylvania division in 1899. By the twentieth century, NYC lines served the Pennsylvania counties of Cambria, Centre, Clarion, Clearfield, Clinton, Crawford, Erie, Indiana, Jefferson, Lycoming, Mercer, Tioga, Venango, and Warren.

While Pennsylvania enjoyed its oil boom in the 1860s, the Lake Shore & Michigan Southern Railway (soon to become part of the New York Central system) extended a branch from Ashtabula, Ohio, to the Pennsylvania towns of Franklin and Oil City. John D. Rockefeller shipped his oil over these tracks to refineries in Cleveland.

The Lake Shore & Michigan Southern Railway also took over several smaller lines built along the southern shore of Lake Erie, which resulted in the placement of this port city on the NYC's main line. In 1877, the New York Central purchased stock that would give it control of the Pittsburgh & Lake Erie Railroad, linking its main line with the river valleys of the Pittsburgh region.

The New York Central's nineteenth-century invasion of the Commonwealth resulted in a long rivalry with the Pennsy. By the twentieth century, both railroads offered high-speed luxury train service between New York City and Chicago with schedules that placed the trains on parallel tracks for a portion of the distance. In 1913, the NYC opened its Grand

Central Terminal in New York City to compete with the magnificent Pennsylvania Station.

Unfortunately, the New York Central and the Pennsy also shared the same twentieth-century problems. Business declined after World War II, resulting in the elimination of scores of intercity and local passenger trains. The two rivals were forced into an uneasy alliance as the ill-fated Penn Central in 1968.

The National New York Central Railroad Museum was founded in 1987 in Elkhart, Indiana, to preserve the histories of the NYC, the Lake Shore & Michigan Southern Railway, and other affiliates. There is also a New York Central System Historical Society in Cleveland, Ohio.

Rail Stories of the Region

The Philadelphia & Erie Railroad

From the mid-1830s, another idea stirring the imaginations of certain Philadelphia entrepreneurs was the possibility of connecting Philadelphia via rail with Erie. Promoters reasoned that such a route running diagonally across the Commonwealth would be the most convenient link between a Great Lakes port and an East Coast metropolis and could not fail to pull a great deal of Midwest trade in Philadelphia's direction. But standing in the way were miles of uncleared, undeveloped wilderness between Sunbury and Erie, not to mention the mountains that would rob the proposed railroad of much efficiency if they had to be negotiated with inclined planes.

As early as 1834, newspaper accounts proposed routes roughly following the west branch of the Susquehanna toward Erie. In 1836, the citizens of Warren County petitioned the Commonwealth for just such a railroad in the hopes that it would run through their county seat. Businessmen in Erie also favored the plan.

In 1837, the Pennsylvania legislature authorized the incorporation of the Sunbury & Erie Railroad Company. At the time, Sunbury was already a hub of transportation, conveniently located at the junction of the Susquehanna River's northern and western branches. And keeping "Philadelphia" out of the railroad's name also meant that technically the project would not be competing with the Commonwealth's State Works.

Edward Miller conducted a survey of the terrain in north-central and northwestern Pennsylvania, and in 1839, he recommended that a railroad be built from Erie to Lock Haven, where goods could be transported to the State Works canal on the west branch of the Susquehanna. Construction began the following year, when a short portion of the route west of Warren was graded.

Unfortunately, that was all the work completed on this railroad for about a dozen years. In his history of the Philadelphia & Erie Railroad, published in 1975, Homer Tope Rosenberger wrote, "The Sunbury and Erie Railroad Company was sleeping during the 1840s." Pennsylvania was suffering economically in the wake of the panic of 1837 and the failure of the Philadelphia-based Bank of the United States. In 1844, the railroad lost a key promoter with the death of Nicholas Biddle, who had also been president of the bank. In the same decade, some of the demand for the Philadelphia-to-Erie connection was addressed by the official incorporation of the Pennsylvania Railroad and its plans for an all-rail line to Pittsburgh, with a projected branch to Erie.

Businessmen in Warren and Erie kept the project alive, and in 1853, after the route was resurveyed, construction began between Milton and Williamsport. It is likely that the rails were manufactured by the Montour Iron Company in nearby Danville. In 1855, tracks were constructed between Milton and Sunbury, where the railroad touched the remains of the Danville & Pottsville Rail Road, as well as the Baltimore & Susquehanna Rail Road, which had since become the Northern Central Railway.

The railroad's more local promoters, Thomas Struthers and Gen. Thomas L. Kane, caused the original route over the mountains to be abandoned and a new one to be adopted—a poor decision that prevented this railroad from ever achieving its potential. The new route climbed two summits that could be negotiated only by lighter trains, which increased the cost of operations. It also lay too far north of rich bituminous coal deposits and well-timbered land.

The Sunbury & Erie Railroad officially became the Philadelphia & Erie Railroad in 1861 and was leased by the Pennsylvania Railroad the following year, making it one of the first of the Pennsy's many acquisitions. In 1864, the final portion of this railroad was completed, and it finally became possible for trains to run from Philadelphia to Erie in two days.

That same decade, the Philadelphia & Erie Railroad fostered the development of its own little railroad town at Renovo, where the Susquehanna River runs through a scenic, narrow valley in the mountains of Clinton County. Here the railroad's locomotives were maintained and workers resided. In 1869, construction of the Renovo House, a large hotel attached to the train station, made the remote town something of a resort.

Philadelphia and Its Environs, a travel book published in 1875, stated, "It is a resort just suited to the hunter and fisher."

Due to the early delays in construction and the change in the planned route, the Philadelphia & Erie Railroad never did make Erie a major port on the Great Lakes or capture much Midwest trade for Philadelphia. According to Rosenberger, it did, however, open much virtually uninhabited wilderness in north-central and northwestern Pennsylvania to economic development and the lumber industry, and it served as a connecting railroad for other lines.

Logging Railroads

Those hiking the forests of north-central Pennsylvania are likely to find themselves using old railroad grades, where it is not unusual to find the occasional discarded spike or some other rusted fragment of the logging railroads that once hauled felled trees to the area's sawmills and transformed Pennsylvania's early lumber industry into big business. The fascinating story of the Commonwealth's logging railroads was researched and told in great detail in the 1970s in a fourteen-volume series collectively titled *The Logging Railroad Era of Lumbering in Pennsylvania,* by Walter C. Casler, Benjamin F. G. Kline Jr., and Thomas T. Taber III.

Until the mid-nineteenth century, lumber was processed in the forests of Pennsylvania in small family-operated mills powered by water. Williamsport became America's lumber capital, the place where logs were transported by the current of the Susquehanna River and its tributary streams, which drained thousands of square miles of pine and hemlock forests.

Increasing demand for lumber after the Civil War meant that more timber had to be cut and more lumber had to reach potential markets more quickly and more reliably. Adapting railroads to the lumber industry eliminated the need to clear streams and build dams and booms, also making it possible to transport lumber in all seasons of the year. By the 1880s, thousands of miles of logging railroads were constructed, particularly in Warren, Forest, McKean, Elk, and Potter Counties.

According to Benjamin F. G. Kline Jr., Pennsylvania's first logging railroad was built in Jefferson County in 1864 by a logging operation called Wright and Pier. The manager decided to transform his horsepower-operated, wooden-railed "tramroad" into a genuine railroad operated by locomotive. He and a millwright traveled to Pittsburgh, where they purchased a boiler and steam engine. The millwright then designed and built a locomotive with the help of an eighteen-year-old engineer.

A natural feature called Pulpit Rocks on the line between Keating and Driftwood in the forests of present-day Clinton and Cameron Counties, as illustrated for William B. Sipes's book on the Pennsylvania Railroad, shows evidence of active logging in this area.

WARREN.

The logging industry was also in action in this illustration of Warren for William B. Sipes's book.

Other lumbermen were soon building their own homegrown locomotives, buying needed parts separately or having them made to order at a local foundry or blacksmith shop. The motley results were called "dinkey" locomotives regardless of their size, and the old tram roads became known as "dinkey tram roads." Eventually, a number of manufacturers would produce locomotives for this growing industry, which was also expanded by the invention of the log loader to place timber on railroad cars. Logging locomotives called the Climax and Heisler were manufactured in Pennsylvania. The Shay, which became most popular nationwide, was built in neighboring Ohio.

The precious locomotives were generally used only to take empty cars to a place where lumber was being cut. The locomotives returned alone, while railroad cars loaded with lumber employed the force of gravity controlled by a single brakeman to get the logs to the mill. This thrilling and often hazardous process became known as "wildcatting."

Logging railroads generally had a main line fed by many spurs that were constantly extended to new timber-cutting areas. Narrow-gauge railroads were best adapted to the steep grades and sharp curves required by the region's rugged terrain. Walter C. Casler wrote, "The logging railroad operated in all kinds of weather and could go anywhere. It followed the winding course of streams, switchbacked up steep hillsides and crossed over into the next hollow seeking more timber. It went into swamps, and laid its track along the soft, marshy ground and in places often covered with two feet of water." A history of Clarion County by Aaron J. Davis, published in 1887, illustrated how completely logging railroads had transformed the industry in a very short time. Davis reported, "The River is no longer the great highway for traffic . . . all the larger firms have sidings and ship their products by the more convenient and always available rail, sending only empty coal boats by water."

In Forest County and southern Warren County, the Wheeler and Dusenbury Lumber Company operated sawmills at Newtown and Endeavor from

A locomotive adapted for the logging industry. RAILROAD MUSEUM OF PENNSYLVANIA

1837 to 1939. Their mills, farms, and lumber camps were linked by approximately fifty miles of logging railroads. The Goodyear Lumber Company, with mills in Galeton and Austin, operated 120 miles of logging railroad served by twenty locomotives between 1878 and 1920.

Truman Dowd ("Teddy") Collins was Pennsylvania's best-known lumberman. Born in 1831, he established nine sawmills in the course of his life, which he spent in north-central Pennsylvania where his business was, rather than some distant city. He built the Sheffield & Tionesta Railroad, which was incorporated as a common carrier in 1900. It followed the path of Tionesta Creek, and after its abandonment in 1943, its grade was much appreciated by fishermen.

The Central Pennsylvania Lumber Company was formed as a subsidiary of the United States Leather Company in 1903. One of the largest lumbering operations in the Commonwealth, it was headquartered in Williamsport and operated sixteen mills. In the early years of the twentieth century, this firm cut half of Pennsylvania's lumber. When its Sheffield mill closed in the early 1940s, the Commonwealth's lumbering industry was essentially over.

Once a lumbering firm was through with a particular piece of real estate, the trees were often completely gone. In his 1887 history of Clarion County, Davis speculated, "It requires no degree of foresight to see . . . that seven years hence Clarion County shall be completely stripped of its pine and oak timber of value." The pitifully denuded tracts were considered worthless by lumber companies and sold back to the Commonwealth at bargain prices. After many years of care and conservation, they have proven to be a great investment. Today, they comprise much of the Allegheny National Forest, established in 1923, as well as many of Pennsylvania's state parks, where hikers now encounter a landscape that looks more like it did during Thomas Jefferson's administration than at the beginning of the Twentieth Century.

Local Chapter of the National Railway Historical Society

The Allegheny National Forest region is home to a single chapter of the National Railway Historical Society known as the Bucktail Chapter, which is affiliated with the Bucksgahuda & Western Railroad of St. Mary's in Elk County. The railroad operates a two-foot-gauge railroad museum in St. Mary's, where members preserve and operate industrial railroad equipment. The railroad got its start in 1966 when members purchased a steam locomotive from Germany. Gradually, they laid track, built facilities, and acquired cars and additional locomotives, including a Shay, or geared locomotive popular with logging railroads. Every year, members hold a Railroaders' Day to celebrate that year's accomplishments. The Bucksgahuda & Western Railroad is located just south of the town on Route 255.

The Region's Railroad Giants

Gen. Thomas L. Kane (1822–1883)

Thomas L. Kane was born into a railroad family. His middle name was Leiper, the surname of his grandfather, the Philadelphian who could claim to have constructed one of the earliest (if not the earliest) railroads in America. Thomas L. Kane's father, however, was a district court judge who instructed Kane in law and awarded him a clerkship.

Outside the Commonwealth, Kane is remembered primarily in Salt Lake City. A personal friend of Brigham Young, he befriended the Mormons, encouraged their expansion in the West, and worked to make them more widely understood and accepted in America. A travel account written by Kane's wife, Elizabeth, remains a widely consulted work on early Mormon life.

As an organizer and agent of the McKean and Elk Land and Improvement Company, Kane explored and studied much of McKean and Elk Counties, finally deciding in 1859 to take up residence; the town was named Kane in his honor. During the Civil War, Kane organized a volunteer regiment consisting of Pennsylvania backwoodsmen from this developing portion of the Commonwealth. Known as the Bucktails, they were distinguished by the deer tails that they wore in their caps.

As a member of the board of trustees of the Sunbury & Erie Railroad, Kane was one of the men who made certain that this promising venture would pass through McKean County and Kane, a move criticized by railroad historians as the reason why this railroad proved to be less successful than it might have been. As early as 1890, M. A. Leeson mentioned in a history of Elk County, "The location of the Philadelphia & Erie Railroad, as at present constructed, has been questioned by a number of engineers."

Kane was also an organizer of the New York, Lake Erie & Western Railroad & Coal Company, which served the town of Bradford. When coal fields were discovered in southern Elk and northern Jefferson Counties, Kane worked with this railroad's engineering department on the various options for extending the line to that part of Pennsylvania. He promoted the daring concept of a bridge across the valley of the Kinzua Creek, even though such a structure would be longer and higher than any other railroad viaduct in the world. Today, Kinzua Viaduct remains a lasting tribute to the economic contribution of Gen. Thomas L. Kane.

Many authors writing about the history of Kinzua Viaduct speculate that Kane personally financed this structure. In a lengthy account of the bridge's construction published in the *Titusville Herald* in 1987, the Rev. W. George Thornton replied, "It is highly likely that the financing of the structure was a corporate and not a personal venture."

Kane died in Philadelphia in 1883 and was buried near the Kane Memorial Chapel in McKean County.

Erastus Corning (1794–1872)

Erastus Corning began his career in his uncle's hardware store. In 1826, he started manufacturing nails, a business he later expanded into the Albany Iron Works, which manufactured railroad spikes and imported iron rails from England for sale to the New York Central Railroad.

In 1835, he organized the Corning Land Company, which purchased two thousand acres along the Chemung River in New York. The chief asset of this piece of real estate was the Chemung Canal, designed to link the southern counties of New York with the Erie Canal. Corning joined forces with other businessmen to build the New York portion of what would become the Tioga Railroad, which opened for business in 1840, connecting this area with the coal fields of Blossburg, Pennsylvania. Ironically, the town named to honor Corning is better known today as the home of Corning, Inc., originally a glass manufacturer that moved to the village in 1868 and had no connection with Erastus Corning.

In the early 1850s, New York had a number of small railroads serving and linking the cities whose growth had been fostered by the Erie Canal. Erastus Corning, who had been president of the Utica & Schenectady Railroad since 1833, urged that a meeting be held in Albany, where he made a motion that these smaller lines be consolidated into a single rail system. He became the chief promoter for the New York Central Consolidation Act passed in 1853 and the first president of the New York Central Railroad (he resigned in 1864). Since Corning had also invested in land in Michigan, he had been one of the buyers of the previously state-owned Michigan Central Railroad, which gave the New York Central through service to Chicago and later became an important component of the NYC system.

In 1867, Corning was more or less ousted from any management role with the New York Central Railroad when Cornelius Vanderbilt voted the huge amount of stock he had acquired and installed a new board of his own choosing. In her biography of Corning, published in 1960, Irene D. Neu summed up Corning's career: "Although Corning used his connection with the Central to promote his mercantile, banking, and manufacturing activities, the scope of those activities reflected benefit on the railroad. He failed to secure for the Central a rail line to New York City, but fifteen years before Vanderbilt took over, Corning had provided his road with western connections that gave it access to Chicago. In every important sense he was the architect of the New York Central."

Cornelius Vanderbilt (1794–1877)

"Gentlemen: You have undertaken to cheat me. I won't sue you, for the law is too slow. I'll ruin you. Yours truly, Cornelius Vanderbilt." These few words of a very brief 1853 letter are cited by virtually every biographer as evidence of the ruthless character of Cornelius Vanderbilt, "the Commodore," remembered primarily as a steamship magnate.

Vanderbilt was born on Staten Island and could boast of little formal education. At the age of sixteen, he acquired a small sailboat and began ferrying passengers between Staten Island and New York City. In 1818, he took a job as a steamboat captain, gaining the expertise that he used to create a steamship route through Central America to take adventurers to the California gold rush.

In the 1850s, he began acquiring stock in the New York & Harlem Railroad, which ran up the east bank of the Hudson River from New York City toward Albany. He next sought control of this railroad's chief competitor, the Hudson River Railroad. Through stock purchases

Cornelius Vanderbilt
LIBRARY OF CONGRESS

he gained control of the New York Central Railroad and then consolidated it with the Hudson River Railroad in 1869. He leased the New York & Harlem Railroad to this new entity in 1872. President of the New York Central since 1867, Vanderbilt ran the line very efficiently, gaining for it the reputation of one of America's leading rail systems.

Perhaps to keep this railroad empire from breaking up after his death, he willed most of his vast estate to only one of his children, William Henry Vanderbilt.

William Henry Vanderbilt (1821–1885)

Cornelius Vanderbilt was disappointed with William's marriage at the early age of nineteen and was convinced that his son was not destined for success in the business world. Therefore, Cornelius exiled William to a quiet farm on Staten Island. William finally gained his father's respect when he successfully reorganized the Staten Island Railroad, a thirteen-mile line that had fallen into receivership through poor management.

Having thus proven himself as a railroad executive on a smaller scale, William Henry Vanderbilt became his father's chief lieutenant. It was William who insisted that his father buy control of the Lake Shore & Michigan Southern Railway and the Michigan Central Railroad. It was also William who was chosen president of the New York Central on his father's death, a position he held until his resignation due to poor health in 1883.

On a December day in 1885, while William was meeting with Robert Garrett, president of the Baltimore & Ohio Railroad, he suddenly slumped forward onto the floor. In five minutes, he was dead of a massive cerebral hemorrhage. Although William's name is not as widely known today as that of his father, there can be no doubt that he was a very capable railroad manager. His inheritance of approximately $90 million had grown to a personal fortune of $200 million by the time of his death.

William Henry Vanderbilt
NATIONAL CYCLOPEDIA OF AMERICAN BIOGRAPHY

Sampling the Region's Railroad History

Williamsport

The town of Williamsport was laid out in 1795, but by 1830, it could boast of only ten brick buildings. So tiny and backward was this woodland hamlet that its designation as county seat aroused bitterness in surrounding communities. Conditions did not begin to improve until after 1833, when Pennsylvania's State Works linked it by canal to other communities on the Susquehanna River.

There had been sawmills in the vicinity of Williamsport since the late eighteenth century, but the canal greatly bolstered the local lumbering industry because it meant that lumber could be more easily shipped from those mills to market. In 1851, the Susquehanna Boom Company constructed Williamsport's most famous feature, a log boom in the Susquehanna River that acted as a floating parking lot where logs could be captured and sorted for their designated mills. Despite occasional damage from floods, the seven-mile boom transformed Williamsport into America's late-nineteenth-century lumber capital, and is the reason why this town is included in the "Sampling" section of the Allegheny National Forest region, even though it is located in Lycoming County.

As early as 1832, Williamsport's citizens proposed a railroad that would link the town with Elmira, New York. Such a railroad would effectively place the Pennsylvania State Works canal in communication with the Chemung Canal, which was itself connected to the famous Erie Canal. Philadelphia businessmen might have liked this idea because it had the potential of tapping the trade of western New York, but the locals looked upon the proposal as a way to make money on the area's deposits of bituminous coal. An article appearing in the January 1832 issue of *Hazard's Register of Pennsylvania* stated, "Indeed, it is now known to be a profitable trade to haul, in the winter season on sleds, our Bituminous coal to that state [New York], and bring a return load of Plaster. Again, every blacksmith's shop will furnish a continued consumption for our coal; and thus steadily promote the interests of the stockholder in this road."

Incorporated in 1832, the Williamsport & Elmira Rail-Road became part of the Northern Central Railway, and subsequently the Pennsylvania Railroad. The Pennsy also absorbed the Sunbury & Erie Railroad, which also ran through Williamsport. In addition, the Philadelphia & Reading Railroad served Williamsport by means of a branch line, making Williamsport a very well connected town.

Williamsport's most famous businessman was Peter Herdic, a native of New York who came to Williamsport in 1853. Besides the lumber industry, Herdic got involved in virtually every other Williamsport business, and even served as mayor. He persuaded the Pennsylvania Railroad to relocate its station somewhat west of Williamsport's main business district, but conveniently adjacent to a luxury hotel he built in 1864. Herdic then sold building lots in this area, where successful businessmen proceeded to build gracious homes. Known today as "Millionaires' Row," this neighborhood on West Fourth Street is now a mixture of restored Victorian properties and mansions long since subdivided into apartments. Peter Herdic's hotel became the Park Home for the elderly in 1940. The commercial complex Herdic built in 1870, hoping it would become Williamsport's new business center, still stands in the 700 block. The renovation of Peter Herdic's house, built in 1854, was completed in 1984, when it was recognized by the Bureau of Historic Preservation as the top project for that year. It is currently open to the public as a restaurant.

The lumber and railroad heritage of Williamsport is best sampled on West Fourth Street at the Lycoming County Historical Society's museum, named after Thomas T. Taber III, a railroad historian and major donor to the museum. This two-story museum has period rooms and exhibits illustrating major aspects of the area's history and industries. The labels for the exhibits dedicated to the lumber industry and logging railroads read as if they were drawn directly from *The Logging Railroad Era of Lumbering in Pennsylvania,* to which Taber contributed.

Much of the museum's lower level is devoted to the LaRue Shempp Model Train Exhibition, a collection of more than three hundred toy trains that was once housed in LaRue Shempp's basement. A Williamsport native, Shempp was employed by the Lycoming County Board of Assistance, but his lifelong passion was collecting toy trains; in fact, he was a charter member of both the Train Collectors Association and the Toy Train Operating Society. Shempp did most of his collecting during the 1940s and 1950s and managed to gather many one-of-a-kind prototype and demonstration models. To prevent his collection from being dispersed by auction after his death, he made arrangements to have it housed in the county museum. Though there are only two operating layouts, the rare and unique toy trains can be studied in well-lit cases donated by local businessmen.

The Tioga Central Railroad

Route 15 connects Williamsport with Route 6, the four-hundred-mile highway connecting all the seats of Pennsylvania's northern tier of counties. In this region, Route 6 winds its way between forested hills, across swift streams, and through prime game lands. It brings vacationers to cabins and rustic motels, and customers to the unpaved parking lots of beloved local watering holes, like the Antlers Inn, a converted roadhouse. Route 6 also more or less connects the artifacts of this region's railroad history.

Route 6 bisects the town of Wellsboro, which has a still-thriving Main Street, where gaslights illuminate a small department store, a hotel built in the 1920s, and a diner. Wellsboro also has a Victorian courthouse next door to a somber red-brick Victorian jail and across the street from a town square with a fountain. One of the square's monuments is decorated with bas-reliefs depicting a steam engine and coal car and is dedicated to John Magee, a founder of the Fall Brook Railway.

The Tioga Central Railroad, a relatively new tourist line handling about twenty thousand passengers per year, operates out of Wellsboro Junction, about three miles north of town. The earliest trains operating on its right-of-way were those of the Tioga Railroad, linking Blossburg with New York's Chemung Canal, a venture later renamed the Blossburg & Corning Railroad (Erastus Corning was one of its early promoters). In 1873, the Blossburg & Corning Railroad merged with the Wellsboro & Lawrenceville Railroad, which had been completed in 1872. The new entity was called the Corning, Cowanesque & Antrim Railway, much of it owned by the Fall Brook Coal Company founded by John Magee and his son Duncan, who had discovered coal on Fall Brook Creek. The Corning, Cowanesque & Antrim Railway officially joined the Fall Brook Railway in 1892 and in due course was absorbed into the New York Central system.

In 1992, well after the NYC had become part of the Penn Central Railroad and subsequently Conrail, rail operations ceased in this area. An organization called Growth Resources of Wellsboro (GROW) purchased the line to create the Wellsboro & Corning Railroad, a freight line, and the Tioga Central passenger excursion line.

The Tioga Central's weekend trips take passengers north to Hammond Lake on the portion of the railroad built in 1872 to haul coal out of Antrim. The train moves from the Marsh Creek Watershed along Crooked Creek and the Tioga-Hammond Wetlands Restoration. Nineteenth-century passengers on the same line would not have enjoyed a view of Hammond Lake; it was built as part of a Susquehanna River flood control project in the wake of Hurricane Agnes. Tourists are encouraged to enjoy the beauty of the scenery; there is no narration except what the conductor provides in response to questions. Passengers often spot osprey, which were reintroduced to the area in 1990 after an absence of more than forty years.

Car 365 Norris Brook is set to depart on a dinner trip on the Tioga Central Railroad. The car was built in 1939 for the Seaboard Railway and was one of the earliest stainless steel cars. R. L. STOVING

The scenery is best observed from the wooden benches of the Ives Run open observation car, a restored Pennsylvania Railroad coach. This is also the best car for those who enjoy the plaintive sound of a train whistle, since it is directly behind the locomotive and the ride includes a lot of grade crossings. In the Tioga Central's club car, rebuilt from a Canadian National Railway open-platform observation car, passengers can purchase hot dogs, packaged snacks, and drinks at the On Track Café.

On Saturday evenings during the tourist season, the Tioga Central runs dinner trains. Richard L. Stoving, president of the tourist line, came up with the idea of recreating the actual dishes and menus of various American railroads famous for their cuisine. Following extensive research, he made arrangements with a chef at nearby Mansfield University to develop enough recipes that passengers on any given dinner trip would have a choice between two main courses served by the same railroad. On nights when the Tioga Central features Baltimore & Ohio Railroad cuisine, passengers might choose to sample the crabcakes the B&O was known for; on New York Central nights, they can taste NYC's famous lobster Newburg. Authentic Pennsylvania Railroad dressing tops the salads on Pennsy nights. To allow sufficient time for leisurely dining, the Tioga Central dinner trains travel much farther north, to the New York State border.

The Pennsylvania Lumber Museum

Farther west on Route 6, past the town of Galeton, which was once known for its busy sawmills, there's a place to sample the life of a "wood hick," or logger, at the recreated logging camp at the Pennsylvania Lumber Museum, administered by the Pennsylvania Historical and Museum Commission on 160 timbered acres in Potter County. Local men who once worked or still work in the lumber industry take visitors there the same way that Philadelphia suburbanites take their out-of-town guests to Valley Forge.

On the edge of a mill pond where logs are floating, the logging camp has an operating sawmill, its floor littered with sawdust from recent demonstrations. The camp also has a reconstructed blacksmith shop, horse barn, and filer's shack, where the loggers would have had their tools sharpened. Tables are set in the mess hall, and the kitchen is furnished with cans of pork and beans. All the buildings are constructed of rough-hewn weathered boards in a way that would make demolition easy when it was time to move on.

Although the typical logging camp would not have had the luxury of an engine house, the Pennsylvania Lumber Museum built one to protect its star exhibit and artifact of logging railroads: a Shay locomotive. Named for its inventor, Ephraim Shay, the Shay locomotive was gear driven, thus making it—like the Climax and Heisler—slow but powerful, to enable it to operate on steep grades and rails hastily laid on rugged and uneven terrain. This particular Shay, used by several lumber companies in West Virginia, was donated by the Penn-York Lumberman's Club.

In an adjoining shed, there's a Barnhart log loader, a device invented to pick up logs and stack them on a railroad car. Several logging cars equipped with distinctively small wheels are also on display.

Residents of the Allegheny National Forest region have a special respect for the Civilian Conservation Corps (CCC), thanks to their role in cleaning up after the logging industry. Created in 1933 during Franklin D. Roosevelt's administration, the CCC enrolled young men for conservation projects nationwide, including road construction, tree planting, and drainage facilitation. The men lived a military life in camps run by the army and sent most of their pay to their families. The Pennsylvania Lumber Museum has a genuine CCC cabin, built in the 1930s, on its grounds. It is one of many memorials that can be found in this region to the men who were responsible for the dams, campsites, and other amenities still used by visitors today.

Kinzua Viaduct

Near the town of Mount Jewett stands one of Pennsylvania's most impressive railroad artifacts: Kinzua (pronounced Kin-zoo) Bridge, or Kinzua Viaduct, built to transport coal from land owned by the New York & Erie Railroad in Elk and Jefferson Counties to Buffalo, New York, where there

The Kinzua Viaduct as seen from the observation platform at Kinzua Bridge State Park. The bridge is currently closed to rail and pedestrian traffic, but the overlook remains open. PENNSYLVANIA DEPARTMENT OF CONSERVATION AND NATURAL RESOURCES

was a ready market for about three million tons of coal per year, as well as excellent facilities for transshipment to the Midwest. As the bird flies, Buffalo was not so far away, so the Erie's local subsidiary, the New York, Lake Erie & Western Railroad & Coal Company, managed to build a structure that enabled trains to "soar" over the valley of Kinzua Creek.

Because the Kinzua Creek flowed through a gorge that was three hundred feet deep and a half mile wide, the railroad had three choices: from the Erie's main line station at Carrolton, New York, it could lay tracks that detoured around the valley, descended into the valley, where they would cross a bridge, or spanned the entire valley on one enormous viaduct.

Gen. Thomas L. Kane promoted the third and boldest choice, and specifications for Kinzua Viaduct were drawn up by the Erie's chief engineer, Octave Chanute. Another member of the self-taught generation of railroad engineers, Chanute had already built bridges across the Missouri

River and the elevated railway system in New York City. A firm called Clarke, Reeves & Company of Phoenixville, Pennsylvania, was tapped to fabricate it.

The resulting viaduct was 301 feet high and 2,051 feet long, about 50 feet higher than the structure in the Peruvian Andes that had previously held the record as world's highest railroad viaduct. Constructed of iron, its twenty spans were supported by towers built on stone foundations. Kinzua Viaduct also gained the nation's respect for having been built in less than four months after its foundations were prepared. It was completed in September 1882.

The bridge immediately became a tourist attraction, and its first bridge tender, Charles Stauffer, became a local daredevil hero who could often be observed climbing the massive structure. In his 1890 history of Mc-Kean County, M. A. Leeson wrote about his exploits: "The first watchman used to inspect three of the twenty towers every day. In the winter of 1883–84, while engaged in his work, the air benumbed his hands, so that he could not cling longer to the braces, and losing his grip, fell sixty-five feet into a deep snowdrift, which saved him. On another occasion some one hailed him from the track, and, forgetting his location, he let go his hold and was falling from the top girts, when a friendly iron brace, within reach, saved his life."

In 1893, a bank robber dying of pneumonia raved in his delirium about $40,000 in gold coin and currency that he had stashed in glass jars buried somewhere near the viaduct. Fortune hunters have searched for the loot for more than a century, but no one has ever reported finding it. The rangers at today's Kinzua Bridge State Park prefer that visitors do not arrive bearing shovels.

In less than two decades, newer and heavier rolling stock meant that Kinzua Viaduct would need to be replaced. The Elmira Bridge Company constructed a new, steel viaduct using the same foundation. Once again, the project was executed as quickly as possible. Demolition of the old viaduct began in May 1900, and trains were running across the new viaduct by the end of that September.

In 1959, Kinzua Viaduct was closed due to declining freight traffic. When the Erie Lackawanna Railroad sold it to a salvager, local citizens lobbied to preserve it as a railroad artifact and tourist attraction. Elisha Kent Kane, grandson of Gen. Thomas L. Kane, was one of the movement's leaders. Kinzua Bridge State Park was created in 1963, and Kinzua Viaduct was placed on the National Register of Historic Civil Engineering Landmarks in 1982.

Kinzua Bridge State Park is located on State Road 3011 several miles off Route 6. Visitors can view the viaduct from a nearby scenic overlook, but the bridge itself was closed to train and pedestrian traffic in 2002, pending repairs.

Kane

Signs welcoming visitors to Kane, Pennsylvania, proclaim this town to be "The Black Cherry Capital of the World." That's black cherry as in hardwood, not fruit. Kane is almost surrounded by the Allegheny National Forest. Sometimes Kane is also called the "Icebox of Pennsylvania" due to the extraordinary amount of snowfall it receives.

Kane's naturally low pollen count and cool summer breezes made it a popular resort during the late nineteenth century. At one time, it had its own railroad hotel, the Thomson House, named after J. Edgar Thomson of the Pennsylvania Railroad. Today, efforts are in progress to preserve the town's transportation history at a museum being developed in its long-unused PRR depot.

Kane's key attraction is presently the Thomas L. Kane Memorial Chapel and Museum, built by the general himself between 1876 and 1878 to be the town's First Presbyterian Church. Today, the chapel is owned by the Church of the Latter Day Saints and functions as a satellite of its world-famous Family History Library. Visitors interested in railroad heritage can admire the statue of Gen. Thomas L. Kane outside the chapel.

The Knox & Kane Railroad

In the 1980s, railroader Sloan Cornell, who had run lines at Blairsville and Gettysburg, became interested in operating a tourist railroad in the Allegheny National Forest that would take passengers for a ride across Kinzua Viaduct. In 1982, the Knox & Kane Railroad acquired tracks up to the bridge and subsequently entered into an agreement with the Pennsylvania Department of Environmental Resources to lease and maintain the structure. The first tourist train crossed the viaduct in 1987.

Although Kinzua Viaduct was closed to all traffic in 2002 pending repair, tourists can board the Knox & Kane Railroad in Kane or more distant Marienville for a round-trip that takes either four hours or all day. Trains proceed over a route completed in the 1880s by the Pittsburgh, Bradford & Buffalo Railroad, which was later taken over by the Pittsburgh & Western Railroad. The Baltimore & Ohio Railroad, which acquired this route in 1902, continued freight service on these tracks until 1982.

After traveling forty-eight miles through the Allegheny National Forest behind a steam or diesel engine, passengers can get a good look at Kinzua Viaduct.

The Knox & Kane Railroad operates a traveling caboose motel, offering an experience that may be unique in America. Tourists can rent the railroad's caboose, which is equipped like a recreational vehicle with self-contained bath and kitchen facilities. They board and load the caboose in Marienville. The caboose is placed on a siding, where it remains for one or two nights. Occupants can enjoy hiking, fishing, and picnicking in the Kinzua Bridge State Park until the train returns to retrieve them.

The Region's Rail Trails

What may be Pennsylvania's best rail trail extends along the floor of Pine Creek Gorge, where a cool Pine Creek flows between forested walls that are home to eagles, herons, hawks, and even coyotes. Now part of the Tioga State Forest, this dramatic gorge is known as the Grand Canyon of

A railroad shed and a short length of track attest to the railroad heritage of the Pine Creek Trail.

Pennsylvania. Formed about twenty thousand years ago when retreating glaciers created a dam that forced Pine Creek to reverse its course and flow south, this gorge is forty-seven miles long and 1,450 feet deep at its southern and deepest end.

The Pine Creek Gorge gained railroad tracks in 1883 when the Jersey Shore, Pine Creek & Buffalo Railroad was constructed to transport timber, coal, and passengers between Wellsboro Junction and Williamsport. This railroad entered the Fall Brook system when it was reorganized in 1892, and later became part of the New York Central and then the Penn Central systems. Conrail ran its last freight train through the canyon in 1988.

Eventually, the Pine Creek Trail will stretch for sixty-two miles from Wellsboro Junction to Jersey Shore, but it is being groomed and opened in phases. Visitors can access the trail at a point just below Route 6 for hiking, nonmotorized biking, or cross-country skiing. A separate equestrian trail runs parallel for about nine miles. The less energetic can enjoy the Pine Creek Trail via covered wagon by signing up for a ride with the Mountain Trail Horse Center, Inc.

Pine Creek Gorge is framed by two state parks, located on its eastern and western rims, respectively. The Leonard Harrison State Park, on the eastern rim, was named after the Wellsboro businessman who developed this immediate area as a public picnic ground called "The Lookout." Work done by the Civilian Conservation Corps to further develop the park is honored by a life-size statue of a CCC recruit poised at the summit. Colton Point State Park, on the western rim, was created on land purchased by the Commonwealth in the early 1900s and developed by the CCC. It is named after local lumberman Henry Colton.

Both state parks have trails descending to the bottom of the gorge, but most visitors just come to stroll along the summit and admire the view. Local residents have been known to arrive in limousines to have their wedding photographs taken. The changing colors of the leaves make the view particularly spectacular in autumn, but the crushed stone path of Pine Creek Trail, visible along the stream, provides an impressive vista all year long. The sight of hikers and bikers moving some eight hundred feet below, where steam locomotives once ran, gives the visitor a real respect for the scale of Pennsylvania's Grand Canyon.

The Clarion/Little Toby Trail runs through Elk and Jefferson Counties along the abandoned Ridgeway & Clearfield branch of the Pennsylvania Railroad. Named for the two rivers it follows, this trail is framed by steep slopes and game lands reminiscent of Pennsylvania's Grand Canyon.

Elsewhere in the region, the Kinzua Bridge Trail utilizes an old Erie line. The Kellettville to Nebraska Trace follows the route of the Sheffield & Tionesta Railroad, part of Teddy Collins's empire.

Following its completion, a project known as the North Country Trail will include a route stretching through eight counties of Pennsylvania as part of a far longer National Scenic Trail that will run from New York to North Dakota. In Pennsylvania, the North Country Trail will cross the Allegheny National Forest in McKean, Forest, and Warren Counties. The Twin Lakes Trail was constructed to link the North Country Trail to the Twin Lakes recreation area in the Allegheny National Forest.

Other rail trails in this region include the Warren/North Warren Bike Trail, the Tidioute Riverside RecTrek Trail, the Clearfield to Grampian Trail, the Railroad Grade Trail, the Lamb's Creek Hike & Bike Trail, and the Mill Creek Trail.

Pocono Mountains and Endless Mountains

Great Railways of the Region

The Erie, the Lackawanna, and the Erie Lackawanna

The New York & Erie Railroad (NY&E) was chartered in 1832 in response to the demands of New York's southern counties for a transportation system to serve their needs and compete with the Erie Canal. Although financial and construction problems delayed its completion for twenty years, opening day on May 14, 1851, was an important event; dignitaries such as Daniel Webster and Millard Fillmore, the president of the United States, were aboard the two trains making their maiden voyage.

The merger of this railroad with another line through Pennsylvania commonly called the Lackawanna was still many years away, but the New York & Erie was already a Pennsylvania railroad in a manner of speaking. Benjamin Wright, an engineer who had worked on both the Erie Canal and the Delaware & Hudson Canal, had mapped a route that took the Erie's tracks into the Commonwealth above Port Jervis, where they ran north along the western shore of the Delaware River to Deposit, a town in New York. From Deposit, the NY&E ran west to the north branch of the Susquehanna River and entered Pennsylvania a second time, above Lanesboro, where the line followed the Susquehanna's "Great Bend" on its way to Binghamton, New York. For the privilege of operating in its jurisdiction, the Commonwealth charged the railroad $10,000 per year.

During the remainder of the nineteenth century and into the twentieth, the Erie's managers were faced with the task of correcting a number of ill-conceived features that placed it at a disadvantage when competing with other railroads. For example, its original terminal points, Piermont on the Hudson and Dunkirk on Lake Erie, were obscure villages. Only after the Erie had obtained access to Buffalo and built a terminal on the west shore of the Hudson River opposite New York in the early 1860s did it cease to be the line that ran through sparsely populated countryside between points to nowhere.

The Erie had also been constructed with rails six feet apart, not four feet, eight and a half inches, which became the standard gauge of other railroads. Attempts to promote its wider cars and capacity for bigger loads could not mitigate the fact that the Erie could not interchange its cars with other railroads. In 1880, it abandoned its broad gauge. Around the same time, the Erie completed a subsidiary called the Chicago & Erie Railroad, giving it access to this Midwest city. In the 1920s, it inaugurated the Erie Limited, a new passenger express between New York and

Passing thru Delaware Water Gap
Lackawanna Railroad

The Lackawanna joined with the Pennsy in making the Poconos accessible for tourism.
RAILROAD MUSEUM OF PENNSYLVANIA

Chicago. Although its fares were cheaper than the New York Central's Twentieth Century Limited and the Pennsy's Broadway Limited, Erie trains took about eight hours longer to complete the trip.

The Erie's poor financial reputation dates from the "Erie Wars" of the 1860s, when it acquired the nickname of the "Scarlet Woman of Wall Street." The story is related by John Steele Gordon in his 1988 book by the same name. Having failed to get the Erie to cooperate with the New York Central, Cornelius Vanderbilt set out to gain control of it by buying stock. The three men who controlled the Erie, Daniel Drew, Jay Gould, and James Fisk, did their best to oblige him by manufacturing thousands of worthless shares and dumping them on the market. "It learned me never to kick a skunk," Vanderbilt is widely reported to have commented.

Having already suffered two bankruptcies in 1875 and 1893, the Erie endured yet another one in 1938, brought on by the Depression. This series of events only enhanced its reputation as the "weary Erie."

The other half of this railroad system was born in the mind of Henry Drinker, a Quaker who purchased a great deal of land in the Lackawanna Valley, which was known for its deposits of anthracite coal. Drinker built the region's first turnpike, the "Old Drinker Road," in 1819. According to Emily C. Blackman's *History of Susquehanna County,* originally published in 1873, in order to satisfy himself that a railroad was possible, "Drinker blazed with an axe a route from the mouth of the Lackawanna, now Pittston, through the unbroken forest, across the lofty Pocono Mountains to the Water Gap, a distance of sixty miles." By 1826, he obtained a charter for the Susquehanna & Delaware Canal & Rail Road, but due to the lack of efficient transportation from the Delaware Water Gap to either Philadelphia or New York at that early date, he was unable to attract sufficient investors.

Drinker tried again after the citizens of Carbondale, hoping to build a railroad from the coal fields north to Oswego and the canals of New York, obtained a charter for the Ligetts' Gap Rail Road in 1832. The Ligetts' Gap plus the Susquehanna & Delaware would have formed a system stretching from the Delaware Water Gap through the Lackawanna Valley to the New York State line, but the financial climate of the late 1830s again spooked potential investors.

From the early 1840s, the Scranton family had been attempting to exploit the area's iron ore and coal deposits with an iron foundry, but their remote location meant that their products had to be shipped by wagon to Pittston and then by canal to Havre de Grace, Maryland. The Scrantons' business was not only saved but greatly expanded by a timely contract for T rails for the nearby Delaware division of the New York & Erie Railroad. In 1847, the Scrantons purchased the old Ligetts' Gap charter, and thanks to their influence, that same year a second company was chartered to build a railroad from the Delaware Water Gap to Cobb's Gap on the Lackawanna: the Delaware & Cobb's Gap Railroad Company. It was merged in 1853 with the old Ligetts' Gap line, which had been renamed the Lackawanna & Western Railroad. The new entity, with George Scranton as its first president, was called the Delaware, Lackawanna & Western Railroad (DL&W), or, in later years, simply the Lackawanna.

The DL&W rapidly began expanding its reach both east and west. In 1868, to obtain access to New York City, DL&W took a perpetual lease on the Morris & Essex Railroad, which ran across northern New Jersey to Hoboken. In 1872, the DL&W began to acquire the Lackawanna & Bloomsburg Railroad, with which it merged the following year. This line, chartered in 1852, ran from Scranton through the Wyoming Valley to

Northumberland, where it connected with the Northern Central Railway, which had become part of the Pennsy system. In 1876, the DL&W corrected a problem it shared with the Erie: it abandoned its six-foot gauge and became a standard-gauge railroad. Much planning made it possible to shut down traffic for only forty-eight hours during the switch.

The DL&W nearly became the eastern division of Jay Gould's railroad empire, which ran from Buffalo to the Rocky Mountains. Gould began buying its stock, but Moses Taylor, then DL&W's dominant stockholder and president of New York's National City Bank, was able to outbid him. Gould was also involved in establishing the New York, Lackawanna & Western Railroad, chartered in 1880 to run from Buffalo to Binghamton. DL&W leased this line in 1882, making the DL&W a through line from New York to Buffalo. Just after the turn of the century, one of DL&W's locomotives became famous as the train appearing in the landmark 1903 film, *The Great Train Robbery*, which was shot along its tracks. One of the railroad's actual engineers made a cameo appearance.

According to Thomas Townsend Taber and Thomas Townsend Taber III, in their 1980 book *The Delaware, Lackawanna & Western Railroad, the Route of the Phoebe Snow, in the Twentieth Century, 1899–1960,* "The 'Twentieth Century' really arrived on the Lackawanna on March 2, 1899 when William Haynes Truesdale assumed the presidency, succeeding the venerable Sam Sloan, who had presided over the destinies of the railroad for thirty-one years since 1868. Mr. Truesdale had previously been Vice President and General Manager of the Chicago, Rock Island, and Pacific Railroad and before that President of the Minneapolis and St. Louis Railroad." In a report issued that year, Truesdale stated his objective of increasing the earning power of the DL&W through rigid economy and physical improvements.

In a move that seemed logical and cost-effective when it took place, in 1960, the DL&W, after seeking a merger with the Nickel Plate Road, merged with the Erie, creating the Erie-Lackawanna Railroad (the hyphen was later dropped). Given that DL&W offered better and faster service, as well as the Erie's long history of bankruptcies, DL&W executives might have expected to dominate the new railroad, but this was not the case. In his 1994 book, *Erie Lackawanna: Death of an American Railroad, 1938–1992,* H. Roger Grant wrote, "The emblem that fireman Truman Knight designed for the Erie-Lackawanna Railroad did more than cleverly incorporate the initials of its corporate name. As a modification of the seven-decade-old Erie diamond herald, Knight's creation suggested that the carrier was more Erie than Lackawanna. He rightly conveyed the image of an Erie-dominated merger; former Erie officials generally held key positions in the new firm until a sweeping administrative reorganization took place in 1963."

Erie Lackawanna became part of the Norfolk & Western Railway's Dereco Corporation in 1968 and continued to operate until 1972, when Hurricane Agnes dumped heavy rains on northern Pennsylvania and southern New York. This unprecedented storm washed out portions of roadbed along two hundred miles of its main line and caused major damage to many of its bridges. Without funds other than its cash flow, the Erie Lackawanna declared bankruptcy.

In 1976, most of Erie Lackawanna became part of Conrail. Properties abandoned by Conrail were sold by trustees to pay taxes and creditors. Today, the Erie Lackawanna Historical Society, headquartered in New Jersey, retains a portion of the railroad's documents on deposit at the University of Akron in Ohio. The Anthracite Railroads Historical Society in Lansdale, Pennsylvania, also interprets the history of this railroad.

The Central Railroad of New Jersey

The Central Railroad of New Jersey (CNJ) was formed in 1849 from two existing railroads: the then bankrupt Elizabethtown & Somerville Railroad and the Somerville & Easton Railroad. The merger was masterminded by John Taylor Johnston, who had become the president of the Elizabethtown & Somerville in 1848 at the age of twenty-eight and was president of the CNJ until 1876.

By 1852, the CNJ was completed to Phillipsburg, on the shore of the Delaware River, and the company purchased its first locomotive, which was called the Pennsylvania. By 1859, the railroad was advertising excursions to Pennsylvania's coal fields (including the attractions of Mauch Chunk) in conjunction with several Pennsylvania railroads, a project that later gave birth to its regular train service to Buffalo and Chicago via Williamsport.

In 1871, the CNJ leased the Lehigh & Susquehanna Railroad from the Lehigh Coal and Navigation Company. This move made it possible for the CNJ to haul coal from the Commonwealth's coal fields across New Jersey to its terminal at Jersey City, where the coal was ferried to New York. It also made the CNJ the route by which the Lehigh Valley Railroad and the DL&W reached New York City. The Lehigh & Susquehanna Railroad brought the CNJ a series of three inclined planes, which hoisted freight cars over Penobscot Mountain. Completed in the 1840s, the Ashley Planes were used until 1948, when twentieth-century diesel locomotives were powerful enough to negotiate regular mountain railroad grades hauling cars filled with coal.

Starting in 1874, the CNJ began a lengthy and close association with the Philadelphia & Reading Railroad, with joint operation of passenger service between Jersey City and Philadelphia. In 1883, Franklin B. Gowen gained control of the CNJ by lease, an agreement that fell apart after the Philadelphia & Reading Railroad went into receivership. Gowen's successor, A. A. McLeod, leased the CNJ a second time and held it until 1893, the date of the Reading's second bankruptcy. In 1901, the Reading Company purchased a controlling interest in the CNJ and the two lines were operated independently but in close cooperation.

The decline in the use of anthracite coal, coupled with financial problems brought on by the Depression, sent the CNJ into receivership in 1939. In 1944, the railroad adopted a new emblem featuring the silhouette of the Statue of Liberty, probably inspired by wartime patriotism as much as by the fact that so many of its facilities were located in Jersey City in sight of this monument. In the 1950s, the CNJ cut costs but faced a new kind of competition with the opening of the New Jersey Turnpike and Newark Airport. Its final filing for bankruptcy came in 1967. All its operations in Pennsylvania ceased in 1972, and it became part of Conrail in 1976, with the state of New Jersey acquiring its passenger services.

Those interested in the history of the Central Railroad of New Jersey may soon be able to visit the new New Jersey Transportation Heritage Center planned for Phillipsburg. Other sources of information include the Central Railroad of New Jersey Historical Society, Inc., in Dunellen, New Jersey, and the Anthracite Railroads Historical Society in Lansdale, Pennsylvania.

The Delaware & Hudson

Thanks to the anthracite deposits they frequently discovered in their travels, William and Maurice Wurts (sometimes spelled Wurtz), two Philadelphia clothing merchants, knew that there were promising coal lands in Pennsylvania's Lackawanna Valley. In 1812, they began acquiring land at good prices in what was then Luzerne County, but by the time they were able to send their first coal shipment to Philadelphia in 1822, they were competing with coal arriving there via the more established Lehigh Canal.

Deciding that there would be a better market for their coal in either New York City or Albany, they established the Delaware & Hudson Canal Company, a project that required authorization from two states. In March 1823, the Pennsylvania legislature authorized Maurice Wurts to improve the Lackawaxen River. That April, the New York legislature permitted the Wurts brothers to build a canal between the Delaware and Hudson Rivers.

To secure the needed funding, Maurice Wurts made some preliminary surveys and hired Benjamin Wright, chief engineer of the Erie Canal, to map the route for a canal that would stretch more than a hundred miles from the Lackawaxen River along the Delaware to Port Jervis, New York, and thence through the valley of Rondout Creek northeastward to the town of Rondout, New York, near Kingston. Wright's map, together with samples of the area's coal shipped from Philadelphia, attracted a sufficient number of New York City investors to finance the canal and build the towns of Carbondale and Honesdale (named after Philip Hone, a mayor of New York City and the first president of the canal company).

Unfortunately, the coal mines near Carbondale were separated from the canal's terminus at Honesdale by the ridge of Moosic Mountain, which was too steep for a canal. Benjamin Wright and his successor, John B. Jervis, engineered a gravity railroad to replace the inefficient wagons and sleds then being used to haul coal. Known simply as the "Gravity," this railroad conquered the ridge with five inclined planes operated by stationary steam engines ascending to Rix's Gap and three planes operated only by gravity descending to Honesdale. The canal and railway system were completed in 1829.

That same year, the Gravity took its place in history as America's first operating railroad to employ a locomotive. Horatio Allen, a young civil engineer who had been making surveys for the system, told the story in 1881 to the *Honesdale Citizen* in an interview that was paraphrased in the 1886 *History of Wayne, Pike and Monroe Counties, Pennsylvania*, edited by Alfred Mathews.

According to Allen, when John B. Jervis discovered that Allen was going to England to study the construction and operation of railroads, he asked Allen to purchase iron for the Gravity's rails, chains for its inclined planes, and three locomotives. Allen ordered one locomotive to be built by Robert Stephenson & Co. and three more from a company located in Stourbridge. In his history of the Delaware & Hudson (D&H), Jim Shaughnessy writes, "A painter in the latter's shop [Foster, Rastrick & Co.] at Stourbridge is said to have detected in the rounded boiler head of the little machine a resemblance to the king of beasts and painted a brilliant likeness on the front of the iron monster," thus acquiring for one of these locomotives its nickname, the "Stourbridge Lion."

When the locomotives began arriving in New York, they were exhibited in the city for the purpose of attracting additional investors before being shipped by canal to Honesdale, where Horatio Allen was waiting. According to Allen's own account, on August 8, 1829, a large crowd came to witness the trial run of the Stourbridge Lion, but no one particularly wanted to chance taking a ride on it. Declaring that there was no need to risk any life other than his own, Allen climbed on board and made a three-mile trip to Seelyville and back.

Many railroad historians have stated that the trial run demonstrated only that the roadbed could not support the locomotive's weight. A passage in the 1886 county history implies that at that date Allen himself was busy contradicting claims that his trial run had been a failure: "As the 'Lion' passed over [the tracks], the weight pressed everything underneath firmly down to its place on the roadbed, with no little creaking and groaning. Beyond this, however, Mr. Allen saw nothing to indicate that the track was unequal to the requirements of the locomotive. The 'Lion' proved to be all that the engineer had expected."

In any case, after a second trial run on September 9, the Stourbridge Lion was taken off the tracks and stored in a shed for about twenty years. Then it was moved to Carbondale, where its boiler was adapted for use in an iron shop, while the railroad tracks were consigned to horsepower. Another one of Allen's locomotives appears to have been shipped to Rondout or possibly Honesdale, where it was also dismantled. The fate of the two other locomotives remains unknown. It was Allen's speculation that his locomotives were scrapped because by the time they arrived, the railroad had been executed as a gravity railroad and they were no longer really needed.

A second gravity railroad was completed in 1850 to transport coal mined by the Pennsylvania Coal Company more than forty miles from Port Griffith on the Susquehanna to the town originally known as Paupack Eddy on the Delaware & Hudson Canal. In 1851, this town's name was changed to Hawley, after Irad Hawley, the first president of the Pennsylvania Coal Company.

In 1847, when the canal system was enlarged, the Delaware & Hudson Canal Company hired John Roebling, a young German immigrant engineer, and acquired some other innovative engineering features in the suspension aqueducts he designed. Roebling had already designed bridges in western Pennsylvania using the principle of wire rope suspension, and he would later take his place in history for designing the Brooklyn Bridge, a grand suspension structure. Once Roebling's aqueducts spanning the Lackawaxen and Delaware were open for business, observers were treated to the spectacle of canal boats floating above rivers on their own water-filled bridges. The D&H had two additional Roebling aqueducts located in New York State.

After 1850, the Delaware & Hudson Canal Company expanded its railroad operations to new mines in the Scranton/Wilkes-Barre area and finally began using genuine locomotive power. By 1870, a branch line joined the D&H at Carbondale with the main line of the Erie at Lanesboro, effectively giving the D&H access to the railroads of New York State as well as New England. In the ensuing years, the D&H constructed and leased railroad lines in New York State and eventually became known as a "bridge line" to Canada. In 1898, in order to save cash, the then obsolete canal was abandoned and so was the famous Gravity, which had since been converted to passenger and excursion service to scenic mountain picnic areas. In 1928, the company's name was changed to the Delaware & Hudson Railroad Corporation.

By the early 1970s, the D&H had been acquired by Dereco Corporation, a subsidiary of Norfolk & Western Railway that also acquired the Erie Lackawanna. Dereco sold the D&H to Guilford Transportation Industries in 1984. After this company filed for bankruptcy for the D&H in 1988, the D&H became part of the Canadian Pacific Railway system, which subsequently formed the Saint Lawrence & Hudson Railroad, a new entity to hold the D&H and other railroads. Today, the history of the D&H is preserved by the Bridge Line Historical Society in Albany and the Wayne County Historical Society in Honesdale.

Rail Stories of the Region

Old Mauch Chunk

The history of Pennsylvania's most famous boomtown began in the drizzling rain on an evening in 1791, when a hunter named Philip Ginter literally stumbled over a lump of anthracite coal on Summit Hill. The next day, he carried it to the community then known as Fort Allen (now Weissport) where he presented it to Jacob Weiss, who ran a lumber business and had been purportedly seeking just such a natural resource.

Weiss organized the Lehigh Coal-Mine Company, but the product he shipped to Philadelphia around 1806 was not a big hit in the fuel market. Business improved during the War of 1812, when Virginia's bituminous coal became prohibitively expensive, but dropped off again when the war was over.

A lucky accident finally revealed the hidden virtues of anthracite, sometimes known as stone coal. Around 1814, Josiah White and Erskine Hazard, who manufactured wire in a factory near the falls of the Schuylkill River, purchased two boatloads of anthracite coal. After spending an entire night trying to get it to burn in the furnace, their workmen finally shut the furnace door and left the mill in frustration. One returned because he had forgotten his jacket and noticed that the door of the furnace was red hot and its interior was glowing with white heat. Eureka. The trick to burning stone coal was to ignite it, shut the furnace, and leave it alone for a while.

White and Hazard sold their Philadelphia business, and in 1818, they founded two other businesses, the Lehigh Navigation Company and the Lehigh Coal Company, which were incorporated as the Lehigh Coal & Navigation Company in 1822. Once the Lehigh River was sufficiently improved for reliable descending navigation, they began shipping increasingly large amounts of what Philadelphians learned to appreciate as some of the best coal America had to offer.

Between the mine at Summit Hill and the Lehigh River port called Mauch Chunk, there was a distance of about nine miles over which coal had to be painstakingly transported in wagons. The entrepreneurs replaced this bottleneck with a gravity railroad system, begun in 1827, that was far less complex but became more famous than the one associated with the D&H.

When the railroad first began operating, mules hauled the empty cars from Mauch Chunk to Summit Hill. After the cars were loaded and ready

Mauch Chunk, as depicted in Eli Bowen's 1852 *Pictorial Sketch-book of Pennsylvania*, with its coal-hauling railroad system.

The fabled Mount Pisgah Plane of Mauch Chunk in the 1875 book *Philadelphia and Its Environs*.

to descend by gravity alone, the mules were led into the lead car, where they were fed, making it possible in later years for what was then called the Summit Hill–Mauch Chunk Railroad to snidely claim that it had offered America's first dining car service.

By 1845, a second track, called the "back track," was added to Mauch Chunk's gravity railroad, making the system a more efficient continuous loop between loading points near Summit Hill and the Lehigh River. The mules were replaced by stationary steam engines at the summits of

Mount Pisgah and Mount Jefferson, which drew railroad cars to their peaks, where they were simply allowed to coast to the base of the next inclined plane.

Between 1845 and 1870, two additional inclined planes were built to haul coal from new mining operations in the Panther Valley to Summit Hill. Since the route that railroad cars had to descend was too steep for a straight line of railroad tracks, the tracks were constructed in a way that

A more developed Mauch Chunk, circa 1875, from *Philadelphia and Its Environs*. Note the parallel railroad and canal.

allowed the cars to zigzag back and forth in order to gradually lose momentum. This local transportation system became known as the Mauch Chunk, Summit Hill & Switchback Railroad. Even after a new Nesquehoning Valley Railroad built in 1871 made this unusual switchback feature obsolete, the name stuck. The entire line was popularly called Mauch Chunk's "Switchback Railroad" until it was torn up in the 1930s.

As business grew for the Lehigh Coal & Navigation Company, so did Mauch Chunk. In July 1829, *Hazard's Register of Pennsylvania* reported, "The town is very flourishing, being at the head of the Lehigh Canal, and the termination of the Mauch Chunk Rail Road. It contains now about 1500 souls, and is fast increasing in population." The thriving community remained a company town until 1831, when the Lehigh Coal & Navigation Company began selling town lots, opening Mauch Chunk to individual enterprise, resulting in even more growth.

To this day, Mauch Chunk's most famous citizen remains Asa Packer, who began his career as a canal boat operator, progressing to shop owner and canal boat builder. Additional enterprises involving the mining and shipping of coal made him a rich man by the 1850s. His Lehigh Valley Railroad made him a legend and broke the transportation monopoly enjoyed by the Lehigh Coal & Navigation Company in the Lehigh Valley.

In 1862, a devastating flood raised the Lehigh River thirty feet, damaging commercial buildings, houses, and canal and railroad alike. Because railroads were easier to rebuild than canals, the managers of the Lehigh Coal & Navigation Company decided to replace part of their system with the extension of a short railroad that they already operated, the Lehigh & Susquehanna Railroad. By 1868, the Lehigh Coal & Navigation Company was running trains on this line between Wilkes-Barre and Easton, and shortly after that, it became the Lehigh & Susquehanna division of the Central Railroad of New Jersey, giving the CNJ permanent access to some of Pennsylvania's best coal fields.

By 1898, the CNJ had also acquired Mauch Chunk's old "Switchback" system, which was no longer hauling coal and had since evolved into a tourist attraction for the river town that had become a vacation resort called the "Switzerland of America." The slow ride up a steep incline followed by a free-fall descent served as a model for America's amusement park roller coasters.

Besides an exciting ride, visitors to Mauch Chunk could explore the great outdoors in an area that had always been physically beautiful. In his 1884 *History of the Counties of Lehigh and Carbon,* Alfred Mathews wrote, "To the eye of the traveler who approaches this unique town from the south, this mountain is the first striking object in the rugged and wild landscape which forms its environment. Following the great sweep of the rushing Lehigh River, it rises as a mighty verdure-clad wall from its very brink, and makes more dark the deep and tortuous gorge through which the river seeks the south, and finally flowing through the Lehigh Gap, emerges from its mountain-pent channel into the broader and sunnier valley, bordered by smaller and more gently sloping hills." A waterfall at a place originally called Moore's Ravine, but later given the more romantic-sounding name of Glen Onoko, was a favorite destination for visitors to Mauch Chunk, and the Lehigh Valley Railroad did its part to make the remote glen accessible by constructing rustic bridges and pathways.

Mauch Chunk went downhill with the coal industry, but local boosters tried to maintain their tourism business by providing a monument and a resting place for the Native American Olympic hero Jim Thorpe, who actually had no connection with the area. In 1954, Mauch Chunk merged with East Mauch Chunk, and the two communities became Jim Thorpe, Pennsylvania.

It took a different kind of attraction, however, to bring the visitors back some thirty years later. Around the 1980s, America's interest in the styles and social history of the late nineteenth century was growing, and so was the number of guests at Asa Packer's mansion built in 1860 and opened to tourists in 1964. It was a rare thing for a historic house to be preserved with virtually all its furnishings intact, but the Packer mansion contained the Packer family's dishes and silverware, their furniture and chandeliers—in short, everything to illustrate the life of a wealthy American family in the Victorian era. Jim Thorpe has been playing up its Victorian heritage ever since, and the town is now a fascinating gateway to the Poconos.

Tourism in the Poconos

Besides valuable deposits of coal, the area today called the Pocono Mountains had been blessed with winding brooks, picturesque waterfalls, and colorful mountain laurel. At a dramatic two-mile gorge called the Delaware Water Gap, where the Delaware River flows through a natural opening in the Blue Ridge Mountains, a Frenchman named Antoine Dutot bought some land. In 1829, he began construction of the Kittatinny House, a hotel purchased and completed by Samuel Snyder in 1832. Accommodations even more quaint and rustic could be found at the homes and boarding houses operated by local farmers. A perfect vacation resort was in the making for the residents of New York and Philadel-

The Delaware Water Gap could be reached from Philadelphia via the Pennsylvania Railroad and the Delaware, Lackawanna & Western Railroad in 1875 when it was illustrated for a book about the Pennsylvania Railroad by William B. Sipes.

phia, but until the area could be reached by rail, a stay in the Poconos involved a two-day trip by stagecoach.

In the 1850s, the Delaware, Lackawanna & Western Railroad expanded its lines from Scranton to what would become East Stroudsburg. Shortly after the turn of the century, the Pennsy and the DL&W joined forces to provide daily service from Philadelphia to Monroe County. Passengers rode the Pennsylvania Railroad to a junction called Manunka Chunk, above the present town of Belvidere, where they changed to DL&W trains. Suddenly, the Poconos were less than a day away and the Delaware Water Gap was poised to become America's second largest inland resort town, after Saratoga Springs.

The DL&W increased the demand for its services through advertising. The railroad published booklets with illustrations and descriptions of resorts along its route, in which hotels and boarding houses were welcome to purchase advertising. The Pennsylvania Railroad also included enticing descriptions of Poconos destinations in its published volumes of summer excursion routes. Its 1903 edition noted that the Delaware Water Gap "affords excellent boating and swimming. A well-laid golf course is a great addition to the Gap and affords opportunities for passing many pleasant hours." In describing the town of Cresco seventeen miles away, the same volume mentioned Buck Hill Falls, where "the clear mountain stream falls nearly two hundred feet in a distance of a half a mile." Tobyhanna was a "delightful mountain hamlet situated on the western slope of the beautiful Pocono Mountains, equidistant from Scranton and Stroudsburg," where "the air is cool, pure, and invigorating, and the surroundings rich in scenic attractions."

One of the Poconos' most well known resorts was founded by a president of the Lehigh Coal & Navigation Company. In 1941, Robert V. White broke ground for Split Rock Lodge, which continues to be one of the most popular resorts in the Poconos. Originally intended as a hunting and fishing retreat for the company's executives, its lodge and cottages were later opened to the public. White was also a skiing enthusiast, and in 1946, he transformed Split Rock into the area's first ski resort.

Tourism in the Poconos survived the demise of railroads and even got a boost in the 1950s from the northeast extension of the Pennsylvania Turnpike, which made the area even more accessible to residents of Philadelphia and its suburbs. However, once auto touring became the norm, people no longer sought out hotels convenient to railroad stations, and the Delaware Water Gap, as well as Stroudsburg and East Stroudsburg, lost business to resorts more remotely and romantically located.

Known today primarily for its honeymoon havens with in-room swimming pools and kitschy bathtubs for two shaped like hearts and champagne glasses, this region is also beginning to rediscover its railroad heritage in towns like Jim Thorpe and Honesdale.

Scranton—the Past and Future Railroad Town?

Thanks to the timely order for iron rails from the New York & Erie Railroad, the Scranton family business was saved and the city of Scranton was able to expand with new streets, more housing for its workers, and mansions for its entrepreneurs. An elegant hotel called the Wyoming House opened in 1852, and by 1853, the Delaware, Lackawanna & Western Railroad chose Scranton for the hub of its operations. Scranton quickly surpassed Carbondale as northeastern Pennsylvania's largest city.

Despite opposition from residents and leaders of nearby Wilkes-Barre, in 1878, Luzerne County was split into Luzerne and Lackawanna Counties. Scranton became a county seat and acquired additional showcase structures, including the stone courthouse, still standing today near the city's center square by the city hall, which boasts a Gothic bell tower and stained-glass windows.

Once served by a number of railroads in addition to the DL&W, Scranton went into sharp decline following World War II, together with the anthracite coal mining and railroad industries. All passenger service ceased in the 1970s, and the magnificent Lackawanna Station was closed and boarded up.

Currently under discussion is the issue of restoring passenger rail service from Scranton or Stroudsburg through New Jersey to Newark or even New York on the former DL&W route. The Lackawanna County Railroad Authority, established in 1985, reports that rail service would alleviate the traffic for commuters on I-80, resulting in lower air pollution. County officials hope that passenger trains would also bring more tourists to the area.

A federal feasibility study is currently under way. In 2001, the New Jersey Department of Transportation purchased the Lackawanna Cutoff, the old railroad bed that would become part of this new system. Depending on the availability of funding, trains could again be entering Scranton sometime between 2003 and 2006.

Phoebe Snow

How does one take a coal-hauling railroad and give it an aura of class, grace, even glamour? William H. Truesdale's answer was Phoebe Snow, an advertising icon as widely recognized at the turn of the last century as the Pillsbury Doughboy and Betty Crocker are today.

Phoebe Snow was created by the DL&W's advertising agency, Calkins and Holden. She was a pretty young lady who wore her hair swept up beneath a fashionably enormous hat. She always wore white linen and she spoke in rhyme, her most famous verses being a comment about her attire and a compliment to the cleanliness of the anthracite-burning DL&W:

Says Phoebe Snow
About to go
Upon a trip
To Buffalo:
"My gown stays white
From morn till night
Upon the road of anthracite."

Phoebe Snow, the advertising icon of the DL&W. RAILROAD MUSEUM OF PENNSYLVANIA

Phoebe's image appeared on advertising placards in New York City's elevated trains and in magazines likely to be read by those considering a trip to the Poconos, or any other destination served by the DL&W. In his 1979 book, *Phoebe Snow: The Lady and the Train,* Don Dorflinger noted that within a decade Phoebe had increased the number of DL&W passengers by 80 percent.

Ever since Phoebe was conceived, people have argued over whether or not she was a "real" person. Her face and figure were created by an artist whose images were inspired by the photographs of a model who posed on, in, and around DL&W trains. The model was an actress named Marion Murray who had played a part in *The Great Train Robbery* movie.

The original Phoebe Snow campaign lasted from 1903 until World War I, but Phoebe reappeared in 1942 in military uniform. In 1949, the name "Phoebe Snow" was attached to a DL&W passenger streamliner fitted for comfort, but powered by diesel. It ran between Hoboken, New Jersey (New York City), Scranton, and Buffalo. Marion Murray was on hand for the inaugural celebrations.

Phoebe Snow the train survived the merger with the Erie until 1962. The name was revived the next year, and the train continued to run between New York and Chicago until 1966.

Local Chapters of the National Railway Historical Society

Although it does not consider itself a "Steamtown chapter," the Lackawanna & Wyoming Valley Chapter of the National Railway Historical Society does work closely with the National Park Service, many of its members serving as employees, volunteers, or directors at the Steamtown National Historic Site. They operate a snack stand at the railroad station in Moscow, Pennsylvania, which is the destination for Steamtown rail excursions from Memorial Day to Halloween. Some of the money earned provides funding for the Boston & Maine Railroad steam locomotive Number 3713, which is currently being restored at the Steamtown shops. The chapter also sponsors a Christmas tree at Steamtown's annual festival of trees held each December.

Chartered in 1973, the chapter publishes a newsletter called *Laurel Lines* and a very popular calendar. Its regular meetings feature educational entertainment. The chapter also sponsors occasional excursions and other activities.

The Pocono Mountains Chapter of the National Railway Historical Society leased the Tobyhanna railroad station from the Lackawanna County Railroad Authority in 1993 and began restoration of this 1908 building, which is sometimes open to the public on weekends. This chapter also offers educational entertainment at its meetings and occasional excursions, as well as activities such as model train shows that attract hundreds of people. Its publication is called the *Phoebe Flash*.

The Region's Railroad Giants

John Taylor Johnston (1820–1893)

John Taylor Johnston went into the railroad business after discovering he did not want to be a lawyer. To his new career he brought a college education from New York University and a legal education from the Yale Law School.

In 1848, he became president of the financially shaky Elizabethtown & Somerville Railroad, then in the hands of a banking firm called Boorman, Johnston & Co. Johnston consolidated his line with the Somerville & Easton Railroad, forming the nucleus of the Central Railroad of New Jersey and stepping into the role of its first president.

Johnston increased the stature of the CNJ and its importance to the region through his acquisition of the Lehigh & Susquehanna Railroad, with its access to Pennsylvania's coal fields. Johnston also fostered the development of suburbs between Jersey City and Somerville with frequent passenger train service and attractive stations.

Johnston had primarily invested in his own railroad. The financial reverses of the CNJ after the panic of 1873 brought about the loss of his personal fortune. He resigned in 1876 just before the CNJ went into receivership in 1877, after crippling strikes in the coal and railroad industries.

Johnston had always had an interest in aesthetics. Today, he is remembered not so much as a railroad executive as a patron of the arts. His suburban stations included landscaped parks, and he initiated a program of prizes awarded to the stationmaster whose grounds looked the best. Johnston had been elected the first president of New York's Metropolitan Museum of Art in 1870, and he became its largest subscriber in 1871 with a contribution of $10,000. Together with William T. Blodgett, he financed the acquisition of the Dutch and Flemish paintings that would form the core of the museum's early collection and win its reputation for excellence.

Johnston had also been amassing an unrivaled private collection of paintings, which he displayed in galleries open to the public. After he lost his money, the 1876 sale of his art collection was the first great sale of art in New York City.

Samuel Sloan (1817–1907)

Samuel Sloan (not to be confused with the Philadelphia architect with the same name) entered the commercial workplace at the age of fourteen after withdrawing from Columbia College Preparatory School following the death of his father. After two years with one merchant, he joined another firm, where he worked his way up to the rank of partner, then head of the company.

Around the middle of the nineteenth century, he began investing in railroads, which may have resulted in his election to the board of directors of the Hudson River Railroad in 1855. Later that year, he was elected president, a position he retained for nine years. Besides guiding the business through the Civil War, he improved the railroad's physical plant and installed telegraph service.

Samuel Sloan lost his job after Cornelius Vanderbilt acquired enough stock in the Hudson River Railroad to make himself president and install his son as vice president. In 1865, Sloan declined Vanderbilt's offer to take over as president of the New York & Harlem Railroad.

Thanks to the influence of Sloan's close and influential friend Moses Taylor, president of New York's National City Bank, Sloan became president of the DL&W in 1867, where he remained until 1899. He transformed this line from a Pennsylvania coal road to a general freight carrier with connections to the Hudson River, Lake Ontario, and Buffalo. He also acquired coal lands and expanded the railroad's market for coal in the greater New York City area with the lease of the Morris & Essex Railroad. He attempted to merge the DL&W with the CNJ, but the merger failed. It was Sloan who brought the DL&W into the modern railroad world by converting the system from its old six-foot gauge to standard gauge in 1876.

In his 1977 book, *The Delaware, Lackawanna & Western Railroad, the Road of Anthracite, in the Nineteenth Century, 1828–1899,* Thomas Townsend Taber depicted Sloan as thrifty, private, and very religious. Taber wrote, "He did not approve of railroad men working on the Sabbath. During his tenure of office the fewest possible number of trains ran on Sunday, and they were only milk, newspaper and mail trains."

William H. Truesdale (1851–1935)

Starting out in 1869 as a clerk, William H. Truesdale worked his way through various positions in different aspects of railroading before he became president of the Minneapolis & St. Louis Railway in 1887. During the 1890s, he worked in executive positions for the Chicago, Rock Island & Pacific Railway.

In 1899, he accepted an appointment as president of the Delaware, Lackawanna & Western Railroad. According to Thomas Townsend Taber and Thomas Townsend Taber III, in their 1980 book, *The Delaware, Lackawanna & Western Railroad, the Route of the Phoebe Snow, in the Twentieth Century, 1899–1960*, "As soon as Mr. Truesdale assumed the Presidency, he started immediately on a program of great improvements. He was by nature a builder—and he built well."

Truesdale began by welding what had been a loose network of individual lines into what the Tabers called "one solid, homogeneous railroad." It was probably no accident that on his watch, the line acquired a new nickname consisting of a single word, the Lackawanna, rather than a combination of initials. Truesdale built some of its most outstanding and attractive engineering features and structures, including the Tunkhannock Viaduct and the architecturally sophisticated passenger stations at Hoboken, Scranton, and Buffalo.

Truesdale also inaugurated one of the most successful and clever advertising campaigns America would see during the twentieth century. Phoebe Snow, the fictional passenger in the immaculate white linen dress who traveled the road of anthracite, was an image that lingered for more than half of the twentieth century, personifying the mystique of railroad travel.

Sampling the Region's Railroad History

Jim Thorpe

The very first thing that visitors see when they enter the town of Jim Thorpe is the business end of a Central Railroad of New Jersey diesel locomotive, proudly bearing the CNJ Statue of Liberty emblem. The locomotive stands at the head of a collection of rolling stock from various Pennsylvania railroads parked near what was once the CNJ station in old Mauch Chunk.

This brick building, considered one of the finest passenger facilities built by the CNJ, was constructed in 1868 and remained in service until 1963, officially closing in 1972, somewhat prior to Jim Thorpe's Victorian renaissance. Today, it serves as the local visitor center, where tourists can gather brochures and information, and sometimes its parking lot is the only place they can park their cars, since this town saw most of its growth before the invention of the automobile and suffers from a critical lack of parking spaces.

The old Central Railroad of New Jersey station in Jim Thorpe is now the home of Yesterday's Train Today and a good place to pick up visitor information.

The CNJ station is also where visitors can board what Rail Tours, Inc., refers to as "Yesterday's Train Today." Incorporated in 1962, Rail Tours, Inc., operates several passenger coaches of 1920s vintage on a route that was part of the Nesquehoning Valley Railroad, which once served anthracite mines from Nesquehoning to Hauto and was leased to the CNJ in 1871. The standard ride offered on weekends lasts about forty minutes and takes visitors a distance of about eight miles along a route that can be hemmed in with thick foliage during the summer. Longer rides to Lake Hauto are sometimes operated, but the organization's most popular rides are its autumn Flaming Foliage Rambles, when Yesterday's Train Today travels thirty-three miles to Hometown, Pennsylvania, and crosses the 161-foot Hometown Trestle. Seasonal themed rides are also available.

The second floor of Jim Thorpe's CNJ station houses the headquarters of the Switch Back Gravity Railroad Foundation, an organization established in 1986 and dedicated to providing the town with a much more exciting train ride, if it can succeed in restoring Jim Thorpe's historic Switchback Railroad. In 2000, due to difficulty in obtaining funding for its ambitious plan, the group adopted a phased approach that would initially restore the inclined plane once used to haul cars to the summit of Mount Pisgah. The top of this mountain, currently littered with railroad ties and metal parts, could potentially be furnished with a replica engine house that would also serve as a museum. Until the organization is able to proceed with its plans, the best way to experience the old Switchback is to view a working model at Jim Thorpe's Mauch Chunk Museum and Cultural Center and explore the rail trail that follows its route, which can sometimes be done by bus on the occasional tours sponsored by the foundation.

Visitors to Jim Thorpe interested in model trains need to visit the Hooven Mercantile Company Building near the CNJ station, where the second floor houses the Old Mauch Chunk HO-Scale Model Train Display, owned and operated by the Heery family. Here model locomotives representing various Pennsylvania railroads haul as many as fifty cars around a thousand feet of track that winds it way through an extensive cityscape. Although the layout itself is named after Mauch Chunk, some of its structures are modeled after buildings located in nearby Allentown. Adding variety to the layout are its vehicles other than trains, like the tiny fire engine and ambulance that race endlessly around the block. Recorded music sets the mood with tunes like Perry Como's "Toyland" and "I've Been Working on the Railroad" sung by the Mitch Miller chorus. The ceiling lights are periodically dimmed so that visitors can see the lights in the buildings come on, but even though the night scene includes a burning building, it is pretty tame compared to the extravaganza in Shartlesville.

Just up the hill from the CNJ station is the attraction that brought tourists back to Jim Thorpe, the mansion built in 1860 for Asa Packer, president of the Lehigh Valley Railroad. This three-story Italianate residence was designed by architect Samuel Sloan of Philadelphia. In 1912, the house, together with all its period furnishings, became the property of the borough of Mauch Chunk following the death of Packer's daughter Mary Packer Cummings. For many years, it languished vacant until the locals realized what a treasure they had on their hands. Opened to the public in 1964, it became increasingly popular in the 1980s as Americans rediscovered the charm of Victorian times.

Its popularity sparked the restoration and reuse of other Jim Thorpe buildings of similar vintage, making the town even more popular with antiquarians than with railroad buffs. Just next door to Asa Packer's mansion, a bed and breakfast operates in the former residence of Packer's son Harry. This flamboyant brick structure, constructed in 1874, is so quintessentially Victorian that it was chosen as the model for the haunted mansion at Disney World. The bed and breakfast is currently popular for its murder mystery weekends.

Farther up Jim Thorpe's main street (called Broadway) is the town's most unlikely tourist attraction, the Old Jail Museum, which served as the Carbon County jail until 1995. This hulking and forbidding structure was considered a model correctional institution when it was built in 1871, and it earned its place in railroad history between the years 1877 and 1879 when a total of seven convicted Molly Maguires were hanged here. After leading a group around its twenty-eight narrow cells and a dark and gloomy dungeon not recommended for the claustrophobic, one guide paused beneath the jail's reconstructed gallows and related the sad ending to the story of the Molly Maguires. She characterized Franklin B. Gowen as a "greedy man" who cut the pay of the poor miners, but mentioned nothing about the assaults and assassinations that the Molly Maguires had perpetrated. The tour ended at cell #17, where an indelible ghostly handprint was purportedly made on the wall by a condemned Molly Maguire as a testament to his innocence.

Steamtown and Scranton's Railroad Heritage

In 1986, Congress created Steamtown National Historic Site, which opened in Scranton in 1995 following an expenditure of $66 million on the old DL&W rail yards. Its stated purpose was to interpret the evolution of steam railroading throughout the United States, but many Scranton residents hoped Steamtown would also stimulate the local economy by bringing in tourists likely to stay overnight.

Steamtown was and remains a fusion of two components. Its structures were more or less abandoned between 1902 and 1912 as William Truesdale diverted repair work to shops in locations other than Scranton, some of them being later adapted to service diesel locomotives. Steamtown's collection of locomotives, passenger cars, and cabooses was once the private collection of Nelson Blount of Bellows Falls, Vermont; it was relocated to Scranton during the mid-1980s by the subsequently bankrupted Steamtown Foundation.

Steamtown could not have become part of the National Park Service had its mission been limited to telling the story of a single railroad, but the history of the DL&W is not neglected in its exhibitions, which reflect the lives and times of both William Truesdale and Phoebe Snow. The broader mission of the site is accomplished by exhibits focusing on railroad technology in general, such as the actual working of a coal-burning steam engine. In the site's massive roundhouse, which circles a fully functioning turntable, visitors can watch workers as they restore locomotives and passenger cars and prepare the excursion locomotives for their daily rounds.

In the height of tourist season, there's always something going on at Steamtown. There are ranger-led tours of the shops, two-hour train excursions to Moscow, Pennsylvania, on the DL&W main line, and living history programs in which interpreters play the roles of railroad characters ranging from switchmen to executives to hobos. From time to time, a locomotive is moved from the roundhouse to the turntable to introduce visitors to the routines of its maintenance. The schedule seems designed to invite guests to stay all day. For lunch, they can cross a bridge spanning the tracks separating Steamtown from the Steamtown Mall and its food court.

The heart of Steamtown.

Each year, Steamtown hosts RailCamp, an event sponsored by the National Railway Historical Society. Young people selected by lottery spend time touring and working at the site to learn the basics of railroad preservation.

Steamtown tends to overpower Scranton's other rail heritage attraction, the Lackawanna Coal Mine, whose visitors ride electric "lokies" down an old mine slope hundreds of feet below ground. Visitors learn about the mining experience and its methods, or "life and hard coal times," as the advertising literature states.

Scranton's prettiest railroad artifact is the new hotel at the old Lackawanna Station, which is also a tribute to the wealth that was once created by the combination of coal mines and railroads. Completed in 1908 by New York architect Kenneth Murchison, this Renaissance-style train station was the crowning glory of William H. Truesdale's plan to upgrade passenger stations all along the DL&W's route. Scranton and its Lackawanna Station were important enough that several departments of the DL&W corporate headquarters were relocated there from New York. In the early 1980s, it was hoped that the building's restoration would spark revitalization in Scranton's downtown.

Scranton's Lackawanna Station, now a hotel. RADISSON LACKAWANNA STATION HOTEL

Constructed of sandstone, the front facade of the Lackawanna Station is faced with limestone and decorated with columns and pilasters, as well as a huge clock framed by eagles. Its most impressive area is its Grand Lobby, where opulence starts at the mosaic tile floor, extends up walls that are faced with sienna marble, and culminates in a barrel-vaulted ceiling made of stained glass open to a skylight above. Faience panels installed just above eye level depict scenes along the route of the DL&W between Hoboken and Buffalo. The best way to drink in the atmosphere is to take a seat at the restaurant now occupying half of the lobby or take a tour led by a ranger from nearby Steamtown.

The former offices of the station's upper levels have been converted into hotel rooms that allow guests to experience modern luxury together with traces of the past, like the original hardware on the windows and the wooden benches from the Grand Lobby's waiting room days, which are now positioned by the elevators. A room at the rear of the Lackawanna Station gives guests a view of the trains making regular excursions from Steamtown.

Erie Relics in the Endless Mountains

The steep hills and deep creek beds near Pennsylvania's border with New York in the eastern part of the Commonwealth are known as the Endless Mountains. Residents of isolated villages like Lanesboro enjoy pretty scenery that hasn't changed much since Emily Blackman described the area in her 1873 *History of Susquehanna County:* "The vicinity of Lanesboro, and especially that of Cascade Creek, was a favorite resort for parties of pleasure. Its trout were unsurpassed, and its falls a charming feature of otherwise picturesque scenery. . . . As late as 1846, the town consisted of but one hotel, the mills, one store, and a cluster of houses."

Minus the mills and hotel, Lanesboro still has a cluster of houses, some of them now huddled beneath a massive stone railroad viaduct constructed as part of the westward expansion of the New York & Erie Railroad. Known as the Starrucca Viaduct because it spans Starrucca Creek, when new it was the most expensive bridge ever built and one of the last to be built of stone masonry. Today, it is believed to be the Commonwealth's oldest stone viaduct still in use.

The valley carved by Starrucca Creek is a quarter mile wide, more than a hundred feet deep, and directly in the route chosen for the Erie between the Delaware and Susquehanna Valleys. Since it was too deep to traverse with an embankment, the Erie's managers chose engineer Julius W. Adams to design the bridge and James P. Kirkwood to supervise construction. They built a bridge of seventeen arches, 1,040 feet long, and wide enough to be eventually double-tracked. Although the northern end of Starrucca Viaduct is about twelve feet higher than the southern end, the arches were designed to make the bridge look perfectly level.

Starrucca Viaduct was built in a surprisingly short period of time. Beginning in August 1847, as many as eight hundred men labored on the bridge, making it ready for its first locomotive by December 1848.

An article about the scenery along the route of the Erie appearing in the July 1850 edition of *Harper's New Monthly*

The Starrucca Viaduct, completed in 1848, is still standing and still in use.

The Starrucca Viaduct as depicted for the July 1850 issue of *Harper's New Monthly Magazine*.

A relic of the Erie Railroad in the town of Susquehanna, this building, purported to be the first brick passenger station in North America, now houses a restaurant called the Iron Horse Saloon.

Magazine applauded the railroad for its "triumphs of art over the most formidable obstacles, which nature has, at almost every step, raised against the iron-clad intruders into her loveliest recesses." Starrucca Viaduct, it continued, was "simple in its design, but symmetrical and beautiful . . . altogether the noblest piece of work upon the whole line of the road."

Expensive though it may have been, Starrucca Viaduct must certainly have paid for itself in its more than a century and a half of continuous use. It was designated a National Historic Civil Engineering Landmark in 1973 and placed on the National Register of Historic Places in 1975. It is still used by freight trains.

In her history of Susquehanna County, Blackman also mentioned a nearby town called Susquehanna: "During the construction of the great works of the Erie Railroad at this point, it became quite a business place," even drawing off some of the former business of Lanesboro. Modern Susquehanna remains a bigger town than modern Lanesboro, with a bigger business district and its own Erie artifact, a sizeable depot said by some to be the first brick passenger station in North America, built in 1863 and placed on the National Register of Historic Places in 1978. The structure that once included a dining hall for Erie passengers now houses a restaurant called the Iron Horse Saloon as well as a banquet hall and a meeting place for the local Church of the Latter Day Saints. An Erie emblem still decorates its walls.

Tunkhannock Viaduct

At Nicholson, Pennsylvania, another Endless Mountain valley is spanned by another viaduct constructed as part of an early-twentieth-century improvement program to increase the capacity and operating efficiency of the DL&W. To eliminate curves and thus save time on passenger schedules, the railroad relocated its Hoboken-to-Buffalo line boldly along hillsides. The project required two viaducts, one over Martin's Creek and a far larger one over Tunkhannock Creek.

Designed by Abraham B. Cohen, Tunkhannock Viaduct is 240 feet high and 2,375 feet long. It was built of reinforced concrete and consists of ten 180-foot arches plus an additional two abutment arches anchoring it to its approaches. Work began in 1912, and the structure was completed in 1915. Tunkhannock Viaduct was listed on the National Register of Historic Places in 1977 after having been designated a National Historic Civil Engineering Landmark in 1975. Like Starrucca Viaduct, it is also still in use, with Canadian Pacific Railway freights crossing it daily.

While visitors sometimes have trouble locating Starrucca Viaduct, which is off the beaten path, Tunkhannock Viaduct, at more than double

In Nicholson, it's impossible to miss the reinforced concrete Roman-looking Tunkhannock Viaduct.

the size, is hard to miss. It dominates the skyline of the valley over which it soars and makes the humble buildings of Nicholson look like a model train layout. However, since it first appeared, it has earned compliments for the graceful appearance achieved by arches inspired by classical or Roman architecture and a surface scored to resemble masonry. When people unfamiliar with railroad history see the Tunkhannock Viaduct for the first time, many think it's a reproduction of a Roman aqueduct—which may have been precisely what its architect had in mind.

Honesdale, Hawley, and Lackawaxen

In Honesdale, the headquarters building for the Delaware & Hudson Canal Company is still open for business on Main Street, where it now serves as the museum for the Wayne County Historical Society. The small brick building has housed the historical society since 1923 and has been open to the public since 1939. It has been expanded several times, including the recent addition of a small brick building that was formerly a county surveyor's office before it was moved to the spot in 1981.

The historical society's exhibition interprets the history of the D&H from 1828 to 1898 and includes a replica of the Stourbridge Lion built by D&H employees in 1932, positioned so that its painted lion face is peering through a window at passersby on Main Street. A passenger car named the Eclipse gives visitors an opportunity to sit in one of its upholstered seats beneath a stenciled ceiling while being entertained by a video production on the history of the Gravity. Images of some of the D&H's founders round out the display, including a model for a statue of Horatio Allen that might have been erected in Honesdale's park except for the exigencies of the Depression.

Behind the museum in the area that used to be the busy terminus of both the D&H Canal and the Gravity railroad, there are still railroad tracks where the Stourbridge Line tourist railroad boards its passengers. Operated by the Wayne County Chamber of Commerce, its trains travel from Honesdale to Hawley or Lackawaxen. Besides its popular Great Train Robbery runs and a fall foliage expedition, the Stourbridge Line offers a dinner theatre excursion and a Bavarian Festival trip. The scenery frequently includes deer and even bears along the rural route on the Lackawaxen River, as well as glimpses of the remains of the old D&H Canal and stonework of the gravity railroad built by the Pennsylvania Coal Company.

When the ride includes a stopover in Hawley, passengers can explore this town that saw new growth as a tourist destination after 1925, when the Pennsylvania Power & Light Company dammed Wallenpaupack Creek to create hydroelectric power. The company also created Pennsylvania's largest man-made lake, which still attracts many tourists for its fishing, boating, and other water recreation opportunities. Downtown Hawley's Bingham Park, donated to the borough by the family of Albert W. Bingham in 1929, used to be a basin for the canal system. Just down the road, visitors can view the Pioneer

Tracks now used by the Stourbridge Line in Honesdale. The artifact on the left is a railroad snowplow.

Coach, a passenger car that was used on the Pennsylvania Coal Company's gravity railroad.

Stourbridge Line passengers disembarking at the village of Lackawaxen can view and tour the artifact of the D&H Canal now known as the Delaware Aqueduct or the Roebling Bridge. It has spanned the Delaware ever since the beginning of canal season in 1848. This structure is the only surviving example of the four suspension aqueducts designed by John Roebling. Roebling's suspension design was particularly suitable for this location because it allowed for a larger span and fewer piers, which meant fewer impediments to timber being floated down the Delaware. This would alleviate some of the conflict between the coal and lumber industries that had previously arisen when rafts of logs rammed coal boats and vice versa.

The Roebling Bridge continued to be used as an aqueduct until 1898, when the canal was closed and drained. It was then converted to a private

An artifact of the Delaware & Hudson Canal Company has been reconstructed in Lackawaxen. This structure celebrates the challenge of building a canal across the Delaware River. Visitors can imagine what it was like when it was filled with water and barges.

toll bridge. The National Park Service purchased the artifact in 1980 to become part of its Upper Delaware Scenic and Recreational River project. In 1995, those portions of the aqueduct that had been dismantled as unnecessary for a toll bridge were reconstructed so that it would look more like what Roebling had originally designed.

Visitors can use the bridge to cross the Delaware River, which is surprisingly narrow this far north. On the New York side, they can visit the toll house that was added in 1900 and view some photos and other materials relating to the structure's history as both aqueduct and toll bridge. They can also watch cars cross the one-lane structure, most of their drivers unaware that this narrow passage with sides too high to see over was once filled with water and boats loaded with coal heading for New York.

The Region's Rail Trails

Mauch Chunk's old Switchback Railroad lives on as the Switch Back Trail, an eighteen-mile loop with a number of access points. The best place to start a Switch Back trek is not on the trail at all, but in downtown Jim Thorpe at the Mauch Chunk Museum and Cultural Center, where a well-crafted operating model of the original railroad illustrates the Switchback's route and demonstrates how it worked.

Hikers can reach the trail from Packer Street at a point past the Packer mansion, where the Switchback Depot and the Grand View Hotel used to be. Be warned that this is a steep hill. Hikers can also start the loop in the town of Summit Hill, which grew up around the area's original mine. The site of the engine house for Mount Jefferson's inclined plane is marked by some concrete slabs near a Summit Hill cemetery.

Those seeking more of a nature walk than a hike will prefer the gently sloping topography called the "home stretch" because cars once returned to Mauch Chunk over its tracks. Not far from the parking lot of pleasant Mauch Chunk Lake Park, a replica Switchback car has been installed for inspection.

The town of Jim Thorpe marks the southern end of Lehigh Gorge State Park, administered by the Pennsylvania Department of Conservation and Natural Resources. Lying along the Lehigh River, it is located in the Audubon's Lehigh Reach of the Delaware and Lehigh Natural Heritage Corridor, extending between the Pennsylvania towns of Wilkes-Barre and Bristol along the routes of the Lehigh & Susquehanna Railroad and the Lehigh and Delaware Canals.

The big attraction on the Lehigh River is whitewater rafting and canoeing, which are at their best from late March through June. Jim Thorpe has a number of licensed outfitters who provide water crafts, guides, and safety equipment to visitors of various skill levels.

The Lehigh Gorge's scenery continues to attract a crowd, just as it did a century ago, but modern visitors have to make do without certain amenities that their ancestors enjoyed. The Hotel Wahnetah, with its wilderness dance pavilion and tennis courts, was closed after a number of fires during the 1910s, effectively ending the resort era in the gorge. Gone too are the rustic bridges and railings that once guided guests to Glen Onoko.

A modern Glen Onoko excursion begins with a drive through Lehigh Gorge State Park along a dirt road that runs parallel to railroad tracks still in use. A number of artifacts along the road, like an old iron bridge, attest to the use of this route by other railroads in times gone by. A new bridge allows cars to cross the Lehigh to reach a small parking lot near where the Hotel Wahnetah used to stand.

Signs leading to the trail are emblazoned with warnings that there have been serious injuries and even deaths along the rocky and narrow trail. The cliff on the opposite side of the river has an intriguing hole that can be identified as a railroad tunnel because of the way it is lined up with a still-standing pier that must have once supported a bridge. These are the remains of the CNJ route to the hotel. So romantic an artifact can't help but draw its share of explorers, and despite a mound of dirt partially blocking the tunnel's other entrance, hikers can sometimes be spotted peering out of the hole down the sheer drop to the river.

CNJ artifacts along the Lehigh Gorge State Park Trail: an old railroad tunnel and the pier for a viaduct across the Lehigh River.

Only the stouthearted can endure the entire distance of about a mile and a half to Glen Onoko, where there are actually two waterfalls. The first waterfall is about forty feet high; water plunges straight down for half the distance then tumbles over rocky steps the rest of the way. At the second waterfall, the stream pours over a wide ledge with enough overhang to make the water appear to be coming out of nowhere. The now remote Glen Onoko waterfalls are some of the biggest in the entire Poconos region.

The D&H Rail Trail runs from the town of Simpson to Lanesboro and the Starrucca Viaduct along the old roadbed of the D&H's Jefferson branch. It forms a recreation system with the eight-mile O&W Road Trail, which also begins in Simpson and runs parallel to the D&H, but on the east side of the Lackawanna River to Stillwater Lake, along the former route of the New York, Ontario & Western Railroad out of Scranton. Access points can be found in Simpson, Forest City, and Thompson. Extensions are in the works that will take hikers north to the New York border and south to the Scranton/Wilkes-Barre area. There are paths to a summit where rail beds for the D&H's Gravity railroad are still visible.

The Endless Mountain Riding Trail, which was once the Lackawanna & Montrose branch of the DL&W, can also be found in this region.

The Laurel Highlands

Great Railways of the Region

The Baltimore & Ohio

Baltimore's business leaders, who were no less threatened by the Erie Canal than the leaders of Philadelphia, made Baltimore the scene of familiar discussions regarding the relative merits of canals and railroads during the winter of 1826–27. A committee took relatively little time to recommend proceeding with a railroad rather than a canal, and the business leaders proposed a line across the Allegheny Mountains, with its western terminus suggested by its proposed name: the Baltimore & Ohio Railway Company. The Baltimore & Ohio Railroad Company became its official name once the entity was incorporated by Maryland's legislature on February 28, 1827.

In his 1987 book, *History of the Baltimore and Ohio Railroad,* John F. Stover related how construction began on the Fourth of July in 1828. Charles Carroll, one of Baltimore's most respected senior citizens, broke ground, proclaiming that this act was the second most important, after signing the Declaration of Independence, of his long life. Members of the Free and Accepted Masons positioned the B&O's "first stone," the sort of granite block also called a "sleeper," used by early engineers to support a railroad's rails.

By June 1830, horses were pulling railroad cars between Baltimore and Ellicott's Mills. By December 1831, the line was operating between Baltimore and Frederick, and a little later, the railroad opened a branch between Baltimore and Washington. By 1842, the B&O's main line west followed the Potomac River valley to Cumberland, and its next logical goal was Pittsburgh.

Not long after Horatio Allen tested the Stourbridge Lion in 1829, B&O began operating locomotives. Engineers at the Canton Iron Works built the experimental locomotive named the Tom Thumb, which was tested by B&O executives on a thirteen-mile run in 1830. Although Tom Thumb later lost a famous race against a horse, B&O management decided that steam was the motive power of the future for railroads. In August 1832, *Hazard's Register of Pennsylvania* reported that an anthracite-burning locomotive built in York, Pennsylvania, had been tested on the B&O, where it had conveyed seven railroad cars between Baltimore and Ellicott's Mills.

Back in 1828, B&O had obtained permission from Pennsylvania to lay its tracks through the Commonwealth, provided that its line was completed by 1843. In 1839, the Pennsylvania legislature extended the completion date to 1847, but before that year arrived, at a time when it appeared that B&O had settled on a route through Pittsburgh, a number of Pennsylvania business leaders began to express second thoughts. Residents of southwestern Pennsylvania were generally ready to welcome the B&O, but Pennsylvanians residing east of the Alleghenies argued that the State Works would lose valuable traffic and Philadelphia would lose Pittsburgh's trade to Baltimore.

In 1846, Pennsylvania's governor signed a bill giving B&O the right to build from Cumberland, Maryland, to Pittsburgh, but it contained an amendment that made the bill null and void if within fifteen months the Pennsylvania Railroad obtained a certain amount of cash and had under contract a specified number of railroad miles. The Pennsy met these conditions, giving B&O no choice but to reach the Ohio River by a route running south of the Mason-Dixon Line.

The B&O main line west was therefore extended through Grafton, Virginia, to Wheeling (now in West Virginia, but then also in Virginia) by 1852. After a second line was built between Grafton and Parkersburg, the B&O extended its reach to the cities of Cincinnati, East St. Louis, and Chicago by the 1870s. In 1871, it entered Pittsburgh by leasing another railroad.

In 1886, B&O opened a line linking Baltimore and Philadelphia via Wilmington. It acquired trackage rights over the Philadelphia & Reading Railroad and the Central Railroad of New Jersey, giving its freight and passengers access to Jersey City, just across the Hudson from New York. The B&O expanded in western Pennsylvania during the early 1890s by acquiring control of other railroads operating there, including the Pittsburgh & Western Railroad.

While this competitor grew and expanded, the Pennsylvania Railroad had been busy purchasing B&O stock, resulting in the increasing representation of Pennsy executives on the B&O board until they effectively controlled the railroad. In 1901, the Pennsy took direct control of the B&O by requesting the resignation of its president, John K. Cowen, and replacing him with Leonor F. Loree.

Despite declines in both revenue and traffic during the Depression, the B&O remained profitable through most of the 1950s. In 1963, the more profitable Chesapeake & Ohio Railway took control, folding the B&O into an eleven-thousand-mile "Chessie" system stretching from the Atlantic to the Mississippi and the Great Lakes. B&O subsequently became part of CSX Corporation, which was created by the merger of the Chessie system with Seaboard Coast Line Industries. Today, the B&O

Railroad Museum in Baltimore preserves and interprets the history of the B&O and other mid-Atlantic regional railroads, including the Chesapeake & Ohio Railway and the Western Maryland Railway. There is also a Baltimore & Ohio Railroad Society in Baltimore.

Rail Stories of the Region

Pennsylvania's System in the West

News that construction work was beginning on the Erie Canal in 1817, followed the next year by news of the completion of the National Road from Baltimore to the Ohio River, could hardly have been welcome in Pittsburgh. Where was its link to the eastern seaboard, Pittsburgh's citizens wanted to know?

Their answer came in 1824 in the form of legislation appointing canal commissioners to examine various possible routes for a canal from the eastern part of Pennsylvania through natural waterways to Pittsburgh. A second act created a second commission in 1825 whose deliberations called for one canal between Middletown and the mouth of the Juniata River and another along the Allegheny River from Pittsburgh to the mouth of the Kiskiminetas River.

Construction began in 1826, even though it was at that time unclear how to join the two canals that would be separated by a chain of well-timbered mountains drained by unnavigable streams. In 1828, the same year that the legislature authorized construction to begin on a railroad between Philadelphia and Columbia, its members also authorized a railroad that would somehow manage to get freight and passengers across the Allegheny Mountains. Moncure Robinson was chosen to determine its route.

The portion of the State Works that would connect the Susquehanna River with the Allegheny Mountains consisted of two divisions. The eastern terminus of the eastern division was changed from Middletown to Columbia in order to join the railroad planned to terminate in that town. It was designed to follow the eastern shore of the Susquehanna and employed aqueducts to cross the streams that emptied into the river. The Juniata division began at Duncan's Island, where the Juniata joined the Susquehanna, and its western terminus was eventually extended to Hollidaysburg, 127 miles away.

By the mid-1830s, other canal divisions were added to the State Works main line, including the Susquehanna division between Duncan's Island

and Northumberland, the north branch division between Northumberland and Pittston, and the west branch division between Northumberland and Farrandville. Along the Commonwealth's eastern border, the Delaware division linked Bristol near Philadelphia with the Lehigh Canal at Easton.

While the canal commissioners were overseeing various excavations, their railroad engineers were locating the Allegheny Portage Railroad. This thirty-seven-mile double-tracked rail system opened in 1834 and included ten inclined planes, five on either side of the summit of the Allegheny Ridge. At first, horses moved its cars along the level portions of track between the planes, where the cars were hauled upward by stationary steam engines, but the horses were gradually replaced by steam locomotives.

A trip on the Allegheny Portage Railroad introduced the passenger to several groundbreaking engineering features, including America's first railroad tunnel, which was more than nine hundred feet long and twenty feet wide. A stone arch bridge over the Little Conemaugh River was reputed to be America's most perfectly constructed arch and drew many sightseers until it was destroyed by the Johnstown Flood in 1889.

The engineers of the day also came up with canal boats cleverly constructed in detachable sections that could be hoisted onto railroad cars and

This sketch illustrates how vessels were moved from canals onto inclined planes. It is taken from William Bender Wilson's 1899 *History of the Pennsylvania Railroad Company*, but it also appeared in many other publications.

The Conemaugh Viaduct from William Bender Wilson's 1899 *History of the Pennsylvania Railroad Company*.

then reassembled on the other side of the mountains. These eliminated the time wasted in unloading the boats and transferring their freight to railroad cars, but they failed to save enough time to make the State Works competitive with other transportation systems being proposed or constructed.

By 1840, the Commonwealth had conducted further surveys for a railroad that did not incorporate inclined planes, and in 1855, a system called the New Portage Railroad was opened to traffic. Most historians have concluded that the $2.5 million spent on its construction was a huge waste of taxpayer money because the railroad was being built at the same time that the Commonwealth was negotiating the sale of the entire State Works to the Pennsylvania Railroad, which would very quickly dismantle the railroad once the Pennsy had established its own mountain route.

When the Pennsylvania Railroad purchased the State Works in 1857, the deal included the Commonwealth's entire system of canals. At first, the railroad tried to honor the obligation placed upon it by Pennsylvania's legislature to keep most of the canal system in good repair and operating condition. However, as the nineteenth century progressed, the canals consistently earned less in tolls than the cost required to keep them repaired, and by about 1900, they were closed and abandoned.

The Logan House

Although the Pennsylvania Railroad managers planned a system that would carry passengers between Philadelphia and Pittsburgh more rapidly than the old State Works combination of railroads and canals, it was clear that they would still need a place for passengers to rest and refresh themselves along the way. In Altoona, the town the railroad built to house its repair shops, the Pennsy built the Logan House, a hotel named after an Indian leader well known in central Pennsylvania who had taken the British name Logan from James Logan, William Penn's secretary.

The Pennsylvania Railroad's Logan House in Altoona, as depicted in *Philadelphia and Its Environs* in 1875.

The Pennsylvania Railroad station in Altoona as it looked in 1875 in an illustration for William B. Sipes's book about the Pennsylvania Railroad.

Completed in 1855, the fine hotel constructed right beside the Altoona station was Italianate in style. It was four stories high and stretched for two hundred feet literally along the railroad tracks. It was luxuriously furnished with red carpeting, upholstered furniture, gas lights, and a veranda where guests could socialize. According to William B. Sipes in his 1875 book on the Pennsylvania Railroad, "This house has become a model for many similar institutions in all parts of the country."

The successful Logan House was expanded by seventy rooms in 1872. Its distinguished guests included Andrew Carnegie, Ulysses S. Grant, Rutherford B. Hayes, William Howard Taft, and Abraham Lincoln's wife and children, who came to escape the heat of Washington, D.C.

Sipes's book also suggests that the Logan House would have been popular with early rail fans:

Immediately in front of the Logan House is an open station, built entirely of iron, elaborately ornamented, and paved with slate flagging, under which all passenger trains over the road stop. From the veranda of the hotel a view is had of this entire station, and probably at no other place in America can such an immense amount of railroad travel and traffic be seen. At almost every hour of the day and night trains are arriving and departing, carrying passengers from all parts of the country, and thousands of tons of freight go rushing by to the marts of trade and commerce. The clang of the engine-bell never ceases; and, to the man unfamiliar with the science of railroading, inextricable confusion would seem to exist. But so far from this being the case, the most perfect system prevails, and the immense business of the road is transacted with precision and regularity.

Even those who did not stay overnight could enjoy the amenities of the hotel's dining room. When a train stopped, its passengers were typically accorded twenty minutes for a meal, an allotment capably met by the staff at the Logan House. Altoona residents patronized the Logan House for weddings and other functions, and everyone enjoyed the vanilla ice cream that was made from an exclusive recipe.

The Logan House was razed in 1931.

The South Pennsylvania Railroad

A war of titans waged during the 1880s by the Pennsy and the New York Central left Pennsylvania with a number of monumental railroad artifacts. It also brought J. P. Morgan, one of America's leading bankers, into Pennsylvania's railroad history as the man who finally negotiated peace.

In a 1969 article published in the *Pennsylvania Magazine of History and Biography* titled "Crisis of Rugged Individualism," Albro Martin noted that hostilities began with a genuine need for a railroad on the west shore of the Hudson River that would open the Catskill resort area in upstate New York and for through service to Boston for passengers from Philadelphia, Baltimore, and Washington, D.C., who wished to avoid New York City. Attempts made to fill this need during the 1870s were hampered by the nation's financial condition following the panic of 1873.

The 1880s saw the birth of a line called the New York, West Shore & Buffalo Railroad, commonly known as the West Shore. While this railroad had problems paying its bills, it was successful enough to arouse the suspicions of William Henry Vanderbilt, president of the New York Central, which operated what would become a competing line on the Hudson's opposite shore. Suspecting that the West Shore was truly being assisted and controlled by his arch-rival, the Pennsylvania Railroad, Vanderbilt decided to build a railroad that would directly compete with the Pennsy's main line.

Among his allies in this endeavor, Vanderbilt could claim Franklin B. Gowen, whose Philadelphia & Reading Railroad stood to gain a friendly connection to the west. Andrew Carnegie also strongly favored the idea of a railroad that would compete with the Pennsy for the output of his steel mills and even offered to raise $5 million for the project in Pittsburgh. Robert H. Sayre, of the Lehigh Valley Railroad, agreed to be responsible for operating this company line.

In 1884 and 1885, construction work progressed on the railroad that was commonly called the South Penn, because it would be located south of the Pennsy's route through the Juniata Valley between Harrisburg and a connection with the Pittsburgh & Lake Erie Railroad, then under Vanderbilt's control. Workers began with its engineering features, which included piers for a bridge over the Susquehanna and a series of tunnels that would enable its trains to run *through* the Allegheny Mountains.

J. P. Morgan, whose recommendations guided many foreign investors, was not pleased to witness this degree of competition within the industry, which was certain to depress profits for both railroads and kill the market for their securities. Morgan initiated what has come to be known as the Corsair Compact, a meeting held in July 1885 aboard his yacht, the *Corsair*, among Pennsy and New York Central executives. The unusual meeting place may have been chosen because New York City was then enduring a heat wave, but it has also been suggested that Morgan chose his yacht so that no one could storm out in anger.

The gentlemen agreed that the PRR would sell its West Shore stock to buyers who would lease this railroad to the NYC and purchase the South Penn at a price that would cover construction work already completed. This deal would give each railroad control over the line that had threatened competition. In addition, the Pennsy would acquire the Beech Creek Railroad, a coal-hauler financed by Vanderbilt interests that ran roughly from Williamsport to Clearfield over tracks that were more or less parallel to the Pennsy's Philadelphia & Erie Railroad.

Pennsylvania's Supreme Court stepped in to prevent the PRR from taking possession of the Beech Creek or South Penn. The PRR-affiliated Cumberland Valley Railroad and the Baltimore & Ohio Railroad acquired pieces of the South Penn project after it was sold at foreclosure in 1890. However, neither ever did anything significant with the property.

The Corsair Compact made J. P. Morgan America's most powerful financier, the man who could bring order and stability to the railroad industry. In his article, Martin commented, "The settlement of 1885 was the first great achievement of American finance capitalism. It would be neatly dramatic to say that finance capitalism in the United States was actually born on the afterdeck of the *Corsair* that hot July afternoon."

The big loser in the Corsair Compact was the Philadelphia & Reading, which had already spent significant cash improving its facilities in Philadelphia and Harrisburg in anticipation of the increased traffic the South Penn promised to bring. The deal negotiated by Morgan also resulted in preventing the Reading from ever becoming a real trunk line.

The abandoned South Penn project left Pennsylvania with nine unfinished tunnels, several bridge piers in the Susquehanna River, and miles of graded roadbed. Schemes to revive the project came and went, but it was the unlikely setting of the Great Depression that brought action. A state representative from Washington County, a state planner, and a lobbyist for the trucking industry were out for a late-night snack in Harrisburg in January 1935. In the climate of Roosevelt's New Deal, the Commonwealth was looking for large public-works projects to help stem unemployment. Gazing at the South Penn bridge piers, one of the three men asked, Why not a toll highway over the old roadbed?

The inspiring bridge piers remain abandoned in the river, but six of the South Penn's tunnels became tunnels for the Pennsylvania Turnpike, which also incorporated portions of the abandoned South Penn railroad bed. Thus, as George H. Burgess and Miles C. Kennedy wrote in their 1949 history of the PRR, the Pennsy finally did see considerable competition from the South Penn route, but in the form of cars and trucks traveling the Pennsylvania Turnpike.

Railroads and the Johnstown Flood

The growth and success of Johnstown began in 1831, when the first barge successfully made a voyage from Johnstown to Pittsburgh through the canal that had been constructed as part of the western division of the Commonwealth's State Works transportation system. The backwoods trading center founded in 1794 had a population of more than three thousand by 1840. After the Pennsylvania Railroad laid its tracks through the town during the 1850s, Johnstown acquired its major growth industry, the Cambria Iron Company, and later additional rail service from the B&O via its Somerset & Cambria branch. By the fateful year of 1889, nearly thirty thousand people were living in and around Johnstown.

Back in the days when Johnstown depended on the State Works canal, the Pennsylvania legislature had approved funding for a mountaintop reservoir miles above the town to keep the canal in business during the summer when it was in danger of running dry. Construction began in

Busy industrial Johnstown as it looked prior to the flood in an illustration for a book on the Pennsylvania Railroad by William B. Sipes.

1838, but not long after the South Fork Dam was finished, trains were able to run all the way from Philadelphia to Pittsburgh, making both the dam and the canal obsolete.

The dam remained neglected until 1879, when it was purchased by Benjamin F. Ruff, who planned to use it as the main attraction for his South Fork Fishing and Hunting Club, a resort intended to draw the wealthy of Pittsburgh away from their mountain retreats in Cresson. The club's members soon included such notables as Andrew Carnegie, Henry Clay Frick, Philander Chase Knox, Robert Pitcairn, and Andrew Mellon.

The South Fork Dam had been constructed to harness the area's spring rains, but it proved unequal to the storm that hit the Laurel Highlands late in May 1889. In his 1968 book about the Johnstown Flood, David McCullough describes several warnings made by persons at the South Fork Fishing and Hunting Club that the dam was in imminent danger of giving way—warnings that reached Johnstown despite storm damage to the telegraph lines. After 4:07 P.M. on May 31, twenty million tons of water came crashing down the Little Conemaugh Valley with what some survivors described as a "roar like thunder."

McCullough also describes the heroic ride of railroad engineer John Hess, who was seated inside Engine Number 1124 about a half mile from the East Conemaugh railroad yards. Upon hearing what sounded like a hurricane, Hess immediately put on steam and headed for East Conemaugh with the flood right behind him, his whistle tied down and shrieking. McCullough wrote, "A locomotive whistle going without letup meant one thing on the railroad, and to everyone who lived near the railroad. It meant there was something very wrong."

Most folks interpreted the whistle as an urgent message to get out of the way. Passengers on a train delayed in East Conemaugh heard it and may have witnessed Hess leap from his locomotive. A conductor ran along the halted cars shouting for everyone to head for the hills.

Survivors and historians would produce many accounts of the sixty-foot wall of water traveling as fast as forty miles per hour toward Johnstown, sweeping everything in its path into a deadly torrent of debris. More than 2,200 people lost their lives, while many of the survivors were rendered homeless and even temporarily destitute due to the destruction of the factories where they had been employed.

The Pennsylvania Railroad lost 24 passenger cars, 561 freight cars, 34 locomotives, miles of track, and a number of bridges. One of the flood's earlier casualties was the Conemaugh Viaduct, which had spanned the Little Conemaugh with a single arch since its completion in 1833 and become a local landmark. The brick roundhouse at East Conemaugh was crushed, and the cars in adjacent yards were scattered about like toys. The most horrific scene of the tragedy was enacted at the railroad bridge over the Conemaugh River in Johnstown, where a fire started, consuming the debris trapped by the bridge's stone arches together with corpses and survivors of the surging waters who had become stranded at the bridge.

Robert Pitcairn, superintendent of the Pennsy's western division, had been notified of danger via telegram when the initial warning reached Johnstown. He had ordered that his private railroad car be attached to an eastbound train, but the train was halted several miles west of Johnstown. He and its other passengers watched in horror as debris and bodies began floating down the Conemaugh River below the train tracks and did what they could to rescue survivors.

Back in Pittsburgh, Pitcairn called for contributions to help the victims. The PRR contributed cash, and its Pittsburgh depot and yards became the collection headquarters for food, supplies, and volunteers bound for Johnstown by railroad. McCullough commented, "For all its highhanded ways, for all the evils people attributed to it, in a crisis the railroad had been worth more than any other organization, including the state."

Local Chapter of the National Railway Historical Society

Altoona might have lost the Railroad Museum of Pennsylvania to Strasburg, but its rail fans were not going to give up on having their own railroad museum to preserve and interpret Altoona's heritage as a railroad town. The organization originally known as the Altoona Railway Museum

Club when it was organized in 1965 became the Horseshoe Curve Chapter of the National Railway Historical Society in 1968. After the Railroaders Memorial Museum, Inc., was established as a nonprofit corporation in the early 1970s, members continued to contribute to the museum's development, and they still support its projects today.

The Horseshoe Curve Chapter owns a collection of rolling stock that includes a PRR business car called the Duquesne, which was built in Altoona in 1929, and the Union League Club Parlor car, also built in 1929. Its members recently refurbished a siding in Altoona for storage. The chapter's activities include excursions like Moonlight at the Curve, where a decorated Horseshoe Curve is open for night photography, as well as summer and autumn excursions in southern Blair County on the Everett Railroad, in conjunction with the Roaring Spring Historical Society. Its monthly newsletter is called the *Coal Bucket*.

The Region's Railroad Giants

Benjamin Henry Latrobe (1806–1878)

Benjamin Henry Latrobe joined the Baltimore & Ohio Railroad in 1830 as a surveyor's rodman, a rather humble position for a man who had previously practiced law, most recently with his brother, who had been counsel for this railroad. The career change into engineering worked well for Latrobe, who rose through the B&O ranks. By 1839, he had located B&O's main route between Harpers Ferry and Cumberland.

He also managed the survey for the B&O route between Baltimore and Washington, which included the Thomas Viaduct over the Patapsco River, named for Philip Thomas, first president of the railroad. This granite bridge, over six hundred feet long, was completed in 1835 and was later hailed as one of the finest examples of railroad architecture in America.

Latrobe was appointed chief engineer for the B&O in 1842, when its main line was completed to Cumberland. He retained this position while taking on a number of other responsibilities, including the position of president and later chief engineer for the Pittsburgh & Connellsville Railroad. In 1871, Latrobe had the honor of driving in the golden spike that connected the Pittsburgh & Connellsville Railroad with the B&O.

John Work Garrett (1820–1884)

John Work Garrett went to work for his father, a Baltimore merchant, after attending two years at Lafayette College in Pennsylvania. During the late 1840s, the Garrett family expanded its business operations by starting a bank and purchasing real estate, making the Garrett family quite wealthy by the time the Civil War started.

The Garrett family became early investors in Baltimore & Ohio stock, and by 1855, John Work Garrett was elected to the railroad's board of directors. A report that he prepared on the railroad's finances made such a positive impression that not only were his suggestions adopted as guiding principles for the railroad, but Garrett was elected the company's president in 1858.

During the Civil War, Garrett kept his railroad loyal to the Union, to the dismay of Maryland's Southern sympathizers. Business was excellent for the B&O in spite of the war, and by 1865, Garrett could report great increases in both passenger and freight traffic.

Although Garrett continued expanding the B&O westward after the war, he relinquished plans to expand the railroad into a southern rail system due to com-

John Work Garrett
LIBRARY OF CONGRESS

petition from other railroads, including the Pennsy. B&O never rivaled the New York Central or the PRR in assets or revenue, but Garrett did succeed in tripling its mileage by the time of his death in 1884.

Robert Garrett (1847–1896)

John Work Garrett's son Robert tried to run away from home to join Confederate general Robert E. Lee's army, but his father persuaded him to enter Princeton instead. He graduated in 1867 and took his place in the bank started by his grandfather, where he learned about finance.

In 1871, he was finally able to follow General Lee—as president of the Valley Railroad of Virginia. After the Valley Railroad became part of the B&O system, Garrett became a vice president of the B&O.

He became acting president of B&O in 1884 after John Work Garrett fell ill following his wife's fatal injury in a carriage accident. He presided over the extension of the B&O from Baltimore to Philadelphia, a project that his father had started. However, in his 1987 history of the B&O, author John F. Stover commented, "Robert Garrett was not the dominant, forceful, and aggressive figure that his father had been. John Work Garrett had served a long and useful apprenticeship under the stern eyes of the first Robert Garrett in the 1830s and 1840s. The younger Robert had had too much given to him and really earned very few of the several advancements presented to him in the 1870s and 1880s."

While traveling in England, Garrett heard that J. P. Morgan, the powerful financier and railroad czar with whom B&O was negotiating for capital, might insist on some say in the selection of the railroad's officers. Possibly fearing that he would lose his presidency anyway, Garrett resigned in 1887, claiming that he was acting on the advice of his physician.

Robert Garrett is remembered in Baltimore not for his brief stint as B&O president, but as the man who brought Frederick Law Olmsted to lay out its Mount Vernon and Washington Squares. Garrett also gave this upscale neighborhood copies of some fountains on the Champs-Elysées and a statue of George Peabody for its Peabody Institute.

Sampling the Region's Railroad History

The Allegheny Portage Railroad

Moncure Robinson was the man chosen by the Commonwealth's canal commissioners as engineer for the proposed Allegheny Portage Railroad. Through most of the spring and summer of 1829, he worked on its original survey and came up with a proposal for a system of stationary steam engines operating inclined planes, with locomotives hauling cars along the level stretches between them.

Although Robinson was no longer associated with the Allegheny Portage Railroad during the period when it was actually built, he must have been as encouraged as the rest of Pennsylvania's citizens to hear that its construction was nearing completion. In August 1833, *Hazard's Register of Pennsylvania* reported, "Many of the rails are laid upon the section of the road which we visited, and preparations for laying the residue are in rapid progress." When inclined plane Number 10 was set in motion for a trial run, a letter from Hollidaysburg reprinted in *Hazard's Register of Pennsylvania* in March 1834 contained the news, "The working of the ropes and machinery gave great satisfaction, not only to the officers on the road, but to a large number of spectators who had assembled to witness the first efforts of steam power upon the rugged Allegheny."

Later that month, the *Pittsburgh Gazette* announced, "We have today the pleasure to announce the arrival of the first lot of goods, by way of

the Portage Rail Road." The amount of time it had taken for that particular shipment to make its historic journey from Philadelphia was thirteen
days, but the operators of the State Works would later trim the length of
a typical freight shipment to about four days.

For about twenty years, canal boats reaching their connection with the
portage railroad were floated onto railroad cars, hauled out of the water,
and sent by horse or locomotive to the first of the railroad's inclined
planes. There workers hitched them three at a time to the cables that
hauled them up the inclined plane at a rate of about four miles per hour.

By the time the Pennsylvania Railroad purchased the State Works, the
Allegheny Portage Railroad had already been superseded by the New
Portage Railroad. The Pennsy pulled up the newer portage railroad's iron
rails for use on another line and sent the large stone sleepers that had
supported the rails of the original portage railroad to Altoona, to be used
in the construction of the company's shops. A few missed sleepers were
all that remained on the grassy hills as evidence of this system's existence.

The portage railroad faded from America's collective consciousness
until a 1927 legislative act created a commission and appropriated cash to
erect a monument in its memory. The monument, which was shaped like
a step pyramid and built of some of the few remaining stone sleepers, was
erected at what was once the base of plane Number 6, placing it only a
few feet from the then busy William Penn Highway, a few miles east of
Cresson. A brochure about the portage railroad published by the PRR at
about that time contains a photograph of Pennsylvania's governor John S.
Fisher with a group of railroad executives at the monument's dedication.

A better attempt to preserve and interpret the history of the portage
railroad was undertaken in 1964 by the National Park Service at the
Allegheny Portage Railroad National Historic Site, which now occupies
the summit of the Allegheny Ridge. At the heart of its historic district
stands the Lemon House, built around 1832 by Samuel Lemon and his
wife, Jean, when this enterprising couple learned that the Allegheny
Portage Railroad would be constructed over that particular mountaintop.
During the years that the railroad operated, the Lemon House served as a
tavern. The National Park Service purchased the house in 1969 and furnished it to suggest life around 1840, during the railroad's heyday.

The Allegheny Portage Railroad National Historic Site has a small portion of reconstructed railroad track and a reconstructed engine house at
the summit of plane Number 6. While the reconstructed engine house
serves the practical purpose of protecting the remains of the original
structure at this site, it also contains models demonstrating how the
planes were operated. From a nearby observation deck, visitors can make

The tavern built by Samuel Lemon at the summit of the Allegheny Ridge has been restored as part of the Allegheny Portage Railroad National Historic Site.

Reconstructed tracks lead to the Engine House Interpretive Center, where visitors to the Allegheny Portage Railroad National Historic Site learn how canal boats were once hauled over the Allegheny Ridge.

out a skew arch built in 1834 to allow a turnpike to cross over the portage railroad. At the base of this hill, just out of sight, stands the 1927 monument to the portage railroad.

The old Staple Bend Tunnel, which had been part of the Allegheny Portage Railroad system, is located more than seventeen miles away, but it is still considered part of the Allegheny Portage Railroad National Historic Site. Built in 1831–32, it was the first railroad tunnel constructed in America. Like the remains of the portage railroad, it remained remote and unsung for many years after it was no longer needed or used. The Pennsy's brochure about the portage railroad published in 1930 described the tunnel at that time as "abandoned, isolated and reclaimed by the wilderness," despite its being the "only Allegheny Portage Railroad structure of any consequence that has defied time and the elements for nearly a century."

The National Park Service reopened the tunnel to visitors in 2001. After getting driving instructions to its parking lot at the site's visitor center, those wanting to see it still have to negotiate a two-mile trail before they can explore its recesses.

Charles Dickens Travels

Inefficient and inconvenient as it may have been, Pennsylvania's Allegheny Portage Railroad did guarantee its passengers an interesting trip. Charles Dickens, the British author, described his own experience in *American Notes,* a work originally published sometime during the 1860s:

> Occasionally the rails are laid on the extreme verge of a giddy precipice; and looking from the carriage window, the traveler gazes sheer down, without a stone or scrap of fence between, into the mountains depths below. The journey is very carefully made, however; only two carriages traveling together; and, while proper precautions are taken, is not to be dreaded for its dangers.
>
> It was very pretty, traveling thus at a rapid pace along the heights of the mountain in a keen wind, to look down into a valley full of light and softness; catching glimpses, through the tree-tops, of scattered cabins; children running to the doors; dogs bursting out to bark, whom we could see without hearing; terrified pigs scampering homeward; families sitting out in their rude gardens; cows gazing upward with a stupid indifference; men in their shirtsleeves, looking on at their unfinished houses, planning out tomorrow's work; and we riding onward, high above them, like a whirlwind.

Train Spotters' Heaven at Gallitzin and Cresson

The National Park Service also provides directions to the tunnel complex at the small town of Gallitzin, Pennsylvania. Industrial development got its start in this region during the middle of the nineteenth century when the Pennsylvania Railroad located its mountain division here and built the highest tunnels that railroad would ever construct.

After the Pennsy's new line had reached the foot of the Allegheny Mountains in 1850, work began on the Allegheny Tunnel. The firm of E. Rutter & Sons was responsible for the job, which sometimes occupied up to five hundred men working with picks, shovels, and black powder. The double-track tunnel they constructed was over 3,000 feet long and open to traffic in 1854. By the turn of the century, the Pennsy's tracks across the Allegheny Mountains had become the busiest mountain line in the world, and a second parallel tunnel was added to the mountain in 1904.

These two tunnels joined a third, which the Commonwealth had already constructed at the same location as part of its New Portage Railroad, built to eliminate the inclined planes of the old one. The PRR also used this tunnel. In fact, the Pennsy widened it prior to building its second tunnel, another measure to speed traffic through the mountains. The tunnels remained unchanged until 1994–95, when Conrail took on a major enlargement project for two of them, to improve clearance and allow higher "double-stack" trains.

What has come to be known as Gallitzin's Tunnels Park is not very large, but it does offer benches for rail fans who want to settle in for a lengthy train-spotting session. Those inclined to remain overnight can check into a bed and breakfast just across the tracks that has a deck overlooking the tunnels. A 1942 Pennsy steel caboose houses an information center where visitors can pick up a schedule of trains that regularly pass through the tunnels.

At the information center or at a small museum just a few steps away, visitors can also obtain a copy of a poem written by Joan Grimes Kowalski in 1993 as a tribute to the tunnels' history. It reads, in part:

> When the tunnel was completed,
>   long and heavy trains could roar
> Between the markets in the west
>   and the cities near the shore.
> Goods and people traveled quickly,
>   all were suitably impressed
> For the tunnel at Gallitzin
>   linked the land from east to west.

Train spotters are equally, if not more, fond of the nearby town of Cresson, where trains have been rolling down a long, straight stretch of tracks since the Pennsylvania Railroad laid them. The Pennsy also graced Cresson with a resort hotel at the suggestion of Dr. Robert Mont-

When this illustration was made for the 1875 edition of *The Pennsylvania Railroad* by William B. Sipes, Cresson was a summer resort for the wealthy, where cool breezes could be enjoyed on the verandas of fine hotels.

gomery Smith Jackson, who recommended the area's springs of healthful mineral water. Pittsburgh business leaders like Andrew Carnegie constructed their private mountain retreats in Cresson in the years prior to the South Fork Fishing and Hunting Club offering them an alternative with a water view.

Cresson draws a different crowd now with its train-spotting observation platform and gazebo on Front Street. The railroad hotels are gone, but Cresson still has an establishment called the Station Inn, which is popular not for its amenities but for its proximity to the tracks. Many of its guests like to set up their camera equipment on its porch and are not the least bit bothered by the sound of freight trains passing just 150 feet from their bedroom windows during the night.

Horseshoe Curve

Spotting trains at Gallitzin or Cresson does not begin to compare with spotting trains at Horseshoe Curve, the engineering wonder that has attracted tourists since the day it was opened for business on February 15,

Horseshoe Curve, a tourist attraction since it opened, as it appeared in *Philadelphia and Its Environs* in 1875.

1854. This is the place where passengers can see both ends of the train in which they are riding and spectators outside can watch while a train bends itself into a U shape as it ascends or descends the tracks that hug the side of the mountain.

Engineer Herman Haupt assisted chief engineer J. Edgar Thomson in designing this feature, which solved an important problem on the route of the Pennsylvania Railroad between Harrisburg and Pittsburgh. The enormous curve, which is eighteen hundred feet across, allowed trains to negotiate the Allegheny Ridge at a lower grade than elsewhere by following the valley of Burgoon Run, a stream that it crosses with its enormous curve. The western end of the curve is 122 feet higher than its eastern end, and with a grade of 1.8 percent, passengers on a long train can easily see how much higher or lower the front or rear of their train is as it ascends or descends.

During World War II, Horseshoe Curve became so important in America's east-west transportation and national defense that it was among the targets of eight Nazi spies armed with explosives who sneaked into the United States via submarine in 1942. When the FBI foiled their plot, the eight spies were arrested and tried by a military court; six of them were executed.

There had long been a public park at the curve, and passenger trains sometimes stopped there, but a paved road to the site built in 1932 made the curve a lot more accessible. In 1992, America's Industrial Heritage Project funded a number of visitor amenities, including a visitor center and an inclined plane connecting the center with the park at trackside. The Altoona Railroaders Memorial Museum took over management, staffing, and maintenance.

Once they get off the inclined plane, visitors can appreciate a magnificent vista of Altoona's reservoir system and the road that winds back to town. In 2002, work had begun to trim back the trees at the curve to make the view even better, as well as make it easier to watch for approaching trains.

Visitors to Horseshoe Curve can see a watchman's shanty dating from around 1900 and a GP9 general-purpose diesel freight locomotive. The diesel is an ironic exhibit, since it was the Pennsy's evolution to lower maintenance diesel power that so adversely affected the economic life of Altoona. This particular locomotive succeeds an Altoona-built steam passenger locomotive, Class K4s Number 1361, that had been at the curve since 1957 but was removed by Conrail in 1985 to be restored to operating condition.

More than a hundred thousand visitors per year mount the plane or the stairs to the curve, many of them toting sophisticated camera equipment. Everyone waits quietly for the sound of an approaching train. The faint echo of a horn causes visitors to glance east and west, trying to determine the direction of the sound. Excitement mounts as a faint rumble grows louder and finally a locomotive appears. Those not snapping photographs wave to the train or lift their children up for a better look. Some cover their ears because the sharp curve causes the train's wheels to make a screeching din on the rails. As the train passes from view, visitors smile and nod at their fellows, convinced they've shared a very special experience. Then most of them settle down to wait for just one more train.

Altoona and Its Railroaders Memorial Museum

In 1849, several years before Pennsy trains could proceed by rail all the way from Philadelphia to Pittsburgh, the Pennsylvania Railroad chose the site for Altoona. In her 1999 book titled *Altoona and the Pennsylvania Railroad*, Betty Wagner Loeb mentioned that the land had been purchased discreetly in the name of a Philadelphia merchant who donated it to the railroad. Loeb suggested that the name "Altoona" had been derived from either the Cherokee word meaning "high lands of great value" or a railway center in Germany called Altona.

The railroad shops of Altoona as depicted in the *Pictorial Sketch-book of Pennsylvania*.

In 1850, construction began on the town's first roundhouse and repair facilities, and the city grew quickly, its population rising to more than ten thousand by 1870. Altoona's skilled workers, many of whom were immigrants, built and repaired not only locomotives but everything needed to run the railroad. By the 1920s, more than fifteen thousand workers labored in Altoona's shops, their lives regulated by the factory whistles that summoned them to work and announced their breaks and quitting times. Just as the Pennsy was known as the standard railroad of the world, Altoona was then the nation's standard for a railroad town.

The Pennsy began converting from steam to diesel and electric power, resulting in a reduction of the workforce. Programs were shut down during the 1950s, and older shop buildings were sold or demolished after Pennsy's merger with the New York Central in 1968.

As railroad jobs were disappearing from Altoona, citizens intent upon creating the Altoona Railroaders Memorial Museum issued a Statement of Purpose declaring their intention to "honor the railroad workers and their significant contributions to the culture and development of the railroad industry and to preserve this rich heritage for the education, enjoyment, and enrichment of present and future generations." During the 1990s, PRR's former Master Mechanics Building, built in 1882 and among the oldest of the town's remaining machine shops, which had most recently housed Conrail's Allegheny division offices, was converted

Workers at the Altoona Roundhouse in the 1930s. COLLECTION OF DAVID E. BERRY

Altoona Roundhouse in the 1950s. COLLECTION OF DAVID E. BERRY

to house the new museum's exhibits, a theatre, a library, and administrative offices.

Hard-core, die-hard rail fans who like museums with lots of locomotives and rolling stock, where they can absorb tons of technical information, may be disappointed in the Altoona Railroaders Memorial Museum, but the key to understanding and appreciating the place is in its name. This is a railroaders' museum, not a railroad museum. The focus is not on how a railroad worked, but how people worked on the railroad.

As visitors move from one exhibit space to the next, they activate a series of sound, light, and video performances in which various railroad characters share information about working in this company-dominated town between 1920 and 1940. A newsboy appears at a newsstand to welcome them to town. An executive in a carpeted corporate office discusses the business of railroading as if they were important stockholders. At Kelly's, visitors take a seat at the bar to eavesdrop on the after-hours conversation of blue-collar workers in a setting that could be made more realistic only if the mannequin representing Kelly really served drinks.

Other interactive exhibits introduce visitors to the skills used in the shops and yards. They can even open drawers and inspect the tools that various kinds of workers used.

Still other exhibits recall local history. On a replica of the Twelfth Street Bridge, which connected the shops with residential areas, a mannequin reminds them that when crossing the windy bridge, country girls grabbed their skirts while city girls hung onto their hats. Another exhibit recalls the wreck of a circus train during the 1890s, an event still remembered in Altoona because of the excitement that ensued when wild and exotic animals got loose.

In the autumn of 2001, officials of the Altoona Railroaders Memorial Museum inaugurated the construction of a roundhouse to exhibit some prize rolling stock, including K4s Locomotive Number 1361, which used to be on display at Horseshoe Curve and is being stored at Steamtown. Instead of using shovels to break ground, the officials drove in railroad spikes.

The museum is probably busiest in the fall during a celebration called Railfest, in which the museum and its Horseshoe Curve site offer special programs and excursions. Other railroad heritage sites within easy traveling distance, including the East Broad Top Railroad and the Bellefonte Historical Railroad, also participate. The annual Gallitzin Tunnelsfest is held concurrently.

Pennsylvania's newest tourist destination for rail fans: the Railroaders Memorial Museum in Altoona. KYLE R. WEAVER

The inclined plane at Johnstown, purported to be the world's steepest. CAMBRIA COUNTY TRANSIT AUTHORITY

Artifacts of the Johnstown Flood

Johnstown recovered from its devastating flood, and this industrial community continued to grow as the Cambria Iron Company evolved into the Cambria Steel Company, which was purchased by Bethlehem Steel in 1923, until setbacks in the steel industry finally forced the community to seek growth in other areas. Today, Johnstown is recovering, thanks to its new high-technology industries and industrial heritage tourism. The town's two main tourist attractions consist of the Johnstown Flood Museum, operated by the Johnstown Area Heritage Association downtown in a former Carnegie library, and an inclined plane built in 1891. Both were inspired by the flood, and both make Johnstown an interesting detour for rail fans exploring the Altoona area.

The Johnstown Flood Museum uses objects to tell the story of the flood and the area's railroad history in the main exhibit area. The entire rear wall of this space supports a bas-relief representing the debris that got stuck and burned at Johnstown's railroad bridge, in which the largest identifiable object is a steam locomotive. The museum uses two productions to add human perspective and demonstrate how the flood captured America's attention and held it for more than a century. The theatre at the museum runs a film made on the hundredth anniversary of the flood in 1989. It won an Academy Award for best documentary short subject. Without too many high-tech special effects, the film captures the suddenness and shock of the disaster and the scope of its devastation. The other production can be viewed on the museum's top floor in a space that seems to have originally functioned as a nineteenth-century gymnasium. Visitors put on 3-D glasses to view a multimedia presentation based on old stereopticon images made right after the flood. They are evidence of how the scene at Johnstown touched the hearts of Americans in a way not duplicated until September 11, 2001.

Johnstown's inclined plane was once a kind of commuter railroad linking Johnstown and Westmont, a suburb built by the Cambria Iron Company on a hill above the city, out of harm's way. It became the preferred location for the mansions of the company's executives. With a grade of 71.9 percent, Johnstown's inclined plane claims to hold the record as the world's steepest.

The plane was closed in 1962 after most of the town's residents found it more convenient to make this trip by automobile, but it was restored and later enhanced with an observation deck, a visitor center, and a summit restaurant. Local officials now estimate that 120,000 visitors ride the plane each year.

The East Broad Top Railroad

The East Broad Top (EBT) Railroad was constructed during the 1870s to link several coal mining towns to the Pennsy's main line. Locomotives hauled both freight and passengers on its narrow-gauge tracks until revenue losses forced it to reduce operations during the 1950s, culminating in the line's abandonment in 1956.

The train station at Orbisonia, where visitors board the East Broad Top Railroad to Colgate Grove.

About an hour before the tourists board the East Broad Top, its steam locomotive is taken from the roundhouse to the turntable to a track, where it is loaded with coal.

The history of this short line would be completely unremarkable except that its yards and structures were abandoned with much of their equipment intact, making it possible for the modern East Broad Top Railroad to promote itself as "the most complete, authentic rail site in North America." In an article called "Save This Railroad," published in *American Heritage of Invention & Technology* in 1995, John H. White commented, "Father Time locked the front door and walked away four decades ago, leaving behind the kind of package that industrial historians dream about finding."

For whatever reason, the Kovalchick Salvage Company, which acquired the railroad following its abandonment, failed to pull up its rails and knock down its buildings. During the 1960 bicentennial celebration of the town of Orbisonia, where the East Broad Top is located, the Kovalchick family even repaired some of its tracks and ran one of its old steam engines. Public response demanded that the rides be continued.

Although a declining number of passengers makes it uncertain whether the EBT will continue to operate trains after 2002, the East Broad Top Railroad offered a fifty-minute ride to Colgate Grove through an area called the Aughwick Valley. Visitors were invited to bring food and disembark for a picnic. The site was popular with both families and rail fans, who could be seen arriving about an hour before the first scheduled excursion so they could set up their cameras outside the old roundhouse. There they could watch while the EBT locomotive to be used that day was taken out amid great gusts of steam and loaded with coal. They could also wander alone among the complex's ghostly old buildings, peering through the broken windows at the equipment still housed inside.

Waynesburg & Washington Engine Number 4

The region once had another narrow-gauge railroad that linked Waynesburg in Greene County to a connection with the Pennsy in the town of Washington in Washington County. Unlike the East Broad Top, this line is gone, but a key artifact remains at the Greene County Historical Society's museum.

An engine that once ran on the narrow-gauge Waynesburg & Washington Railroad is now at the museum of the Greene County Historical Society. JAMES D. WEINSCHENKER

In an article for *The Keystone* published in 2001, James Weinschenker told the history of Number 4, a locomotive used primarily to haul freight on the Waynesburg & Washington (W&W) Railroad from 1916 to 1933. The Pennsylvania Railroad refurbished Number 4 in 1958 for display at the Greene County Fairgrounds, where it remained in open display for seventeen years.

After the Greene County Historical Society obtained the old "county poor farm" to serve as a museum, Number 4 was moved to the site and restored by railroad buffs in 1977–78. In 2000, Number 4 was cosmetically restored a second time and displayed at the local fall festival. The engine remains on the museum's grounds, where volunteers are now planning to restore it to operating condition.

Youngwood

Although Youngwood was never on the Pennsy's main line, it was connected with the PRR by a branch that ran from Greensburg to Uniontown, which took it through the towns of Youngwood and Scottdale. Constructed in 1902 and saved from destruction in 1982, the PRR's passenger and freight station in Youngwood now houses a museum and archives containing hundreds of photographs and artifacts. Visitors can examine a model train display and sometimes take a ride on the Westmoreland Heritage Railroad over tracks that once served twenty-one coal mines.

The Region's Rail Trails

In between the Allegheny Portage Railroad National Historic Site and its Staple Bend Tunnel area, visitors can find the intriguingly named Ghost Town Trail, which incorporates sixteen miles of railbed in the Blacklick Creek Valley of Cambria and Indiana Counties. Its name commemorates Wehrum and Bracken, two coal-mining towns that were abandoned during the 1930s. The rail trail is jointly operated by the Cambria County Conservation and Recreation Authority and Indiana County Parks.

Hikers of the Ghost Town Trail pass by the remains of the Eliza Furnace complex of dwellings and commercial and industrial buildings, which operated between 1846 and 1849. Today the furnace is considered one of the most well-preserved hot blast iron furnaces in Pennsylvania. The Ghost Town Trail also lies adjacent to the Blacklick Valley Natural Area. At Dilltown, the Dillweed Bed and Breakfast and Trailside Shop caters to trail users.

The Youghiogheny River Trail (pronounced Yock-ah-gain-ee) is a forty-three-mile stretch that was once part of the Pittsburgh & Lake Erie Railroad line between McKeesport and Connellsville on the west side of the river with the same Indian name. An organization established in 1991 called the Regional Trail Corporation, with representatives from Allegheny, Fayette, and Westmoreland Counties, purchased the right-of-way for this trail in 1992.

Its artifacts include a number of original mileposts, some of which were recently cleaned and restored by Boy Scouts. New amenities are planned for the Youghiogheny River Trail, as well as side trails to connect it with local parks and historic sites.

The Allegheny Trail Alliance will incorporate the Youghiogheny River Trail in an ambitious trails network that is now in the works and will stretch for hundreds of miles—from Pittsburgh to Cumberland, Maryland, and finally to Washington, D.C., by means of the Chesapeake & Ohio (C&O) Canal National Historical Park. Hikers and bikers will be able to move between urban and wilderness settings on a right-of-way free of motor vehicles that will utilize old railroad engineering features such as tunnels and viaducts.

The Lower Trail (Lower is pronounced to rhyme with "power"), connecting Williamsburg in Blair County with Alexandria in Huntington County along the Frankstown branch of the Juniata River, is eleven miles long and covers ground that was once part of both the State Works canal system and the Petersburg branch of the Pennsylvania Railroad. It meanders past canal artifacts like the remains of locks and a locktender's house, as well as railroad bridges.

Other rail trails in this region include the Trail of Transportation, the Five Star Trail, and the Jim Mayer Riverwalk Trail.

SECTION SEVEN

Pittsburgh Area

Great Railways of the Region

The Pittsburgh & Lake Erie

The Pittsburgh & Lake Erie (P&LE) Railroad was chartered in 1875, somewhat later than the other major lines in Pennsylvania's railroad history. It was the brainchild of Pittsburgh businessman William McCreery, who stated his intention to affiliate the P&LE with the B&O, which had gained entry to Pittsburgh in 1871, hoping that these allied railroads would give the Pennsy some serious competition.

Construction started in May 1877, and that fall William H. Vanderbilt purchased $300,000 worth of stock. While the capital was a welcome boost for the P&LE, it also portended that this line would become affiliated with the New York Central system, not the B&O. P&LE's initial line was built from Pittsburgh to Youngstown, Ohio, a town that was already connected to Vanderbilt's Lake Shore & Michigan Southern Railway via the latter railroad's Mahoning Coal Railroad, running from Youngstown to Ashtabula on Lake Erie.

The P&LE general office and passenger station were located on the south bank of the Monongahela River, opposite downtown Pittsburgh. Operations began in February 1879 without fanfare or festivities, shortly after tracks were laid under the Monongahela suspension bridge that linked the P&LE's South Side facilities with Pittsburgh. P&LE trains ran at water level on the banks of the Monongahela, Ohio, Beaver, and Mahoning Rivers, serving many of the heavy industries located in this area. Eventually P&LE, nicknamed the "Little Giant," would operate two hundred miles of railroad in six Pennsylvania counties as well as the few miles from the Ohio border to Youngstown.

It was easy to predict that P&LE business would benefit by an extension to the region south of Pittsburgh, where coal was roasted into coke in ovens near the mines. Vanderbilt advanced the funds to construct what would become an important feeder, a line called the Pittsburgh, McKeesport & Youghiogheny Railroad. This railroad opened in 1883, connecting Pittsburgh to Connellsville along the Monongahela and Youghiogheny Rivers. It would subsequently give the P&LE a connection to Baltimore when the Western Maryland Railway built a line from Cumberland to Connellsville.

In his 1980 book, *The Pittsburgh and Lake Erie Railroad*, Harold H. McLean suggests that Vanderbilt had plans to make both these railroads important links in his proposed South Penn system. To ensure cooperation from the P&LE, around this time Vanderbilt bought enough additional stock to control the railroad and make it a permanent part of the New York Central system, though it would always operate as a separate corporation.

Although the P&LE's terminal was not downtown, its location at the corner of Smithfield and Carson Streets placed it at an important transportation junction. The Smithfield Street Bridge linked this neighborhood to Pittsburgh proper, while the city's oldest inclined plane provided access to Pittsburgh's Mount Washington suburbs. The P&LE terminal was also near the Pennsylvania Railroad's Birmingham Station, which served its Pittsburgh, Cincinnati, Chicago & St. Louis Railway, or Panhandle, lines.

P&LE replaced its modest two-story passenger station with a far grander depot and office complex designed by architect William George Burns and completed in 1901. This station, which continues to be this railroad's key artifact, has since become the keystone of a massive redevelopment project in this area and an inviting destination for tourists and Pittsburgh area residents.

Although P&LE suffered declines in passenger miles through most of the twentieth century, its efficient freight operations in highly industrialized river valleys kept earning profits. In fact, after it became a controlled subsidiary of the Penn Central Railroad, P&LE lent the Penn Central surplus cash.

After being permitted to drop out of the Penn Central system when Conrail was formed in 1976, P&LE continued to operate until it was doomed by heavy losses in the steel industry during the 1980s. Part of the railroad was sold to CSX Corporation in 1991, and the rest was assigned to CSX in 1992, when P&LE finally ceased operations.

The Wabash-Pittsburgh Terminal—
Later the Pittsburgh & West Virginia

Before he died in 1892, Jay Gould had taken control of a number of midwestern, southwestern, and western railroads in pursuit of his dream of controlling a transcontinental railroad. One of the key parts of this network was the Wabash Railroad, which ran principally through Indiana and Illinois, connecting the Mississippi River, Chicago, and St. Louis with Toledo. His son George Jay Gould continued the acquisitions, ending up with a gap of about two hundred miles between the Western Maryland Railway, which he had acquired, and the Wheeling & Lake Erie Railroad, which he controlled. His solution was the Wabash Railroad–

backed Wabash-Pittsburgh Terminal Railway (WPT), incorporated in 1904, to extend from Pittsburgh Junction, Ohio, to the Golden Triangle of downtown Pittsburgh, territory that was long dominated by the Pennsylvania Railroad and that the Pennsy would not be eager to share.

In their 1989 book, *The Pittsburgh & West Virginia Railway*, Howard V. Worley Jr. and William N. Poellot Jr. tell how this line was secretly planned and authorized. Joseph Ramsay, ostensibly president of the Pittsburgh & Mansfield Railroad streetcar line, secretly worked for George Jay Gould. Early in 1900, while claiming that he was only visiting friends, he scouted the route by which the WPT would enter town. Ramsay also worked to introduce legislation authorizing a railroad bridge over the Monongahela River, allowing everyone to assume it would be used by his streetcars. The Pennsy was sufficiently convinced that Gould's Wabash system would never enter Pittsburgh, so in 1902, the railroad signed agreements allowing the WPT to cross its tracks in ten locations between Pittsburgh and its Wheeling & Lake Erie Railroad connection. George Jay Gould himself refrained from visiting Pittsburgh until July 1903.

Even after Gould's plans became evident, the executives of other railroads serving Pittsburgh consoled themselves that all the good routes into the city had already been taken. However, Gould's engineer James Patterson managed to build a main line along the tops of ridges and hills with more than 150 bridges and numerous tunnels, including the tunnel through Mount Washington that brought the WPT tracks to its downtown neobaroque, flatiron, ten-story terminal, which became known locally as the Pittsburgh Wabash Station or the Palace Depot.

Joseph Ramsay became the WPT's first president and was on hand to ride his private car into town on opening day on June 1, 1904. Unfortunately, when scheduled operations began about a month later, the first train left Pittsburgh with only a single passenger, and competitors were doing everything they could to see that this railroad would never do much better.

At the turn of the century, Gould had had the support of Andrew Carnegie, who deplored the PRR's pricing policies when it came to shipping the products of his mills. Carnegie had signed a tonnage agreement with Gould, but this did not prevent Carnegie from selling his steel mills to J. P. Morgan, placing the agreement in limbo and making freight prospects uncertain for the WPT.

Following the panic of 1907, WPT's deficits mounted. In 1908, the comapny was unable to pay the interest due on its first mortgage and the railroad entered receivership that May.

New owners acquired the WPT in 1916 after a court ordered the sale of its assets and property. These investors, led by J. N. Wallace, brought the railroad new ideas and operating plans, together with a new identity. The Wabash-Pittsburgh Terminal became the Pittsburgh & West Virginia (P&WV) Railway in 1917. In 1928, P&WV was authorized to extend its line to Connellsville. Operations began on these tracks in 1931, giving P&WV a connection with the Western Maryland Railway, whose rails reached Connellsville in 1912. While the economic conditions of the 1930s marked the beginning of a long struggle to keep the P&WV in business, it became a fast through gateway for hauling freight between the Midwest and the East Coast.

In March 1946, one of the most disastrous fires in the history of Pittsburgh burned for forty-two hours at this railroad's downtown freight terminal. In 1949, all the downtown facilities built for the Wabash-Pittsburgh Terminal, including the Palace Depot, were razed, to make room for the new buildings planned for Pittsburgh's renaissance of its Golden Triangle. Around the same time, the railroad's bridge across the Monongahela River was removed and its tunnel through Mount Washington was abandoned and sealed.

In 1964, the P&WV became the Pittsburgh division of the Norfolk & Western Railway, which has since become Norfolk Southern Corporation.

Rail Stories of the Region

Pennsylvania's System in Pittsburgh

The legislation passed in 1826 that authorized Pennsylvania's canals in the western portion of the Commonwealth also provided for a canal that would run from Pittsburgh along the Allegheny River to a junction with the Kiskiminetas River. Construction was somewhat delayed due to controversy on how the canal would approach the city that had grown at the point of land where the Allegheny and Monongahela Rivers met, sometimes called the Golden Triangle. The decision of whether the canal would be constructed on the north or south bank of the Allegheny was really a matter of choosing whether the commercial activity that would evolve around its basin would benefit the city of Pittsburgh or the borough called Allegheny, just north of the river.

It was eventually decided that the canal would enter Allegheny (the borough), where its main line would cross the Allegheny River by aqueduct to Pittsburgh, but an extension would give canal boat operators the option of proceeding to another basin on the north shore, from which they could pass through locks to the Allegheny River. After considering three different routes for the canal through Pittsburgh proper, Pittsburgh's two city councils agreed that the canal would be built along what is now Eleventh Street to Liberty Avenue, then along the present Grant Street, passing beneath the obstacle of Grant's Hill through a tunnel, and continuing through several locks to the Monongahela River.

Guns were fired from the artillery and thousands of spectators watched on November 10, 1829, when the aqueduct was filled with water and three packet boats maneuvered into Pittsburgh. At 1,140 feet long, this particular aqueduct was the longest in Pennsylvania's State Works, but it leaked and later had to be rebuilt. John Roebling was chosen for the job and replaced it with an early example of the wire suspension bridges for which he would become famous.

The canal's other expensive and challenging engineering feature, the 810-foot tunnel beneath Grant's Hill, was intended to take canal boats to where the Chesapeake & Ohio Canal was expected to enter the city. The tunnel was completed in 1831, but it also leaked and both of its ends were frequently damaged by earth slides.

Over the next twenty years, as Americans acknowledged the superiority of railroads over canals, expensive repairs to Pittsburgh's canal became increasingly difficult to justify. The Chesapeake & Ohio Canal never did reach Pittsburgh, making the tunnel a particular liability. By the 1850s, canal operations ceased and the locks, canal basins, and tunnel were gradually filled in.

The Pittsburgh canal made the news a few more times during the twentieth century when construction workers excavating to erect modern buildings occasionally came across its relics. In 1911, men working on the Pittsburgh and Allegheny Telephone Company building found the remains of an old canal boat, and in 1967, the tunnel itself was rediscovered by those working on a building for United States Steel.

The Pennsy or the Baltimore & Ohio?

Pittsburgh's canal did not operate long, but it did promote the growth of Pittsburgh's iron and glass industries, making rail service more desirable to residents of the city. In 1846, the very year that Pennsylvania's legislature was considering an act to "incorporate the Pennsylvania Central Railroad Company," it was also struggling with the key issue of whether to give the Baltimore & Ohio Railroad one more chance to reach Pittsburgh, since it had failed to make its charter's original deadline.

Residents of both Pittsburgh and Baltimore favored giving the B&O more time since the railroad was going to reach the Ohio River at some point, which might as well be Pittsburgh. They argued that constructing the B&O line would cost the Commonwealth nothing. B&O also had tracks on the ground, while it remained to be seen whether a Pennsylvania railroad would ever be more than a concept. Philadelphians, however, insisted that the prospect of B&O service to Pittsburgh would sink the State Works and also scare investors away from the proposed Pennsylvania railroad project. With all the trade of the West then flowing into Baltimore, Philadelphia itself would face ruin.

Legislation enacted that year permitted both railroads to proceed, but gave the new Pennsylvania Railroad Company an advantage. If the Pennsy secured $3 million in stock subscriptions by the end of July 1847 and constructed fifteen miles of railroad at each end of its line, the B&O would lose its Pennsylvania charter.

The Pennsylvania Railroad met these requirements, and its remaining construction work progressed rapidly under the leadership of J. Edgar Thomson. By 1852, trains could run between Philadelphia and Pittsburgh, though they had to use portions of both the old and new portage railroads built by the Commonwealth until the Pennsy's mountain division was completed in 1854. In the Pittsburgh area, Pennsy tracks roughly followed the course of Turtle Creek and ended at the railroad's first downtown station, located at Twelfth Street and Liberty Avenue.

B&O got a second chance at Pittsburgh's rail traffic in 1864 when plans were made to extend the little Pittsburgh & Connellsville Railroad, chartered in 1837, to Cumberland, Maryland, and connect with the B&O. Thomas A. Scott, then president of the PRR, not only got the charter repealed for the Pittsburgh & Connellsville Railroad, but also secured legislation allowing a new entity that would be controlled by the Pennsy to take it over. When both bills passed in the wee hours of an April morning, one senator expressed his disgust for the power that the Pennsy was by then able to wield with his often quoted acid inquiry, "Mr. Speaker, may we now go Scott free?"

In 1871, the B&O finally succeeded in leasing the Pittsburgh & Connellsville Railroad, after it had been completed to Cumberland and gained independent access to Pittsburgh. By that time, it was clear that no latecomer would truly rival the Pennsy's importance to Pittsburgh, with its connections to destinations in all directions through its branches, including the Pittsburgh, Fort Wayne & Chicago Railway; the Pittsburgh, Cincinnati, Chicago & St. Louis Railroad (known as the Pennsy's Panhandle lines); the Pittsburgh, Virginia & Charleston Railway; the Western Pennsylvania Railroad; and the Allegheny Valley Railroad.

The Pittsburgh Riots

In a book titled *History of Allegheny County, Pennsylvania,* published in 1889, the anonymous author wrote, "All cities have riots, at some time in their history, and Pittsburgh had her share in 1877. It was chiefly remarkable for the amount of property destroyed, and for the utter paralysis that overcame the local authorities in attempting to put it down. The total of the property destroyed was valued at three millions of dollars, and all this destruction was wrought during the quiet of a beautiful Sunday in July." The 1877 riot was part of America's first national labor uprising, which erupted simultaneously in many other cities and towns, but has since come to be generally associated with Pittsburgh and the Pennsylvania Railroad.

In 1877, at a time when railroads were still recovering from the depression triggered by the panic of 1873, the Pennsy announced a 10 percent cut in wages for all officers and employees. Management was also experimenting with other cost-cutting measures, such as "double-heading," or joining two freight trains into one, essentially downsizing by eliminating available jobs for railroad workers.

Three days after a riot started among equally disgruntled B&O railroad workers in Martinsburg, West Virginia, on July 19, 1877, several Pennsy crews refused to take out their trains. Other Pittsburgh workers, both employed and unemployed, soon joined them at the freight yard, where they succeeded in causing a sheriff and his posse, who had been summoned by Pennsy executives, to back down. After the local militiamen who were called in joined the strike, fresh troops were transported from Philadelphia. The situation worsened when these Philadelphians opened fire upon hearing what sounded like either pistol shots or explosions, killing twenty people and wounding many more. The troops retreated to the roundhouse, but the mob set fire to the Pennsy's freight yard and rammed flaming cars down the tracks to flush out the soldiers, who again opened fire. At that point, according to the *History of Allegheny County, Pennsylvania,* "Every thief, every loafer, every idler, every ill-disposed creature, seeing the opportunity offered for plunder, jumped at the unwonted chance, and at once began the work of looting."

The ultimate loss to the PRR included virtually all its Pittsburgh terminal facilities, including its passenger station, two roundhouses, machine shops, and 125 locomotives. The Pennsy filed claims against Allegheny County for property damage amounting to $2,312,000.

The strikers had inflicted their anger and frustration on the very railroad that was so important to the city. The published *History of Allegheny County, Pennsylvania* advanced the theory that the general population of Pittsburgh might have concluded that the Pennsy was no longer according their city the proper respect: "From the very start the Pennsylvania road had persisted in treating Pittsburgh, not as the western terminus of the line, but as a mere way-station on its route to the west. The city, until within a few years past, was unable to profit by the advantages of its position. The railroad rates discriminated against it at nearly every point, and it was cheaper to ship grain and other western produce from Chicago to Philadelphia and New York than to Pittsburgh."

At the time it occurred, newspapers suggested that the strike might signal the start of a new civil war in America, between labor and capital. It did indeed foster union development and led many to conclude that if the railroad needed the government's protection from its own workers, perhaps it needed some government regulation as well.

One Last Main Line for Pittsburgh

In 1912, when the first freight train traveled a new route from Pittsburgh to Baltimore over an extension of the Western Maryland Railway to Connellsville, the achievement was welcomed and applauded in both cities and all the towns in between. No one knew it at the time, but this extension was the last significant piece of mainline railroad to be constructed in the continental United States.

Acquisition of the Western Maryland Railway had been an important step in George Jay Gould's dream to control a transcontinental railroad network, the dream that also brought his Wabash-Pittsburgh Terminal Railway into Pittsburgh. In 1902, working quietly through an organization called the Fuller Syndicate with the authorization of Baltimore's city council, Gould purchased the interest that the city of Baltimore had held in this railroad in the form of mortgages. Gould began construction in 1903 on an extension that would follow the Potomac to Cumberland. With numerous bridges and more than two miles of tunnels, the line proved to be expensive, and the Western Maryland Railway entered receivership in 1908, together with Gould's Wabash-Pittsburgh Terminal and his Wheeling & Lake Erie Railroad.

Once the Western Maryland Railway was free of Gould and out of receivership, its simple extension to Connellsville brought it a trade and traffic partner in the P&LE, which was by that time part of the New York

Central system. The connection between these railroads forged a new Great Lakes to Seaboard system that was suddenly a real competitor for the B&O.

The fact that the Western Maryland Railway's new tracks ran parallel to those of the B&O in many places brought about the eventual demise of this line. Although the Western Maryland Railway may have had the better route, the CSX Corporation abandoned it after absorbing what was then called the Connellsville subdivision in the mid-1970s. Parts of the western end of the Western Maryland Railway are now being converted into rail trails, except for that portion being used by the Western Maryland Scenic Railroad.

Railroads and Pittsburgh's Renaissance

No one knows exactly how the section of Pittsburgh bounded by the Allegheny River, the Monongahela River, and Grant Street came to be called Pittsburgh's Golden Triangle. This piece of real estate is certainly triangular, but it hasn't always been a very appealing place. When the Writers' Program of the Work Projects Administration published its *Guide*

Pittsburgh, the "western terminus of the Pennsylvania Railroad," in William B. Sipes's 1875 book on the railroad.

to the Keystone State in 1940, its authors observed, "The triangle formed by the rivers is packed with smoke-grimed buildings; from the manufacturing establishments come clouds of devastating smoke that unite with the river fog to form Pittsburgh's traditional nuisance, 'smog.'"

The smoke and the grime were a product of, and a kind of tribute to, the many successful industries in and around Pittsburgh, including Andrew Carnegie's Edgar Thomson Steel Works, the H.J. Heinz food processing operations, Alcoa, and PPG, or Pittsburgh Plate Glass. Making the atmosphere even less wholesome were the railroad facilities that dominated the triangle, including the massive freight operations of the Pennsylvania Railroad, which embraced the terminal facilities of the Wabash-Pittsburgh Terminal, later the P&WV.

By the mid-twentieth century, architectural styles had changed and even the railroads' spectacular stations, designed to surround passengers with opulence, looked dated and old. Two of them, Theodore C. Link's flatiron Wabash Terminal and the B&O passenger station designed by Frank Furness, had already been torn down, and Pittsburghers seemed inclined to sacrifice even more Victorian landmarks. For a while, it seemed that even the Allegheny County Courthouse and Jail, designed by Henry Hobson Richardson, would be replaced by a hotel.

The massive renovation project that would become known as Pittsburgh's Renaissance was led by Mayor David Lawrence and the influential banker Richard King Mellon. As a member of the PRR board of directors, Mellon was particularly influential in gaining the support of the reluctant Pennsy.

In 1950, demolition began on everything at the western end of the Golden Triangle, except for its few remaining eighteenth-century structures and the nondescript building housing the Pittsburgh Press. The empty space was filled in by an office complex called Gateway Center and new buildings for Alcoa and United States Steel.

There had been a number of suggestions about what to locate at the extreme point of land where the rivers meet. Statues and futuristic office centers were rejected in favor of a fountain tapping an underground water source that spouted water three hundred feet into the air, just beyond the preserved outline of old Fort Duquesne.

A second redevelopment project of the Golden Triangle was undertaken in the 1980s. Grant Street was essentially rebuilt, and Pittsburgh got a "light-rail transit line," or a combination subway/surface line that proved to be very successful and has since been expanded. Although the first renaissance obliterated quite a few railroad artifacts, the second one brought rail service back to Pittsburgh, even utilizing a few remaining railroad artifacts, such as the Pennsy's Panhandle Division Bridge, over which light-rail transit cars now travel to Station Square and points south.

Local Chapters of the National Railway Historical Society

The Beaver Valley Junction Chapter of the National Railway Historical Society was founded by rail fans in the Conway area to preserve Beaver County's railroad heritage. They operate a museum in Mahoningtown, where they are restoring and reerecting a century-old B&O railroad tower and two cabooses. Since the tower is one of the last of the B&O towers still standing, it is expected to become the centerpiece of the museum site. The chapter holds regular meetings that feature educational entertainment, and it offers occasional excursions. Sometimes the two activities are combined, like the time the chapter members conducted a monthly meeting in the middle of the Kiski River Bridge while aboard the Kiski Junction Railroad. Their regular newsletter is called the *Beaver Valley Highball.*

The Pittsburgh Chapter of the National Railway Historical Society also holds regular meetings with educational entertainment. Their special excursions can take members to Cresson for trackside observation or for rides on the Kiski Junction Railroad. This chapter's publication is called the *Keystone Newsletter.*

The Region's Railroad Giants

Andrew Carnegie (1835–1919)

The name Andrew Carnegie is as synonymous with Pittsburgh as it is with the phrase "self-made man." Carnegie was born in Scotland and immigrated with his family to the town called Allegheny in 1848. Slum housing was all they could afford while Carnegie's father labored to support them in a textile factory. At the age of twelve, Carnegie was put to work in the same factory as a "bobbin boy."

Carnegie's rise to wealth and fame began when he was promoted from a subsequent job of delivering telegrams to telegraph operator. He so impressed Thomas A. Scott that this Pennsylvania Railroad executive hired him as private secretary. Carnegie spent twelve years working for the Pennsy, where he acquired his business and management skills. When Scott was promoted, Carnegie was appointed to Scott's former position of superintendent of the western division, where he remained until 1865.

Scott also introduced Carnegie to the art of stock investment. Carnegie sold railroad bonds in Europe and invested in a telegraph company that was purchased at a profit by Western Union. He also organized the Pullman Palace Car Company with George Pullman.

Carnegie is best remembered for the steel plant he constructed to employ the new, quick, cheap Bessemer process. Located along the Pennsy's tracks, Carnegie's plant was named the Edgar Thomson Works after the president of the PRR, which Carnegie hoped would become his biggest customer. Carnegie's efficient company soon became the world's largest producer of steel.

Carnegie frequently found himself at odds with the Pennsy, whose rates he claimed discriminated against Pennsylvania's businesses in favor of those located farther away. Determined to break its

Andrew Carnegie
LIBRARY OF CONGRESS

transportation monopoly, he supported the South Pennsylvania Railroad project and later formed the Bessemer & Lake Erie Railroad, mainly out of a deteriorating line that ran from a town north of Pittsburgh to Conneaut, Ohio. Once the Pennsy management realized that Carnegie was serious about developing his acquisition into a competing railroad with connections to other major lines, it backed down and cut his rates.

Carnegie Steel became the United States Steel Corporation in 1901 when J. P. Morgan bought Carnegie out, a deal that also made Carnegie one of the world's richest men. Regarding himself as the trustee, not the owner, of this fortune, Carnegie devoted himself to philanthropy, providing opportunities for those who could and would grasp them. Carnegie is remembered today for the many libraries he founded—nearly two thousand in the United States.

Robert Pitcairn (1836–1909)

Robert Pitcairn was another Scot whose family immigrated to the Pittsburgh area, where he and Andrew Carnegie became boyhood friends. Carnegie got Pitcairn a job as a telegram messenger (Pitcairn was also later promoted to operator) and later a position as a ticket agent in Cresson.

Pitcairn rose in the Pennsy ranks, becoming superintendent of the division between Harrisburg and Altoona. When Carnegie left the PRR in 1865 to go into business for himself, Pitcairn succeeded him as superintendent of the entire western division. Pitcairn is sometimes blamed for the destruction of the great railroad strike of 1877 because his policies during times of general depression had been perceived as harsh by the angered workers.

Pitcairn found another friend in George Westinghouse, whom he assisted in organizing the company that would manufacture air brakes for trains. It was Pitcairn's investments in Westinghouse that helped him amass a personal fortune.

Jay Gould (1836–1892)

Just as Carnegie personifies the self-made man, Jay Gould is sometimes depicted as the archetype evil robber baron, though modern business historians are lately beginning to rehabilitate his reputation. Like Carnegie, Gould was a man of humble background; his parents were farmers in upstate New York, and Gould worked at his father's store before he was able to start a business as a self-taught surveyor.

Gould's robber-baron image was born in the days when he joined forces with James Fisk and Daniel Drew in the Erie War to prevent Cornelius Vanderbilt from taking over the New York & Erie Railroad. Gould launched an expansion program at the Erie that forced the Pennsy and the New York Central to expand and compete. Gould blackened his reputation with an effort to corner America's gold supply and was forced out of the Erie's management.

In 1874, Gould acquired the Union Pacific Railroad and worked hard to improve its inefficient operation. During the 1880s, he gained control of a number of midwestern, southwestern, and western railroads in an effort to forge a transcontinental system.

Gould's contemporaries described him as habitually thin and sickly, a condition probably resulting from chronic tuberculosis. He died at home on Fifth Avenue, leaving a will intended to keep his fortune in his family.

George Jay Gould (1864–1923)

By the terms of his father's will, George Jay Gould obtained control of the Gould family millions and about fifteen thousand miles of railroad empire, not to mention his father's interests in the lucrative Western Union Telegraph Company and the Manhattan Elevated Railway. Unlike his self-made father, this Gould had attended private school and had received a seat on the New York Stock Exchange as a gift for his twenty-first birthday.

Gould liked the good things that his money could buy. He was known for his love of parties and the theatre, and particularly for the sport of polo, which he helped to popularize in the United States. His first wife was a stunning actress, and after her death, he married his showgirl mistress, who had already borne him three children.

Gould attempted to realize his father's dream of controlling America's first coast-to-coast rail system. He bought, built, and extended many railroads, culminating in his enormously expensive Wabash-Pittsburgh Terminal Railway project. After the financial panic of 1907, Gould lost railroad after bankrupt railroad, a collapse that caused him to turn from active participation in business to the management of his personal investments.

George Jay Gould
LIBRARY OF CONGRESS

Another blow came in 1916 when his family sued him; they claimed that he had mismanaged his father's estate. Gould made the headlines one last time when he died in France in 1923. Although he died from pneumonia, he had just been visiting the recently discovered tomb of King Tutankhamen in Egypt, causing contemporaries to list him as a victim of "King Tut's Curse."

Sampling the Region's Railroad History

Lorett Treese Travels

The Amtrak train called the Pennsylvanian stops in Paoli at 7:08 A.M., which puts my departure for Pittsburgh on a foggy, drizzling December day slightly before dawn. The train arrives on time at the Paoli station, and the conductor points me to a car less than half full. My fellow passengers are a mix of people commuting to Harrisburg, those making a holiday visit to family in Pittsburgh, and college students returning home to western Pennsylvania for the long semester break. As for me, I'm on board to follow the paths of the old Philadelphia & Columbia Railroad, the State Works rail and canal system, and the Pennsylvania Railroad.

Dawn breaks as we glide through the still green fields of Lancaster County. We cross two sizeable streams, the Big and the Little Conestoga, while automobile traffic on parallel roads grows heavier as we approach Harrisburg. The cooling towers of Three Mile Island are barely visible in the fog, which is, however, not dense enough to prevent planes from landing at Harrisburg's International Airport.

We arrive at Harrisburg, where a scheduled half-hour delay allows time to attach the freight cars we will be hauling west with us. Here we also move from Amtrak's tracks to those of Norfolk Southern Corporation. Unfortunately, the regular bulletin from Norfolk Southern Corporation that warns the conductor of anything he might need to be aware of on the road ahead has not yet arrived, and we sit for an additional half hour while the conductor tries to get it faxed. An Amtrak employee patiently explains the problem in each passenger car and says something promising about making up the lost time.

I don't believe her for a minute, but not until my return trip do I learn she was sincere. The conductor on my eastbound Three Rivers train made a similar promise after our departure from Pittsburgh was held up nearly fifty minutes, and to my delight, we did speed along between Lewistown and Harrisburg, reaching the state capital nearly on time and my own destination of Paoli a few minutes early.

The waters of the Susquehanna glimmer silver, reflecting the fog, when we cross Rockville Bridge. I lean against the window and can make out the piers of an earlier bridge just beneath the surface in the river below.

The body of water on the right side of the car suddenly gets narrower as we leave the Susquehanna Valley for the banks of the Juniata River. At first we are moving as fast as the cars and trucks on Route 322, on the river's opposite shore, and then we speed up and begin to pass them.

After we proceed through Lewistown, where no one gets on or off the train, I am certain that I recognize the gorge known as Jack's Narrows from what I have seen and read in travel guides written a century ago promoting the scenery along the Pennsy's route. It is still a desolate place best experienced from the comfort of a passenger car. Mountains rise up on either side of the river—at this time of the year their slopes painted only with the gray of tree trunks, the brown of fallen leaves, and the dark green of rhododendrons and ferns. I spot something moving and my imagination wants to think it was a bear.

William B. Sipes, in his 1875 book *The Pennsylvania Railroad*, described Jack's Narrows as "wild and rugged in appearance," noting that the area had been named for Jack Anderson, a pre-Revolutionary hunter.

When we near Huntingdon, a group of passengers asks the conductor, "Where's Horseshoe Curve?" He doesn't know, but another conductor returns to explain that we'll reach it about ten minutes after Altoona. We stop in Altoona within sight of the Altoona Railroaders Memorial Museum, just beyond the museum's collection of rolling stock. There are two pedestrian bridges over the tracks here, and some train spotters are on hand to observe us.

As we leave Altoona, I can tell we are climbing because of the pressure in my ears and the increasing distance between our railroad car and the dwellings in the valley below us; otherwise, the grade is too gentle to be noticed. Here and there, I get a glimpse through the trees of the reservoirs that serve the city of Altoona. I don't need the conductor's announcement that we are at Horseshoe Curve because I can hear the wheels of our car screeching against the rails, the sound that announces an oncoming train to train spotters at this landmark. Today, however, there are no tourists waiting in the cold drizzle, and I miss my chance to wave back to them. I do manage to sight both ends of the train from my seat, and for the first time, I realize that I'm really on a freight train with at least a dozen boxcars trailing our few passenger coaches.

As we approach the Gallitzin Tunnels, I can see the wide ribbon of the new Route 22, which replaced the old William Penn Highway. The conductor does not announce the tunnels as we crash into a blackness that lasts a surprisingly long time. At Cresson, a passing freight train obscures my view of the observation platform, but I recognize the porch of the Station Inn, which is devoid of rail fans today.

According to my map of the Norfolk Southern Corporation's rail system, we are approaching Johnstown by the same route as the 1889 flood, along the Little Conemaugh beyond South Fork. It's difficult to imagine this fairly wide valley pummeled with the contents of a swollen reservoir. After our stop in Johnstown across the street from the Johnstown Flood Museum, we continue along the Conemaugh River, where we surely pass the point at which Robert Pitcairn's train was halted and he was faced with the awful evidence of disaster.

Heading toward Latrobe, there are miles and miles of steep hills, a river bed, the occasional tiny town, and a complete lack of halted vehicles at the grade crossings.

The George Westinghouse Memorial Bridge, soaring over both Turtle Creek and the route of our train, welcomes me to Pittsburgh. The scenery evolves from industrial buildings to suburban homes, and finally, we pull into the city's humble Amtrak station, which seems to have been shoved beneath the old Pennsylvania Railroad building. Outside the door, I find myself standing between two transportation artifacts of different vintage: the rotunda of the turn-of-the-century Pennsy station and a blue historic site marker commemorating the site of Pittsburgh's old canal basin.

It was good to see a lot of freight still moving over the rails on my voyage west. I enjoyed traveling Amtrak much more than driving the Pennsylvania Turnpike. In fact, I find myself wishing I could visit other desirable medium-distance destinations by rail. Erie has that nice lake, and what about the Jersey shore? How about Annapolis or Williamsburg?

I had heard that the trains on some Amtrak routes are equipped with dining cars that serve full menus, and that the high-speed Acela trains have beautiful new café cars that remind one of traveling in Europe. Alas, my Pennsylvanian had an older café car offering only prepared sandwiches and snacks. When I inquired about the turkey, ham, and cheese club sandwich on the menu posted on the wall, the attendant described it as a basic ham and cheese where the ham was made from turkey; in other words, it was a turkey-ham and cheese club sandwich. "Do you want that heated up?" he inquired, pointing to a microwave oven.

"Does that make it taste better?" I wanted to know.

"Well, some."

Perhaps I should have asked what he recommended. Be prepared. Pack a lunch.

Station Square

Pittsburgh's Light Rail Transit Line is an increasingly important and popular part of its public transit system, which is managed by the Port Authority of Allegheny County. The Light Rail Transit Line connects the city's downtown and its South Side, and makes it easy to reach the fifty-two-acre riverfront complex combining retail shops, restaurants, and office space—Station Square.

Light-rail cars heading for Station Square emerge into daylight around First Avenue, near the site of the south end of the State Works canal, under Grant's Hill, and proceed over the Monongahela River on the old PRR Panhandle Division Bridge. Passengers disembark near the busy intersection of Carson and Smithfield Streets beneath a bluff that used to be known as Coal Hill but is now called Mount Washington because George Washington is supposed to have surveyed the Golden Triangle from its summit. The flat plain between Mount Washington and the river was called Birmingham back when it was a busy industrial town of glass factories and ironworks. It is still known as Pittsburgh's ethnic district, where many German, Scots-Irish, and eastern European immigrant workers settled and where their descendants still reside.

At the turn of the last century, when P&LE opened its new passenger station and company headquarters here, this location already had a trolley tunnel under Mount Washington, an inclined plane stretching up its face, and the utilitarian buildings of a rail yard. Because it was an era of stunning and impressive passenger terminals, and perhaps because the Pennsylvania Railroad was building its own stunning and impressive passenger terminal across the river, P&LE chose to grace this particular crossroads with an outstanding example of American architecture.

William George Burns was the architect for the structure begun in 1899 and opened in 1901. He embellished a fairly modest front facade with a fanciful tablet that is still standing on the roof, decorated with classical scrolls that surround a bas-relief of a steam engine emitting clouds of smoke. In the days when the building actually functioned as a train station, visitors entered its vestibule from Smithfield Street and walked down a flight of stairs to its passenger waiting room. As they descended, they were greeted by a stained-glass barrel-vaulted ceiling and what appears to be an extravagant use of marble and gold, but is really faux-painted wood, in this dramatic space decorated by the firm Crossman and Sturdy of Chicago.

Like most other railroads, P&LE suffered a decline in its passenger traffic during the twentieth century, and its passenger terminal might have been demolished, save for the Pittsburgh History & Landmarks Foundation, whose members didn't believe that urban renewal necessarily meant knocking older buildings down. Locally known simply as Landmarks, this organization, led by Arthur Ziegler, was seeking a challenge for the principle of adaptive reuse, or restoring old buildings for different and modern purposes. The P&LE passenger station and headquarters building was surrounded by other interesting P&LE rail yard structures at a waterfront location that looked like it could attract a lot of visitors with its ample parking and an unequaled view of the Pittsburgh skyline. In 1976, contrary to expert advice, Landmarks came to an agreement with the railroad for a grand experiment in urban revitalization.

Landmarks obtained its initial funding from the Allegheny Foundation, a Scaife family charitable trust headed by Richard M. Scaife. The trustees approved the project not just for what it would accomplish in historic preservation, but because it would create jobs and help Pittsburgh grow.

The construction of Station Square began with the restoration of the P&LE waiting room, where the stained-glass ceiling, originally open to a skylight, had been sealed with tar in 1927. The faux surfaces also had to undergo extensive cleaning and retouching in order to restore the orig-

The old P&LE station on Pittsburgh's South Side now houses one of the city's finest restaurants.

inal color scheme. Restaurateur Charles A. (Chuck) Muer then spent millions converting the space into a restaurant called the Grand Concourse, at the time Pittsburgh's largest.

The Grand Concourse is still open, is still a favorite with both residents and tourists, and is still one of the city's best restaurants for fresh fish. Today, people enter the building at ground level, but they can still get the full impact of the waiting room by climbing the stairs and looking down. The room has been furnished in a way that recalls a turn-of-the-century passenger station, where the echoing clatter of restaurant operations seems somehow appropriate for the space.

Most visitors ask for a table on the "porch," once a passenger walkway outside the building proper that has now been enclosed in glass. Here, they can observe traffic on the Smithfield Street bridge as well as the Monongahela River, with the skyline of Pittsburgh as a backdrop. The occasional CSX freight train moving along the tracks between the building and the river only enhances the experience. The Grand Concourse must surely be the best train station restaurant in the Commonwealth.

The old freight house adjacent to the building reopened as a retail and restaurant mall in 1979, and shops now stretch into Commerce Court, the old P&LE central warehouse built in 1917, which also includes office space constructed around a central atrium. Other office space is available in the nearby terminal building (now called the Express House) and on the upper floors of the Landmarks Building, the new name for the old P&LE passenger station and headquarters. Between the P&LE complex and a new hotel, construction continues on Bessemer Court, which will add additional restaurant and entertainment attractions to Station Square, together with a floating boardwalk.

In a book written during the early stages of this project, *Station Square: A Golden Age Revived,* James D. Van Trump of Landmarks presented a history of the site and its restoration. But even its most enthusiastic proponents could not have foreseen the impact Station Square would have on Pittsburgh while it also saved a whole neighborhood of Pennsylvania's railroad history.

Monongahela Incline

The lower end of the Monongahela Incline is located at the same intersection as the main entrance of the Station Square complex. This little inclined plane railroad has been part of Allegheny County's Port Authority transit system since 1964 and part of a daily commute for many people, but it also beckons tourists like an amusement park ride.

The Monongahela Incline, an icon of Pittsburgh.

The Monongahela Incline was the first of many inclined planes that once scaled Mount Washington or Coal Hill. It is said that the German immigrants of this area proposed its construction, which resulted in the development of the top of Mount Washington as a residential district about a quarter century before trolleys opened up Pittsburgh's other suburbs. Assisting John Endres, its chief engineer, were his son-in-law Samuel Diescher and his daughter Caroline, one of America's first female engineers. John Roebling made the cables, and the incline opened in May 1870.

The Monongahela Incline is 635 feet long, and its cars hold about two dozen people at a time. They travel at a speed of six miles per hour, which seems a lot faster on the descending trip, especially as the car gets closer to the roof of the lower terminal.

From 1884 until 1935, the incline had a parallel sister conveyance designed for hauling freight and horses. Older residents of Pittsburgh recall a time when automobiles were loaded on it and lifted to Grandview Avenue, before new roads made it easier to drive to the top of Mount Washington.

An observation platform constructed near the upper station offers the most breathtaking view of the city, from a height of almost four hundred feet. Visitors can gaze down at skyscrapers unobscured by any trace of smoke or smog. At the apex of the Golden Triangle, they can see the outline of Fort Duquesne and, in warmer months, its landmark fountain in operation. They can also see the sports complexes on the north side of the Allegheny River, which is becoming an attractive destination.

The observation deck is also the best place to view another relic of Pittsburgh's railroad history and its old Wabash-Pittsburgh Terminal Railway. Still visible in the waters of the Monongahela River are the piers of the vanished Monongahela River Bridge, sometimes called the Wabash Bridge. This bridge once carried trains from a tunnel through Mount Washington over the river to a complex in the heart of the Golden Triangle, west of Stanwix Street, where modern office buildings now stand. The bridge was torn down in 1948, but its remaining piers play a part in Pittsburgh's annual Three Rivers Arts Festival when they are decorated with pennants.

Duquesne Incline

The Duquesne Incline was Pittsburgh's fourth incline when it opened in 1877. Its tracks followed those of an early coal hoist that had been operating in the same part of the bluff since the 1850s. It was engineered by Samuel Diescher, who had by then become one of the area's foremost incline engineers.

Duquesne Incline. GREATER PITTSBURGH CONVENTION & VISITORS BUREAU

It was closed in 1962 because it needed repairs, but its declining ridership made its operator, the Duquesne Inclined Plane Company, doubt whether the expenses would be justified. Concerned residents of Mount Washington who used the incline organized the nonprofit Society for the Preservation of the Duquesne Incline and launched a fund-raising drive to get it repaired and reopened.

At a length of eight hundred feet, the Duquesne Incline is longer than the Monongahela Incline but less steep. It retains its vintage 1877 cars, which have been restored to reveal their original hardware and carved cherry panels trimmed with oak and maple. The upper station has a small museum, gift shop, and observation deck offering another dramatic view of the Golden Triangle. Like the Monongahela Incline, this one is owned by the Port Authority of Allegheny County.

Riding one or both of Pittsburgh's inclined planes is the best way to gain some understanding of how similar engineering features might have operated on early railroad systems such as the Allegheny Portage Railroad or the Danville & Pottsville Rail Road. Riders can witness the tension on the cable lifting their car and understand why fragile and fraying ropes were abandoned in favor of metal cables. They can admire the precision with which the counterweighted cars operate. They can experience the sensation that Charles Dickens described of witnessing scenes of daily life far enough below to be completely out of earshot. And on a windy day in the part of the car that is open to the elements, they can understand why Dickens chose the word "whirlwind" to describe the ride.

The Pennsy's Old Station

Since about 1851, there has been a Pennsylvania Railroad station in the company's Pittsburgh territory, which began around Eleventh Street and extended for many blocks east in an area along what had earlier been an old road to Philadelphia. The station burned by striking workers in 1877, the third station in that general location, was replaced that same year, but by the turn of the century, PRR president Alexander J. Cassatt decided to replace it with something bigger and better.

Pittsburgh's Union Depot as illustrated for William B. Sipes's 1875 book on the Pennsylvania Railroad.

Daniel Burnham & Co. of Chicago was chosen in 1898 to design the structure. The result was a twelve-story brick and sandstone building—a skyscraper for its time—attached to a fanciful domed rotunda. While serving the utilitarian purpose of sheltering travelers being picked up or dropped off, the rotunda's dimensions made it monumental and its ornamentation lent an Art Nouveau flair to its classical style. Beneath its dome, the sculpted faces of four lovely ladies smiled over the names of the four key cities that Pennsy connected: Chicago, Pittsburgh, Philadelphia, and New York.

Following the decline and demise of the Pennsy, the building was allowed to deteriorate, while Amtrak moved its Pittsburgh passenger station to a smaller space behind it. In 1988, the building saw rebirth as the "Pennsylvanian," its upper-floor offices transformed into apartments and what its leasing company refers to as furnished "corporate homes," where one can find, according to its advertising literature, the "character, grace and splendor" of a previous age.

Daniel Burnham designed a waiting room for this building in the style of the Italian Renaissance, lined with marble and terra-cotta and roofed with a skylight. The waiting room, with all its refurbished ornamentation, still occupies the first floor, but the typical visitor can get nothing but a glimpse of it through its glass front doors. Only those who work in the building can enter, unless they are guests at a function for which the former waiting room can be rented.

The Amtrak station remains tucked beyond the Pennsylvanian, furnished modestly but adequately for the passengers it serves on the three trains that stop there each day. Those three trains, the Capitol Limited, the Three Rivers, and the Pennsylvanian, continue to connect Pittsburgh with the major cities whose names are emblazoned on the rotunda.

The Strip

Around the corner from the Pennsylvanian and the Amtrak station, at the base of Eleventh Street, the old Pennsylvania Railroad's Fort Wayne Bridge is now engulfed in a district in transformation. The eastern portion of this vast construction site has long been called Pittsburgh's "Strip," a name that came from the strip of land between Penn and Liberty Avenues. In 1868, the busy ironworks located there prompted writer James Parton to pen his famous comment comparing Pittsburgh to "hell with the lid off," but Pittsburgh's Strip may soon rival Station Square as a place to dine and enjoy oneself.

An area once dominated by factories, including the original headquarters of the Westinghouse Air-Brake Company, the Strip has been more recently associated with the food distribution industry. Early in the twentieth century, the Pennsylvania Railroad built its produce sheds there, and a sign still identifies the 1926 Pennsylvania Railroad Fruit Auction & Sales Building, which is five blocks long. For many years, the Strip has been the place to go for fresh fruit and vegetables, bread, and Chinese and ethnic foods.

High-tech industries are now choosing to build in this area, while a number of old warehouses are being transformed into restaurants done up in postindustrial chic. The TV chef and restaurateur Lidia Bastianich recently opened her very popular restaurant at Fourteenth and Smallman Streets.

The area's largest tourist attraction is the Senator John Heinz Pittsburgh Regional History Center, located in a building that used to be an icehouse. Its fifteen thousand square feet of exhibition space tell the story of 250 years of social life and industrial development in the region. Railroad artifacts do not dominate this museum, but it would be impossible to interpret the history of Pittsburgh without its transportation history: visitors can find material recalling the 1877 strike, the old Allegheny Portage Railroad, and the first locomotive to reach the city.

Model Railroading in the Pittsburgh Region

Model railroad fans can tour the Miniature Railroad & Village at the Carnegie Science Center, a new museum on the North Side not far from the city's new football stadium. Currently sponsored by Lionel, the layout was established by Charles Bowdish of Brookville, Pennsylvania, in 1920. Its models reflect life in western Pennsylvania from 1890 to 1930, and they occupy 2,300 square feet of display space.

The layout is not the frozen vision of its founder, but rather something that is regularly updated and expanded by museum staff members. Once they select a historic structure they would like to reproduce, they take a series of photos and measurements, then they duplicate the structure in miniature, sometimes using materials as unconventional as the angel-hair pasta that became ivy on one of the homes in the tiny replica of Liverpool Street.

The Miniature Railroad & Village incorporates complexes that illustrate the industries of the Pittsburgh area, including a steel plant, coal-mining equipment, coke ovens, and quarries. Its historic replicas include Roebling's house and workshop, attractions from popular amusement parks in Altoona and Kennywood, and Bowdish's house.

Besides the four or five Lionel trains always in motion, more than a hundred figures are animated by individual motors. People dance and children play on swings, but everyone's favorite animation is the tiny dog that repeatedly lifts his leg against a tree. Guides with flashlights are stationed inside a railing to make sure that visitors miss nothing and realize, as one guide commented, "All of Pittsburgh's history is right here."

Actually, there's even more Pittsburgh history to be seen in nearby Gibsonia at the Western Pennsylvania Model Railroad Museum, where the layouts include a scale model of the tracks between Pittsburgh and Cumberland, Maryland.

Railroad Artifacts Outside Pittsburgh

Although most people would identify Pittsburgh's George Westinghouse as an electrical manufacturer, his invention of the air brake was an important milestone in railroad history. It is said that while riding in a train that collided with another, Westinghouse conceived the idea of a single brake that could be applied by the engineer rather than by brakemen riding on individual cars and would save a lot of lives and train equipment. Westinghouse air brakes were first tested by the Pennsylvania Railroad on its Panhandle lines in the Pittsburgh area.

Westinghouse air brakes were first manufactured in Pittsburgh's Strip district in a modest building still standing at Twenty-fourth Street and Liberty Avenue. Westinghouse then moved production to the handsome new foundries and shops in the model industrial town he laid out in Wilmerding, just a few miles from the Westinghouse Electric Corporation plant in Turtle Creek Valley, which later employed twenty thousand workers.

In Schenley Park in Oakland, there's a marble monument honoring George Westinghouse and his major achievements, but it isn't too easy to find. Pittsburgh's grand memorial to Westinghouse is the bridge that bears his name and carries the old Lincoln Highway, or Route 30, across Turtle Creek Valley. It also spans the mainline Norfolk Southern tracks that used to belong to the Pennsylvania Railroad with what some claim to be the longest concrete arch in the world. Ever since it was erected between 1930 and 1932, the George Westinghouse Memorial Bridge has been the portal to Pittsburgh for those arriving by train, and it was a familiar sight to those who commuted by train to work at the Westinghouse plant.

Geography made the greater Pittsburgh area a region of bridges, and visitors can even find crisscrossing bridges in the Larimer suburb. In 1902–3, William H. Brown, chief engineer of the Pennsylvania Railroad, constructed a stone arch bridge as part of a freight cutoff from the railroad's main line. The stone is actually a facing over a concrete structure, but this bridge closely resembles Brown's Rockville Bridge across the Susquehanna, with which it is nearly contemporary. In 1906, the Lincoln Avenue Bridge was constructed to carry Lincoln Avenue over Washington Boulevard, and its arches were designed for it to fit beneath the earlier railroad bridge.

The Hot Metal Bridge built in 1900 over the Monongahela River is indeed constructed of metal trusses, but it got its name because railroad cars once used it to carry iron smelted on the north shore (that is, hot metal) to mills and furnaces on the south shore. In the years before there was a bridge at this location, it would have been necessary to cool the iron, ferry it across the water, then remelt it.

Like Philadelphia, Pittsburgh has its share of remaining Victorian suburban railroad stations, including one built for the Pennsy in Edgewood. Constructed at the turn of the century in the shingle style, with a brick and shingle facade, this structure is thought to have been designed by Frank Furness or his firm, which would make it the only surviving Furness structure in modern Pittsburgh. It now functions as a commercial building.

Harlansburg Station

Harlansburg never had a real train station, but it now has a building that resembles one and houses the Museum of Transportation, the collection of retired airline pilot Don Barnes. The tracks behind the station lead nowhere, serving instead as necessary foundations for the four railroad cars Barnes collected, including two built during the 1910s for the Pennsylvania Railroad. Two other cars were built in the 1940s for the Santa Fe Railroad and later purchased by the Pennsylvania Railroad. Barnes's railroad memorabilia comes from the various railroads that operated in the region, including the B&O, the Pennsy, the Erie Lackawanna, and the P&LE.

It may look like a railroad station, but the only trains that ever came to Harlansburg are those collected by Don Barnes for his transportation museum. HARLANSBURG STATION

A model railroad layout depicts life and industry in western Pennsylvania. The collection also contains artifacts of other forms of modern transportation, including travel by boat, trolley, air, and even Greyhound buses.

The Kiski Junction Railroad

The town of Schenley in Armstrong County, where the Schenley Distilling Company was formerly located, is now the headquarters of the Kiski Junction Railroad. This operation manages to combine scenic rail touring with regular freight operations primarily for its key customer, the Allegheny Teledyne Specialty Silicon Steel Plant. In fact, passengers riding on weekdays are actually riding on mixed-freight runs.

The Kiski Junction Railroad originated in 1995 with the purchase of a small active freight line from Conrail that had once been part of the Pennsy's Pittsburgh-to-Buffalo line, but saw its first traffic in 1856 as part of the Allegheny Valley Railroad. Its tracks run along the Kiskiminetas River, and passengers can spot canal artifacts. The railroad also owns an 1899 bridge over the Kiskiminetas River.

Passengers ride in a 1925 Pullman coach, an open canopy-covered car, or a caboose pulled by a diesel locomotive. The round-trip lasts either an hour or an hour and a half, and visitors can bring their lunches.

The Region's Rail Trails

The Armstrong Trail is an artifact of the Allegheny Valley Railroad, which was incorporated in 1852 and built between 1853 and 1856 to link Pittsburgh and Kittanning and serve the industries of the Allegheny River Valley, including those producing materials important for manufacturing steel, such as coke and firebrick. After oil was discovered farther north in Pennsylvania, the line was extended toward Oil City in 1868. The railroad went bankrupt attempting to construct a low-grade line to circumvent the Allegheny Mountains, and it was leased to the Pennsylvania Railroad in 1900. Conrail sold parts of the line in 1992 to the Allegheny Valley Land Trust, which is now converting it into a rail trail with the support of the Armstrong Rails-to-Trails Association. Fifty-two miles in length, the Armstrong Trail has numerous trailheads in the towns through which it passes, though there are some breaks in the trail that force users into municipal streets.

Other, shorter rail trails in Armstrong and Butler Counties include the Great Shamokin Path, the Roaring Run Trail, and the Butler Freeport Community Trail, which includes eleven bridges on its route along the Little Buffalo and Buffalo Creeks. The counties of Butler, Beaver, Armstrong, and Lawrence are also traversed by the North Country Scenic Trail. The Stavich Bicycle Trail extends west from New Castle into Ohio.

The Allegheny Trail Alliance is a group of trail organizations determined to link Pittsburgh's Point State Park with Washington, D.C. Its Pittsburgh components with mileage under way include the Three Rivers Heritage Trail and the Steel Valley Trail proposed for the city's waterfront areas. The Montour Trail is another Pittsburgh area trail in the alliance; it swings west into Washington County along the route of the abandoned Montour Railroad, which was chartered in 1877 and once served twenty-seven coal mines.

Pittsburgh's pleasant Oakmont Borough is home to the Arboretum Trail, which is only 1.4 miles long, making it the region's shortest.

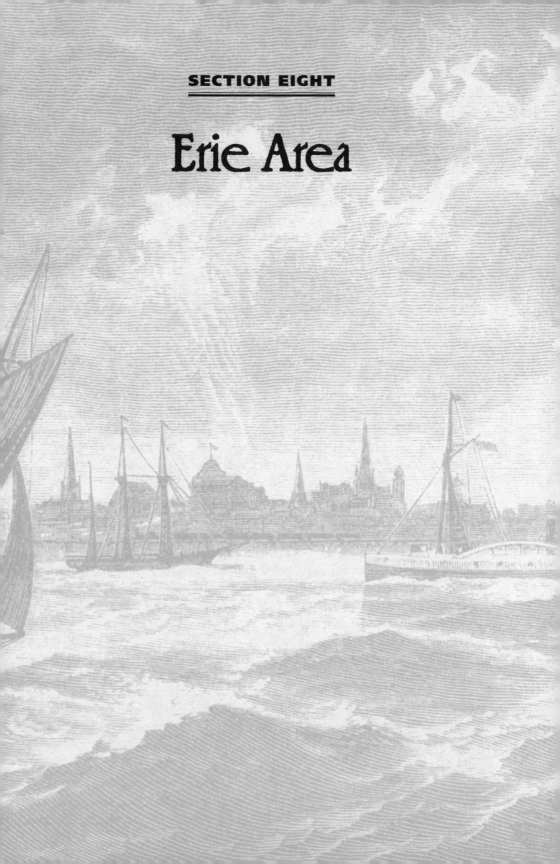

SECTION EIGHT

Erie Area

Great Railways of the Region

The Bessemer & Lake Erie

The earliest ancestor of the Bessemer & Lake Erie (B&LE) Railroad was a short line called the Bear Creek Railroad, chartered in 1865 to move coal from a mine owned by the Mercer Mining and Manufacturing Company to an ancestor of the Erie Lackawanna Railroad. Its name was changed to the Shenango & Allegheny Railroad in 1867. In 1888, the railroad emerged from receivership with yet another name: the Pittsburgh, Shenango & Lake Erie Railroad.

In his 1969 book titled *The Bessemer and Lake Erie Railroad*, Roy C. Beaver describes how its new owners quickly expanded the railroad from a local carrier that served only two counties to a freight line connecting ports on Lake Erie with Allegheny, the borough on Pittsburgh's North Side. This would put the railroad in a position to move iron ore from Michigan and Minnesota to Pittsburgh, where it was used in making steel.

Andrew Carnegie, Pittsburgh's largest steel producer, purchased the Pittsburgh, Shenango & Lake Erie Railroad and transformed it via merger into the Bessemer & Lake Erie Railroad, chartered in 1900, making it essentially a private line for delivering iron ore to his blast furnaces. However, the real value of this north-south B&LE line to Carnegie was probably the fact that it connected with four major railroads in addition to the Pennsy, giving Carnegie, who had long been dissatisfied with the rates of the PRR, new options for moving his steel to market. In a 1975 biography of Carnegie, Harold L. Livesay noted that Pennsy executives became suddenly eager to discuss freight rates after having dismissed Carnegie's previous complaints. Carnegie remained unmoved when they reminded him of his prior connection with the Pennsy and negotiated a rate cut in exchange for a promise that he would not create any more new railroad systems.

The B&LE trains could and did travel to Erie (via the tracks of the railroad called the Nickel Plate Road), but this railroad's principal port on Lake Erie was and is Conneaut, Ohio. In 1898, Andrew Carnegie purchased the entire Conneaut harbor area and modernized its equipment, creating a facility where iron ore could be efficiently transferred from his fleet of ore ships into ore cars. Around the turn of the last century, the railroad expanded its passenger traffic by investing in the development of Conneaut Lake Park, near Meadville, Pennsylvania, which became popular for summer agricultural fairs and other expositions.

When Carnegie sold his steel empire in 1901, the B&LE went with it into the new U.S. Steel Corporation. It remained part of the company for almost a full century and now continues to operate within a company called Great Lakes Transportation LLC, a privately held transportation holding company of rail and water carriers that serves steel-making operations.

The Nickel Plate Road

The New York, Chicago & St. Louis Railroad was born in a bank in 1881 when a group of wealthy capitalists subscribed a substantial amount of cash to build a shorter route between Buffalo and Chicago. This railroad owes its nickname Nickel Plate Road to an Ohio newspaper that dubbed it the "nickel plated railroad" because it had such solid financial backing and lucrative prospects.

The Nickel Plate was constructed in only five hundred days and open for business by October 1882. Just three days later, it was sold to a man working on behalf of William H. Vanderbilt, who installed his own son as its president a few months later.

As it happened, the tracks of the Nickel Plate ran parallel to those of the Lake Shore & Michigan Southern Railway, which Vanderbilt already owned. At the time, many financiers speculated that the Nickel Plate had really been built to force Vanderbilt to buy it or face competition. Vanderbilt allowed the Nickel Plate to operate as part of the New York Central system, but he made certain that it never performed up to its potential.

In 1915, the New York Central Railroad was informed that recent antitrust legislation made it illegal for it to operate parallel lines, causing the railroad to go shopping for friendly buyers. The Nickel Plate became the property of Oris Paxton Van Sweringen and Mantis James Van Sweringen, two bachelor brothers (sometimes called "the Vans") in the real estate business in Ohio who would use its right-of-way for a much needed rapid transit line connecting their suburban development, Shaker Heights, with downtown Cleveland.

With the aid of John Bernet, the Vans also revitalized the Nickel Plate and began to contemplate creating their own railroad empire. They quickly established a seventeen-hundred-mile system through mergers with the Toledo, St. Louis & Western Railroad and the Lake Erie & Western Railroad. Additional leases and acquisitions expanded their system farther, and for a time, it was said by some to be the largest railroad group in the world. Their Nickel Plate emerged as a freight line best known for the speedy transportation of meat and other perishables from Chicago to

Buffalo, where they could be shipped to eastern cities via connecting lines. Although its major terminals were located outside the Common-wealth, a tiny percentage of the Nickel Plate's tracks ran through the neck of land that gave Pennsylvania access to Lake Erie, where the railroad also served the city of Erie and other lakeshore communities.

In the 1950s, the potential merger of the New York Central with the Pennsy inspired the Nickel Plate to seek its own partner. In 1964, it merged with the Norfolk & Western Railway. In 1966, the Nickel Plate Road Historical & Technical Society was formed in Indiana, an organization that continues to preserve and interpret this railroad's history.

Rail Stories of the Region

Rail Transportation and Erie

Erie became famous in 1813 as the scene of Oliver Hazard Perry's victory in the Battle of Lake Erie in America's War of 1812. Erie's natural harbor was a fine one, but as the Midwest became increasingly settled in the early nineteenth century, it was discovered that Erie's harbor was difficult to enter for ships sailing from the west, and the citizens of Erie watched as neighboring Buffalo grew much faster than Pennsylvania's only Great Lakes port.

The 1830s and 1840s saw several attempts to provide Erie with better transportation connections with the rest of the Commonwealth. The 1830s found the locals agitating for a railroad from Erie to Sunbury (which would later become the Philadelphia & Erie Railroad). In 1845, a canal opened, connecting Erie to the Ohio River. The Pittsburgh & Erie Railroad, formed to connect Erie with the B&O, was incorporated in 1846, but failed before it actually built a railroad.

The Erie & North East Railroad was incorporated in 1842 to connect railroads in New York and Ohio. Within a decade, it had constructed a rail line with a section of six-foot gauge; this made it necessary for passengers and freight to change trains in Erie. In 1853, its owners decided to change to standard gauge so that the gauge would be uniform between Cleveland and Buffalo. Many citizens of Erie resented this seemingly sensible business decision because they saw it as something else that would contribute to Buffalo's growth at their expense. It didn't help that this same railroad refused to extend its tracks directly to Erie's harbor.

Erie's Bayfront district, once the city's coal port. ERIE AREA CONVENTION AND VISITORS BUREAU

In a 1974 article for the *Western Pennsylvania Historical Magazine,* Donald A. Grinde Jr. wrote about the "Rippers" of Erie and neighboring communities who proceeded to rip up railroad tracks until the U.S. government threatened to send federal troops in 1854. While the tracks remained ripped, freight and passengers were forced to travel between Erie and Harborcreek by old-fashioned stagecoach or wagon.

A compromise allowed the railroad (which eventually became part of the New York Central system) to build its standard-gauge tracks, provided that Erie's harbor got rail service. The railroad paid the Sunbury & Erie Railroad to take on that task, and Erie became a stop on the Pennsy system when that railroad leased its successor, the Philadelphia & Erie Railroad, in 1862. The PRR also leased another railroad, the Erie & Pittsburgh Railroad, which had opened between New Castle and Erie in 1864 and built a branch to the docks in 1865.

The city of Erie had given the Pennsy 130 acres of bayfront, which the railroad proceeded to seal off with a belt line completed in 1870. This prevented any other railroad from having easy access to the bayfront and may have been one reason why the B&LE's principal Lake Erie port was in the neighboring state of Ohio. The Philadelphia & Erie Railroad developed its waterfront with piers from which grain, coke, lumber, and a great deal of coal were shipped, mainly by a firm called the Anchor Line. In the 1890s and early 1900s, business was very good.

Charles L. Heisler also contributed to Erie's prosperity with a railroad-related business he founded after obtaining a patent in 1892 for a locomotive designed for the logging industry. Heisler locomotives were manufactured in Erie until shortly before the Second World War.

Pennsylvania's Oil Boom

In the 1850s, a Connecticut company was seeking a way to sell the petroleum that was known to exist not far below the ground's surface in northwestern Pennsylvania, where one of the bodies of water was even named Oil Creek. The company hired Benjamin Silliman Jr., a chemistry professor at Yale, who predicted that petroleum would make good fuel for the lamps that lit people's houses.

The company then sent a former railroad conductor, Edwin L. Drake, to Titusville, where he leased land. There, on an August afternoon in 1859, Drake struck oil with a fairly primitive well.

Like California's gold rush, Pennsylvania's oil boom brought a deluge of speculators to the area, and by the end of 1860, the neighborhood was sprouting oil wells. By 1865, a village originally called Cornplanter had grown into a muddy, ramshackle boomtown renamed Oil City.

Suddenly, there was a critical need for better transportation in yet another portion of Pennsylvania. Titusville, which had been a lumbering town, was forty miles from Erie and sixteen miles from Corry, which was served by the Sunbury & Erie Railroad (later the Philadelphia & Erie Railroad) and the Atlantic & Great Western Railway (later part of the Erie Railroad and, still later, the Erie Lackawanna). Both of these railroads, as well as any others that ran anywhere near oil country, quickly built branches to capture a new kind of freight.

In its natural state, Pennsylvania's petroleum was a nasty substance that needed to be deodorized and purified before anyone would choose it over whale oil to light their homes. Oil refineries sprang up in Titusville and also in Pittsburgh, where barrels of oil had been floated via the Allegheny River before the railroads had laid their tracks. In 1862, John D. Rockefeller built his first refinery in Cleveland, which quickly became an important refining city, outstripping the Pennsylvania locations. His Standard Oil group would eventually command a great deal of influence in setting railroad rates for all the nation's major trunk lines.

In northwestern Pennsylvania, the oil boom went bust when the number of wells and the quantity of oil they pumped drove prices down. In the years before the gasoline-powered automobile would create a more lasting demand for petroleum products, better sources of oil would be discovered in other states and foreign countries. Pennsylvania would be left with ghost towns and abandoned railroad tracks, artifacts reflecting the entrepreneurial spirit of those who had scrambled to harness a new source of wealth.

Local Chapters of the National Railway Historical Society

The Shenango-Pymatuning Chapter is headquartered in Greenville, which until recently was the location of the freight car building operations of Trinity Industries. The chapter offers no excursions, but it does operate the Greenville Area Railroad Park and Museum, which welcomes up to four thousand visitors per year. The chapter also often holds railroad theme parties at the park for youngsters in hopes that these will educate them in railroad history and predispose them to become rail fans. The chapter's newsletter is called the *Shenango/604*.

Operating as the Lake Shore Railway Historical Society, the Lake Shore Chapter sponsors regular public programs on various aspects of the railroad industry. It also operates the Lake Shore Railway Museum, which is open to the public for parts of the year and hosts special events, sometimes involving the exhibits themselves, such as the "Dinner in the Diner" on Mother's and Father's Days. The museum has also been the scene of a Civil War battle reenactment, in which Union and Confederate troops take turns attacking and defending the depot. The chapter sponsors occasional excursions on regional scenic railroads and publishes the *Lake Shore Timetable*.

The Region's Railroad Giants

Oris Paxton Van Sweringen (1879–1923) and
Mantis James Van Sweringen (1881–1935)

Locally known as "the Vans," Oris Paxton Van Sweringen and Mantis James Van Sweringen were bachelor brothers who spent their lives as business partners, first in real estate development, then in the railroad industry. Following a childhood in Cleveland with little formal education, the Vans borrowed money to buy land that had been abandoned by a religious sect and developed one of America's first planned suburban communities, which they named Shaker Heights. At the same time that the New York Central Railroad was looking for a friendly new owner for the Nickel Plate, the Vans needed public transportation to connect their suburb with downtown Cleveland. The brothers purchased the Nickel Plate and provided it with the new management necessary to make it a profitable and efficient freight line.

In the early 1920s, they merged two other railroads into the Nickel Plate system. Other acquisitions followed, making the Vans owners of what some call the world's largest railroad group and advocates of a movement to consolidate America's railroads.

In the late 1920s, the prospective Van Sweringen railroad empire fell victim to objections from the Interstate Commerce Commission, which opposed too much integration of separate railroads. The Depression brought on the bankruptcy of one of their acquisitions, and their properties were sold at auction shortly before the death of the younger brother.

Charles Barstow Wright (1822–1898)

Charles Barstow Wright is well known in the Pacific Northwest as the director and president who successfully reorganized the Northern Pacific Railroad in the 1870s. However, Wright was born in Pennsylvania and achieved his first business success in Erie, where he established a business and the area's first bank.

Wright became a director of the Sunbury & Erie Railroad (later the Philadelphia & Erie Railroad) and devoted himself to its completion. Wright was also among the entrepreneurs who sought to furnish Pennsylvania's oil region with rail service. In 1863, he formed a syndicate to build a railroad from Warren to Oil City, which later merged with the Oil Creek Railroad to form the Oil Creek & Allegheny River Railway; it was for a time very profitable.

Sampling the Region's Railroad History

Erie and Today's Transportation

Once Erie had a coal port; today, it has a developing Bayfront district that is described in promotional literature as a "tourist and community cultural center complex." The area is anchored by a 187-foot tower that was built to commemorate Erie's two hundredth birthday. Just down the

Bayfront Highway, special events are held throughout the summer at Liberty Park. The waterfront's major attraction is the U.S. Brig Niagara, a replica of the warship with which Oliver Hazard Perry won the Battle of Lake Erie; it is routinely anchored outside a maritime museum that interprets its story.

Former governor of Pennsylvania Tom Ridge was a key promoter of waterfront development. During his administration, the Commonwealth invested more than $60 million in Erie's bayfront. In 2001, Ridge delivered $3 million in funds to the local port authority for a cruise and ferry boat terminal that will become the largest facility of its kind on the Great Lakes, allowing Erie to plan for ferry service to Canada.

Erie is clearly capitalizing on its maritime heritage and its picturesque location to make itself more of a tourist destination, meaning that boats are in and trains and coal cars are out. However, Amtrak's Lake Shore Limited stops in Erie twice a day on its trips between Chicago and Boston or New York, and a website with images of the Amtrak station includes a plea for extending several other Amtrak corridors to Erie. It's possible that Erie's bayfront might attract more visitors and tourist dollars if it were easier to get to. Currently, Amtrak passengers wait in a modest waiting room at the 1920s vintage Union Station Building on West Fourteenth Street between Peach and Sassafras Streets. This is pretty much the same location where a grander Union Depot, constructed in 1864, once served the Philadelphia & Erie Railroad and the Lake Shore & Michigan Southern Railway, or respectively, the Pennsy and New York Central systems.

Lake Shore Railway Museum

Since 1970, the Lake Shore Railway Historical Society has been operating the Lake Shore Railway Museum in North East, Pennsylvania, where it occupies the old passenger depot built by the New York Central. The museum displays railroad photographs, documents, and memorabilia. Altogether, the society maintains twenty-seven pieces of rolling stock, including an original Heisler fireless steam locomotive, diesel and electric locomotives built at General Electric's Erie plant, a tank car, and refrigerator cars, as well as dining and sleeping cars that are periodically open for tours.

Greenville Area Railroad Park and Museum

The Shenango-Pymatuning Chapter of the National Railway Historical Society operates the Greenville Area Railroad Park and Museum in Greenville, Pennsylvania, which houses railroad artifacts and local historical information, while its major exhibits are parked outdoors. The largest of these is Engine 604, built by the Baldwin Locomotive Works of Philadelphia in 1936; this engine was once active on the Union Railroad. The chapter promotes it as the "only one of its kind"—it is the single remaining and one of the largest switch engines ever built. A coal tender, hopper car, and caboose are displayed at the park, with the engine positioned like a train about to depart. The hopper car was built in Greenville in 1952.

A recently donated railroad flatcar now has a roof and railings that allow it to be rented, with a restored caboose, for private parties. The park also includes replicas of a stationmaster's quarters and a dispatcher's office.

Oil Creek & Titusville Railroad

In 1862, the twenty-seven-mile Oil Creek Railroad was constructed between Corry and Titusville, its original six-foot gauge an indication that its builders intended to do business with the Erie system. However, in 1864, representatives from the New York Central Railroad and the Pennsylvania Railroad jointly purchased most of its stock, placing it in the hands of New York lawyer Samuel J. Tilden as trustee. When the Pennsy's managers discovered that they were not getting the previously agreed-upon amount of traffic from this arrangement, they purchased the New York Central's interest in the railroad and took over.

After being merged into the Oil Creek & Allegheny River Railway in 1868, it connected with the Allegheny Valley Railroad to form a through route between Pittsburgh and Buffalo. Its earnings shrank with the end of the oil boom and the railroad was reorganized, finally making its way into Conrail, which eventually abandoned it.

In 1986, the modern Oil Creek & Titusville Railroad (OC&T) was born with the formation of a historical society that purchased the old tracks and buildings. The first Oil Creek & Titusville excursion train ran that year, and by 1999, the railroad was carrying twenty-five thousand passengers annually.

Passengers can board at the Perry Street Station in Titusville or at the Drake Well Museum for a ride through Pennsylvania's oil boom country. OC&T's two diesel locomotives were built in 1947 and 1950. They haul passenger cars built in 1930 and an open car that allows riders to better spot the bald eagles, deer, and black bears in the state park lands through which the railroad travels. A caboose is available for private parties.

The Oil Creek & Titusville Railroad also operates what it bills as America's only railway post office in a car built in 1927. (The actual sorting of mail by postal employees aboard rolling cars ended in 1977.) Passengers can purchase postcards and actually mail them from the train. An organization called Mayhem, Inc., provides summertime murder mystery dinners with a prize for the passenger who can solve the crime.

The Region's Rail Trails

Those intending to hike the Oil Creek State Park Trail in Venango County are warned to stay off the active railroad tracks and out of the way of the Oil Creek & Titusville Railroad excursion trains. Hikers can begin at the trailhead at Petroleum Centre, where a train station houses historic displays, or at the Drake Well Museum, where reproduction wells are still pumping oil. Although the Oil Creek State Park Trail runs through oil boom country in Oil Creek Gorge, today the scenery again resembles the wilderness that this area was before Edwin L. Drake struck oil. The trail is equipped with historic markers to indicate the vanished sites of Pennsylvania's oil industry.

The Samuel Justus Recreational Trail is also located in Venango County, between the towns of Franklin and Oil City.

In neighboring Crawford County, the Pymatuning State Park Trail is located in one of the Commonwealth's largest state parks near the massive reservoir created by Pymatuning Dam, which was opened in 1934 to regulate the flow of water to the Shenango and Beaver Rivers. Those traveling the Ernst Bike Trail, also located in Crawford County, can explore French Creek and portions of an old canal bed.

CONTACT INFORMATION
FOR REGIONAL SITES

All Regions

Pennsylvania Rails-to-Trails
   Database
www.dcnr.state.pa.us/rails

National Railway Historical Society
National Office and Library
100 N. 17th St.
Philadelphia, PA 19103
215-557-6606
www.nrhs.com
[Local chapters in all regions]

Anthracite Railroads
   Historical Society
P.O. Box 519
Lansdale, PA 19446-0519
http://arhs.railfan.net
[Eastern Pennsylvania regions]

Philadelphia Area
and Lehigh Valley

Lehigh Valley Railroad
   Historical Society
P.O. Box RR
Manchester, NY 14504-0200

New Hope & Ivyland Railroad
P.O. Box 634
West Bridge and Stockton Streets
New Hope, PA 18938
215-862-2332
www.newhoperailroad.com

Reading Terminal Market
12th and Arch Streets
Philadelphia, PA 19107
215-922-2317
www.readingterminalmarket.org

Suburban Station
One Penn Center
Philadelphia, PA 19103
SEPTA information:
   215-580-7800
www.septa.org

The Train Factory
The Franklin Institute
222 North 20th St.
Philadelphia, PA 19103
215-448-1800
http://sln.fi.edu

Thirtieth Street Station
30th and Market Streets
Philadelphia, PA 19104
AMTRAK information:
   215-349-2222
www.amtrak.com

West Chester Railroad
P.O. Box 355
Yorklyn, DE. 19736
610-430-2233
www.westchesterrr.net

Hershey, Gettysburg,
and Dutch Country

Choo Choo Barn
Box 130, Route 741 East
Strasburg, PA 17579
717-687-0464
www.choochoobarn.com

Gettysburg Railroad Station
c/o Main Street Gettysburg, Inc.
59 E. High St.
Gettysburg, PA 17325
717-337-3491
www.mainstreetgettysburg.org
(restoration info)

Gettysburg Convention
   and Visitors Bureau
Gettysburg Railroad Station
35 Carlisle St.
Gettysburg, PA 17325
717-334-6274
www.gettysburg.com

Gettysburg Scenic Railway
160 North Washington St.
Gettysburg, PA 17325
717-334-6932
www.gettysburgrail.com

Harrisburg Transportation Center
4th and Chestnut Streets
Harrisburg, PA 17101
717-232-5241

Hawk Mountain Line
c/o Wanamaker, Kempton
   & Southern Railroad
P.O. Box 24
Route 737
Kempton, PA 19529
610-756-6469
www.kemptontrain.com

Lincoln Train Museum
425 Steinwehr Ave.
Gettysburg, PA 17325
717-334-4100

Manheim Historical Society
P.O. Box 396
88 South Grant Street
Manheim, PA 17545
717-665-7989
www.manheimpa.com

Middletown & Hummelstown
   Railroad
136 Brown St.
Middletown, PA 17057
717-944-4435
www.mhrailroad.com

National Toy Train Museum
300 Paradise Lane
Strasburg, PA 17579
717-687-8976
www.traincollectors.org/toytrain.html

Railroad House of Marietta
280 W. Front St.
Marietta, PA 17547
717-426-4141

Railroad Museum of
   Pennsylvania
P.O. Box 15
Rte. 741
Strasburg, PA 17579
717-687-8628
www.rrmuseumpa.org

Reading Society of
   Model Engineers
P.O. Box 13011
Reading, PA 19612
610-929-5444
www.rsme.org

Roadside America
P.O. Box 2
109 Roadside Dr.
Shartlestville, PA 19554
610-488-6241
www.roadsideamericainc.com

Stewartstown Railroad
P.O. Box 155
Stewartstown, PA 17363
717-993-2936

Strasburg Railroad
P.O. Box 96
Strasburg, PA 17579-0096
717-687-7522
www.strasburgrailroad.com

Western Maryland Railway
  Historical Society
P.O. Box 395
Union Bridge, MD 21791

**Valleys of the Schuylkill
and Susquehanna**

Bellefonte Historical Railroad
West High St.
Bellefonte, PA 16823
814-355-0311
www.bellefontetrain.com

Caboose Lodging in Catawissa
c/o Walt Gosciminski
119 Pine St.
Catawissa, PA 17820
570-356-2675
www.caboosenut.com

Historical Society of
  Berks County
940 Centre Ave.
Reading, PA 19601
610-375-4375

Knoebels Grove
  Amusement Park
P.O. Box 317
Elysburg, PA 17824
570-672-2572
www.knoebels.com

Museum of Anthracite Mining
17th and Pine Streets
Ashland, PA 17921
570-875-4708

Northern Berks/Southern Schuylkill
  Historical Association
Transportation Museum
Penn and Clinton Streets
Port Clinton, PA 19549
610-562-9383

Pioneer Tunnel Coal Mine
  and Steam Train
19th and Oak Streets
Ashland, PA 17921
570-875-3850
www.pioneertunnel.com

Reading Company Technical
  and Historical Society
P.O. Box 15143
Reading, PA 19612-5143
610-372-5513
www.readingrailroad.org

Allegheny National Forest

General Thomas L. Kane Memorial
  Chapel and Museum
30 Chestnut St.
Kane, PA 16735
814-837-9729

Kinzua Bridge State Park
c/o Bendigo State Park
P.O. Box A
Johnsonburg, PA 15845
814-965-2646

Knox & Kane Railroad
P.O. Box 422
Marienville, PA 16239
814-927-6621
www.knoxcanerr.com

Lycoming County Historical Society
Thomas T. Taber Museum
858 West Fourth St.
Williamsport, PA 17701
570-326-3326
www.lycoming.org

New York Central Railroad Museum
P.O. Box 1708
721 South Main St.
Elkhart, IN 46515
574-294-3001
nycrrmuseum.org

New York Central System
  Historical Society
P.O. Box 81184
Cleveland, OH 44181-0184
www.nycshs.org

Pennsylvania Lumber Museum
5660 U.S. 6 West
P.O. Box 239
Galeton, PA 16922
814-435-2652
www.lumbermuseum.org

Tioga Central Railroad
P.O. Box 269
Wellsboro, PA 16901
570-724-0990
www.tiogacentral.com

**Pocono Mountains
and Endless Mountains**

Asa Packer Museum
P.O. Box 108
30 Elk St.
Jim Thorpe, PA 18229
570-325-3229
http://asapackermansionmuseum.
  homestead.com

Bridge Line Historical Society
P.O. Box 13324
Albany, NY 12212
www.bridge-line.org

Central Railroad of New Jersey
  Historical Society
P.O. Box 4226
Dunellen, NJ 08812-4226
www.jcrhs.org

Erie Lackawanna Historical Society
c/o Membership Chairman
279 Eyeland Ave.
Succasunna, NJ 07876
973-927-9808

Hooven Mercantile
  Company Museum
42 Susquehanna St.
Jim Thorpe, PA 18229
570-352-2248

Lackawanna Coal Mine
McDade Park
Scranton, PA 18504
717-963-MINE (6463)
800-238-7245

Mauch Chunk Museum
  and Cultural Center
41 W. Broadway
Jim Thorpe, PA 18229
570-352-9190
www.mauchchunkmuseum.org

Old Jail Museum
128 West Broadway
Jim Thorpe, PA 18229
570-325-5259

Radisson Lackawanna
  Station Hotel
700 Lackawanna Ave.
Scranton, PA 18503
570-342-8300

Rail Tours, Inc.
P.O. Box 285
CNJ Station at Rte. 209
  and Broadway
Jim Thorpe, PA 18229
610-250-0968
570-325-4606
www.railtours-inc.com

Roebling's Delaware Aqueduct
Upper Delaware Scenic and
 Recreational River
RR2 Box 2428
Beach Lake, PA 18405
570-685-4871
www.nps.gov/upde

Steamtown National Historic Site
150 S. Washington Ave.
Scranton, PA 18503
570-340-5200
www.nps.gov/stea

Stourbridge Line
c/o Wayne County Chamber
 of Commerce
303 Commercial St.
Honesdale, PA 18431
570-253-1960
www.waynecountycc.com

Wayne County Historical Society
810 Main St.
Honesdale, PA 18431
570-253-3240
www.waynehistorypa.org

Laurel Highlands

Allegheny Portage Railroad
 National Historic Site
110 Federal Park Rd.
Gallitzin, PA 16641
814-886-6150
www.nps.gov/alpo

Altoona Railroaders
 Memorial Museum
1300 Ninth Ave.
Altoona, PA 16602
814-946-0834

B & O Railroad Museum
901 West Pratt St.
Baltimore, MD 21223
410-752-2490
www.borail.org

Baltimore & Ohio Railroad
 Historical Society
P.O. Box 24225
Baltimore, MD 21227
www.borhs.org

East Broad Top Railroad
P.O. Box 158
Route 994
Meadow Street
Rockhill Furnace, PA 17249
814-447-3011

Gallitzin Tunnels Park, Caboose,
 and Museum
c/o Gallitzin Area Tourist Council
411 Convent St., Suite 20
Gallitzin, PA 16641
814-886-8871

Greene County Historical
 Society and Museum
P.O. Box 127
Waynesburg, PA 15370
724-627-3204

Horseshoe Curve National
 Historic Landmark
1300 Ninth St.
Altoona, PA 16602
814-946-0834

Johnstown Flood Museum
P.O. Box 1889
304 Washington St.
Johnstown, PA 15907
814-539-1889

Johnstown Inclined Plane
711 Edgehill Dr.
Johnstown, PA 15905
814-536-1816
www.inclinedplane.com

Pennsylvania Railroad Technical
  & Historical Society
P.O. Box 712
Altoona, PA 16603-0712
http://prrths.com

Youngwood Historical
  and Railroad Museum
P.O. Box 444
1 Depot St.
Youngwood, PA 15697
724-925-7355

Pittsburgh Area

Duquesne Incline
1220 Grandview Ave.
Pittsburgh, PA 15211
412-381-1665
www.portauthority.org

Harlansburg Station Museum
  of Transportation
West Pittsburgh Rd.
RD1 Box 202A
New Castle, PA 16101
724-652-9002

Kiski Junction Railroad
P.O. Box 48
Schenley, PA 15682
724-295-5577
www.kiskijunction.com

Miniature Railroad and Village
Carnegie Science Center
One Allegheny Ave.
Pittsburgh, PA 15212-5850
412-237-3400
www.carnegiemuseums.org

Monongahela Incline
c/o/ Port Authority of
  Allegheny County
345 Sixth Ave.
Pittsburgh, PA 15222
412-442-2000
www.portauthority.com

Senator John Heinz Pittsburgh
  Regional History Center
1212 Smallman St.
Pittsburgh, PA 15222
412-454-6000
www.pghhistory.org

Station Square
Station Square Drive
Pittsburgh, PA 15219
412-261-1993

Erie Area

Greenville Area Railroad Park
  and Museum
314 Main St.
Greenville, PA 16125
724-588-4009

Lake Shore Railway Museum
31 Wall St.
North East, PA 16428
814-825-2724

Nickel Plate Road Historical
  & Technical Society
P.O. Box 381
New Haven, IN 46774-0381
www.nkphts.org

Oil Creek and Titusville Railroad
7 Elm St.
Oil City, PA 16301
814-676-1733
http://octrr.clarion.edu

BIBLIOGRAPHY

Abendschein, Frederic H. "The Atglen and Susquehanna: Lancaster County's Low Grade," *Journal of the Lancaster County Historical Society* 95, no. 1 (1993): 2–19.

Alexander, Edwin P. *On the Main Line: The Pennsylvania Railroad in the Nineteenth Century.* New York: C.N. Potter, 1971.

——. *The Pennsylvania Railroad, A Pictorial History.* New York: Bonanza Books, 1967.

Alexander, James, Jr. "Where History and Magic Converge: The Railroad Museum of Pennsylvania," *Pennsylvania Heritage* 21, no. 4 (1995): 29–37.

Anderson, Elaine. *The Central Railroad of New Jersey's First 100 Years, 1849–1949.* Easton, PA: Center for Canal History and Technology, 1984.

Archer, Robert F. *A History of the Lehigh Valley Railroad.* Forest Park, IL: Heimburger House Publishing Company, 1977.

Baldwin, Leland Dewitt. *Pittsburgh: The Story of a City.* Pittsburgh, PA: University of Pittsburgh Press, 1937.

Baltzell, E. Digby. *Philadelphia Gentlemen.* Glencoe, IL: Free Press, 1958.

Bates, S.P., Benjamin Whitman, N. W. Russell, R. C. Brown, and F. E. Weakley. *History of Erie County, Pennsylvania.* Chicago, IL: Warner, Beers & Co., 1884.

Beaver, Roy C. *The Bessemer and Lake Erie Railroad, 1869–1969.* San Marino, CA: Golden West Books, 1969.

Bell, Kurt R. "A Railroad Museum of Pennsylvania Retrospective," *Milepost* 18, no. 4 (2000): 11–21.

Bishop, Avard Longley. *The State Works of Pennsylvania.* New Haven, CT: Tuttle, Morehouse & Taylor Press, 1907.

Blackman, Emily C. *History of Susquehanna County, Pennsylvania.* Montrose, PA: Susquehanna County Historical Society and Free Library Association, 1873. Reprint, Baltimore, MD: Regional Publishing Company, 1970.

Bogen, Jules Irwin. *The Anthracite Railroads: A Study in American Railroad Enterprise.* New York: The Ronald Press Company, 1927.

Bowen, Eli. *The Pictorial Sketch-book of Pennsylvania.* Philadelphia, PA: W.P. Hazard, 1852.

Broehl, Wayne G. *The Molly Maguires.* Cambridge, MA: Harvard University Press, 1964.

Brown, John K. *The Baldwin Locomotive Works, 1831–1915.* Baltimore, MD: Johns Hopkins University Press, 1995.

Brumbaugh, Martin G., and Joseph Solomon Walton. *Stories of Pennsylvania or School Readings from Pennsylvania History.* New York: American Book Company, 1897.

Bruno, Malcolm L., and Patrick E. Purcell. "Schuylkill Valley: Route of the Anthracite Express," *National Railway Bulletin* 46, no. 4 (1981): 4–40.

Buck, William J. *History of Montgomery County within the Schuylkill Valley.* Norristown, PA: E.L. Acker, 1859.

Burgess, George H., and Miles C. Kennedy. *Centennial History of the Pennsylvania Railroad Company, 1846–1946.* Philadelphia, PA: Pennsylvania Railroad Company, 1949.

Casler, Walter C., Benjamin F. G. Kilne Jr., and Thomas T. Taber III. *The Logging Railroad Era of Lumbering in Pennsylvania.* 14 vols. Williamsport, PA: Lycoming Printing Co., 1970–1978.

Clark, Malcolm C. "The Birth of an Enterprise: Baldwin Locomotive Works," *Pennsylvania Magazine of History and Biography* 90, no. 4 (1966): 423–444.

Cochran, Thomas Childs. *Railroad Leaders, 1845–1890: The Business Mind in Action.* Cambridge, MA: Harvard University Press, 1953.

Cohen, Charles J. *Rittenhouse Square, Past and Present.* Philadelphia, PA: privately printed, 1922.

Contosta, David R. *Suburb in the City: Chestnut Hill, Philadelphia, 1850–1990.* Columbus, OH: Ohio State University Press, 1992.

Cook, Roger, and Karl Zimmermann. *The Western Maryland Railway: Fireballs and Black Diamonds.* Laury's Station, PA: Garrigues House, 1992.

Cupper, Dan. "America's Dream Highway," *Pennsylvania Heritage* 16, no. 4 (1990): 22–29.

——. *Crossroads of Commerce: The Pennsylvania Railroad Calendar Art of Grif Teller.* Mechanicsburg, PA: Stackpole Books, 2003.

——. *Horseshoe Heritage: The Story of a Great Railroad Landmark.* Halifax, PA: Withers Publishing, 1993.

——. *Railroad Museum of Pennsylvania: Pennsylvania Trail of History Guide.* Mechanicsburg, PA: Stackpole Books, 2002.

——. *Rockville Bridge: Rails across the Susquehanna.* Halifax, PA: Withers Publishing, 2002.

Daughen, Joseph R., and Peter Binzen. *The Wreck of the Penn Central.* Boston, MA: Little, Brown, 1971.

Davis, Aaron J. *History of Clarion County, Pennsylvania.* Syracuse, NY: Mason, 1887.

Davis, Patricia Talbot. *End of the Line: Alexander J. Cassatt and the Pennsylvania Railroad.* New York: Neale Watson Academic Publications, 1978.

Denny, John D. "The Reading and Columbia Railroad," *Journal of the Lancaster County Historical Society* 67, no. 4 (1963): 149–183.

Dickens, Charles. *American Notes.* London: Chapman and Hall, n.d.

Dickson, Paul. "The Great Railroad War of 1877," *American Heritage* 29, no. 2 (1978): 56–61.

Dorflinger, Don. *Phoebe Snow: The Lady and the Train.* Bernardsville, NJ: Hill Press, 1979.

Fisher, Charles E. "The Lehigh Valley Railroad," *Pennsylvania Locomotive Historical Society Bulletin* 42 (1937): 5–36.

Folmar, John Kent, and Ivan W. Saunders. "Some Reflections on Railroad Development in Western Pennsylvania," *Western Pennsylvania Historical Magazine* 65, no. 4 (1982): 363–371.

Folsom, Burton W. *Urban Capitalists: Entrepreneurs and City Growth in Pennsylvania's Lackawanna and Lehigh Regions, 1800–1920.* Baltimore, MD: Johns Hopkins University Press, 1981.

Garforth, Harry. *Rails through Manayunk.* Telford, PA: Silver Brook Junction Publishing Company, 1999.

Gordon, John S. *The Scarlet Woman of Wall Street: Jay Gould, Jim Fisk, Cornelius Vanderbilt, the Erie Railway Wars and the Birth of Wall Street.* New York: Weidenfeld & Nicholson, 1988.

Grant, H. Roger. *Erie Lackawanna: Death of an American Railroad, 1938–1992.* Stanford, CA: Stanford University Press, 1994.

Grinde, Donald A., Jr. "Erie's Railroad War," *Western Pennsylvania Historical Magazine* 57, no. 1 (1974): 15–23.

Hazard, Sameul, ed. *Hazard's Register of Pennsylvania.* Philadelphia, PA: William F. Geddes, 1828–1835.

Henry, M. S. *History of the Lehigh Valley.* Easton, PA: n.p., 1860.

History of Allegheny County, Pennsylvania. Chicago, IL: A. Warner, 1889.

Holton, James L. *The Reading Railroad: History of a Coal Age Empire.* 2 vols. Laury's Station, PA: Garrigues House, 1989–1992.

Ilisevich, Robert D., and Cark K. Burkett. "The Canal through Pittsburgh: Its Development and Character," *Western Pennsylvania Historical Magazine* 68, no. 4 (1985): 351–372.

Kenny, Kevin. *Making Sense of the Molly Maguires.* New York: Oxford University Press, 1998.

Kidney, Walter C. *Pittsburgh's Landmark Architecture: The Historic Buildings of Pittsburgh and Allegheny County.* Pittsburgh, PA: Pittsburgh History and Landmarks Foundation, 1997.

King, Shelden S. *The Route of the Phoebe Snow: A Story of the Delaware, Lackawanna and Western Railroad.* Elmira Heights, NY: author, 1974.

Kiscaden, Lester James. "History of the Strasburg Railroad," *Journal of the Lancaster County Historical Society* 77, no. 1 (1973): 1–25.

Klein, Aaron E. *The New York Central.* New York: Bonanza Books, 1985.

Leason, M. A. *History of the Counties of McKean, Elk, Cameron, and Potter, Pennsylvania.* Chicago, IL: J. H. Beers & Co., 1890.

Livesay, Harold C. *Andrew Carnegie and the Rise of Big Business.* New York: Longman, 2000.

Livingood, James Weston. *The Philadelphia–Baltimore Trade Rivalry, 1780–1860.* Harrisburg, PA: Pennsylvania Historical and Museum Commission, 1947.

Loeb, Betty Wagner. *Altoona and the Pennsylvania Railroad: Between a Roar and a Whimper.* Altoona, PA: Pennsylvania Railroad Technical and Historical Society, 1999.

Lucien, Paul. "Petroleum, What Is It Good For," *American Heritage of Invention and Technology* 7, no. 2 (1991): 56–63.

Martin, Albro. "Crisis of Rugged Individualism: The West Shore South Penn Railroad Affair, 1880–1885," *Pennsylvania Magazine of History and Biography* 93, no. 2 (1969): 218–243.

Mathews, Alfred. *History of the Counties of Lehigh and Carbon in the Commonwealth of Pennsylvania.* Philadelphia, PA: Everts & Richards, 1884.

——. *History of Wayne, Pike and Monroe Counties, Pennsylvania.* Philadelphia, PA: R.T. Peck & Co., 1886.

McClure, Alexander K. *Old Time Notes of Pennsylvania.* Philadelphia, PA: John C. Winston, 1905.

McCullough, David G. *The Johnstown Flood.* New York: Simon and Schuster, [1968] 1987.

McLean, Harold H. *The Pittsburgh and Lake Erie Railroad.* San Marino, CA: Golden West Books, 1980.

Middleton, William. *Landmarks on the Iron Road: Two Centuries of North American Railroad Engineering.* Bloomington, IN: Indiana University Press, 1999.

Moedinger, William M. *The Road to Paradise: The Story of the Rebirth of the Strasburg Rail Road.* Lancaster, PA: The Strasburg Railroad Shop, Inc., 1983.

Morley, Christopher. *Travels in Philadelphia.* Philadelphia, PA: David McKay, circa 1920.

Neu, Irene D. *Erastus Corning: Merchant and Financier, 1794–1872.* Ithaca, NY: Cornell University Press, 1960.

Nolan, J. Bennett. *Southeastern Pennsylvania.* New York: Lewis Historical Publishing Company, 1943.

Oberholtzer, Ellis Paxson. *Philadelphia: A History of the City and Its People.* Philadelphia, PA: S.J. Clarke, 1911.

Ockershausen, Jane. "The Valley that Changed the World," *Pennsylvania Heritage* 21, no. 3 (1995): 12–19.

Pennsylvania Railroad Publicity Bureau. *Allegheny Portage Railroad: Its Place in the Main Line of Public Works of Pennsylvania.* Philadelphia, PA: Pennsylvania Railroad Publicity Bureau, 1930.

Perlman, Alfred E. *Pittsburgh and the P&LE.* New York: Newcomen Society in North America, 1963.

Philadelphia and Its Environs: The Railroad Scenery of Pennsylvania. Philadelphia, PA: J.B. Lippincott, 1875.

Porterfield, James D. *Dining by Rail: The History and Recipes of America's Golden Age of Railroad Cuisine.* New York: St. Martin's Press, 1993.

Powell, H. Benjamin. "Establishing the Anthracite Boomtown of Mauch Chunk," *Pennsylvania History* 41, no. 3 (1974): 249–262.

Rea, Smauel. *How the Pennsylvania Railroad Has Grown.* Philadelphia, PA: Pennsylvania Railroad Co., 1928.

Rehor, John A. *The Nickel Plate Story.* Milwaukee, WI: Kalmbach Publishing Company, 1965.

Ringwalt, J. Luther. *Development of Transportation Systems in the United States.* Philadelphia, PA: n.p., 1888.

Rosenberger, Homer Tope. "How Pittsburgh Gained an Additional Railroad Outlet to the Seaboard," *Pennsylvania History* 35, no. 2 (1968): 109–146.

——. *The Philadelphia and Erie Railroad: Its Place in American Economic History.* Potomac, MD: Fox Hills Press, 1975.

Rupp, I. Daniel. *The History and Topography of Dauphin, Cumberland, Franklin, Bedford, Adams, and Perry Counties, Pennsylvania.* Lancaster, PA: G. Hills, 1846.

Saunders, Richard. *The Railroad Mergers and the Coming of Conrail.* Westport, CT: Greenwood Press, 1978.

Saylor, Roger B. *The Railroads of Pennsylvania.* State College, PA: Bureau of Business Research, College of Business Administration, Pennsylvania State University, 1962.

Schlegel, Marvin Wilson. *Ruler of the Reading: The Life of Franklin B. Gowen, 1836–1889.* Harrisburg, PA: Archives Publishing Company of Pennsylvania, 1947.

Shaughnessy, Jim. *Delaware & Hudson.* Syracuse, NY: Syracuse University Press, 1997.

Simpson, Bill. *Guide to Pennsylvania's Tourist Railroads.* Gretna, LA: Pelican Publishing Company, 1998.

Sipes, William B. *The Pennsylvania Railroad.* Philadelphia, PA: The Passenger Department of the Pennsylvania Railroad Company, 1875.

Smith, George. *History of Delaware County, Pennsylvania.* Philadelphia, PA: H.B. Ashmead, 1862.

Southeastern Pennsylvania Transportation Authority. *Commuter Railroad Service Improvements for a Metropolitan Area.* N.p., 1969.

Stevens, John. *Documents Tending to Prove the Superior Advantages of Rail-Ways and Steam-Carriages over Canal Navigation.* New York: T and J Swords, 1812.

Stover, John F. *History of the Baltimore and Ohio Railroad.* West Lafayette, IN: Purdue University Press, 1987.

——. *The Routledge Historical Atlas of American Railroads.* New York: Routledge, 1999.

Summer Excursion Routes, 1903. Philadelphia, PA: The Passenger Department of the Pennsylvania Railroad Company, 1903.

Swetnam, George. *Pennsylvania Transportation.* Gettysburg, PA: Pennsylvania Historical Association, 1964.

Taber, Thomas Townsend. *The Delaware, Lackawanna & Western Railroad, the Road of Anthracite, in the Nineteenth Century, 1828–1899.* Muncy, PA: author, 1977.

Taber, Thomas Townsend, and Thomas Townsend Taber III. *The Delaware, Lackawanna & Western Railroad, The Route of the Phoebe Snow, in the Twentieth Century, 1899–1960.* Muncy, PA: authors, 1980.

Tatnall, Francis G. "National Railway Historical Society: A Story of Growth," *National Railway Bulletin* 50, no. 5 (1985): 5–7.

Taylor, George Rogers. *The American Railroad Network, 1861–1890.* Cambridge, MA: Harvard University Press, 1956.

Thornton, W. George. "The Kinzua Saga," *Titusville Herald,* 1987 (exact date unrecorded).

Townsend, J. W. *The Old Main Line.* Philadelphia, PA: n.p., [1919] 1922.

Turner, George Edgar. *Victory Rode the Rails: The Strategic Place of the Railroads in the Civil War.* Indianapolis, IN: Bobbs-Merrill, 1953.

Van Trump, James D. *Station Square: A Golden Age Revived.* Pittsburgh, PA: Pittsburgh History and Landmarks Foundation, 1978.

Van Trump, James D., and Arthur P. Zielger Jr. *Landmark Architecture of Allegheny County, Pennsylvania.* Pittsburgh, PA: Pittsburgh History and Landmarks Foundation, 1967.

Vranich, Joseph. *Derailed: What Went Wrong and What to Do about America's Passenger Trains.* New York: St. Martin's Press, 1997.

Ward, James A. "Herman Haupt and the Development of the Pennsylvania Railroad," *Pennsylvania Magazine of History and Biography* 95, no. 1 (1971): 73–97.

——. *J. Edgar Thomson: Master of the Pennsylvania.* Westport, CT: Greenwood Press, 1980.

——. "J. Edgar Thomson and Thomas A. Scott: Symbiotic Partnership," *Pennsylvania Magazine of History and Biography* 100, no. 1 (1976): 37–65.

——. *That Man Haupt, A Biography of Herman Haupt.* Baton Rouge, LA: Louisiana State University Press, 1973.

Weinschenker, James D. "Waynesburg & Washington Engine #4," *The Keystone* 34, no. 1 (2001): 15–17.

White, John H. "Save This Railroad," *American Heritage of Invention & Technology* 11, no. 1 (1995): 40–47.

White, Lynne L. *The Nickel Plate Road.* New York: Newcomen Society in North America, 1954.

Williams, Harold A. *The Western Maryland Railway Story: A Chronicle of the First Century, 1852–1952.* Baltimore, MD: n.p., 1952.

Wilson, William Bender. *History of the Pennsylvania Railroad Company.* Philadelphia, PA: H.T. Coates, 1899.

Worley, Howard V., Jr., and William N. Poellot Jr. *The Pittsburgh & West Virginia Railway.* Halifax, PA: Withers Publishing, 1989.

Writers' Program of the Works Projects Administration in the Commonwealth of Pennsylvania. *Pennsylvania: A Guide to the Keystone State.* New York: Oxford University Press, 1940.

INDEX